With God on All Sides

With God on All Sides

Leadership in a Devout and Diverse America

DOUGLAS A. HICKS

OXFORD

UNIVERSITY PRESS

2009

OXFORD
UNIVERSITY PRESS

Oxford University Press, Inc., publishes works that further
Oxford University's objective of excellence
in research, scholarship, and education.

Oxford New York
Auckland Cape Town Dar es Salaam Hong Kong Karachi
Kuala Lumpur Madrid Melbourne Mexico City Nairobi
New Delhi Shanghai Taipei Toronto

With offices in
Argentina Austria Brazil Chile Czech Republic France Greece
Guatemala Hungary Italy Japan Poland Portugal Singapore
South Korea Switzerland Thailand Turkey Ukraine Vietnam

Copyright © 2009 by Oxford University Press, Inc.

Published by Oxford University Press, Inc.
198 Madison Avenue, New York, NY 10016

www.oup.com

Oxford is a registered trademark of Oxford University Press

Library of Congress Cataloging-in-Publication Data
Hicks, Douglas A.
With God on all sides : leadership in a devout
and diverse America / Douglas A. Hicks.
p. cm.
Includes bibliographical references and index.
ISBN 978-0-19-533717-4
1. Leadership—Religious aspects.
2. Leadership—United States. I. Title.
BL325.L4H53 2009
322´.10973—dc22   2008029266

1 3 5 7 9 8 6 4 2

Printed in the United States of America
on acid-free paper

To Catherine, Noah, and Ada

"Never budge! That's my rule. Never budge in the least!
Not an inch to the west! Not an inch to the east!
I'll stay here, not budging! I can and I will
If it makes you and me and the whole world stand still!"
 —the South-Going Zax, in "The Zax," by Dr. Seuss

Contents

PART I

Scanning the Horizon

1

Introduction

With God on All Sides

───────────────

The dogmas of the quiet past are inadequate to the stormy present.
—Abraham Lincoln

Lincoln's Leadership and Ours

ABRAHAM LINCOLN FOUND IT DEEPLY TROUBLING THAT LEADERS OF BOTH THE
Union and the Confederacy believed God was on their side. Preachers in the
North and the South declared the righteousness of their cause, and they frequently invoked the same biblical texts to opposing ends.[1] Lincoln knew better.
In 1862 he wrote in his journal, "In great contests each party claims to act in
accordance with the will of God. Both *may* be, and one *must* be wrong. God can
not be *for*, and *against* the same thing at the same time."[2]

With this perspective, Lincoln acted firmly to hold the nation together. In
1865, with Union victory nearly ensured, he delivered his second inaugural
address, widely considered to be the greatest example of American public theology. Union supporters in the crowd were ready for a triumphal declaration,
but instead Lincoln delivered an unexpected message. He proclaimed that all of
America had been complicit in the sin of slavery, and all had paid a dear price.
Neither the Union nor the Confederacy was in a position of moral rectitude:

> Both read the same Bible and pray to the same God, and each invokes
> His aid against the other. It may seem strange that any men should
> dare to ask a just God's assistance in wringing their bread from the
> sweat of other men's faces, but let us judge not, that we be not judged.

The prayers of both could not be answered. That of neither has been answered fully. The Almighty has His own purposes.[3]

Lincoln believed that a providential deity was active in history, but he also declared—especially to those he thought were tempted to self-righteousness and vengeance—that no one could fully know the will of God.

If Lincoln encountered claims of God on both sides—the Union and the Confederacy—today we see images of God, faith, and morality on all sides of society. These images are not only political claims but also religious, cultural, and social expressions of God in our public life. Americans disagree on politics, civic affairs, and moral questions, and although the conflicts do not typically result in bloodshed, the disagreements do cause us harm. Although we are not fighting a civil war, we face a stormy present. However, the battle lines rarely run along the boundaries of religious tradition. Some Christians line up against stem cell research; others support it. Evangelicals are split over whether to support the war in Iraq. Social conservatives from a variety of faiths support "traditional values," while liberals in those same traditions urge progressive social reforms. Those who would speak for God indeed stand on many sides.

To make matters more complicated, there is no simple map of the American religious landscape. America is arguably the most religiously diverse nation in the world at any time in history.[4] Christians of all types, sects, and denominations make up about four-fifths of the nation's population. Jews, Buddhists, Muslims, Hindus, Sikhs, Jains, and Confucians now inhabit the United States in appreciable numbers. Every major religion and many smaller ones are represented. Even before the early European explorers arrived, thousands of Native American tribes had highly developed theologies and rituals, and these remain part of our religious landscape. Since the arrival of Europeans, America has also cultivated a number of homegrown traditions such as Mormonism and Christian Science. We are also made up of secularists, humanists, atheists, pagans, and the spiritual-but-not religious. You name it, we have it. Indeed, all of these groups together make up the American "we."

And these diverse Americans express their commitments in widely different ways. For many, though certainly not all, this means using religious language or symbols in public life. Not everyone is happy about this. Supporters of a secular public sphere—whether atheists or religious believers who favor a strict public-private separation—bemoan the fact that "God" seems to be lurking in the wings of every political debate. Nonetheless, as Alexis de Tocqueville noted nearly two centuries ago, religion plays a particular and vital role in American democracy. Now, of course, the breadth of religious belief and practice is far greater than Tocqueville could have imagined.

How we deal with these cacophonous expressions of God in public life is a matter of leadership. Civic and political leaders will help shape the terms in which we navigate our religious differences and commonalities. Leading requires bringing people together despite their varied backgrounds and interests to achieve a common goal. A former White House staffer puts it this way: In politics today, leaders must reach out to citizens "from A to Z—atheists to Zoroastrians."[5]

In this time of anxiety over terrorism and globalization, we need a vision of leadership that draws Americans together for common efforts against international and domestic challenges. Yet too many of our leaders choose divisive politics over inclusive leadership. They prey on our vulnerabilities through fear mongering. Their confrontational language and warlike imagery destabilize our public life. We are distracted from the most important debates in our national conversation.

Religious rhetoric in particular provides ammunition on both—or rather *all* (since there are usually more than two)—sides of what we now call the culture wars. Their arguments may differ, but conservatives and liberals of many kinds claim to have special knowledge of what God wants. Some employ antireligious speech, but in doing so they can be just as dogmatic as those they criticize; the attempt to remove God from the public sphere can also be pursued with fanaticism. Deeply held beliefs on all sides and from all parties too often fuel discord, distrust, and social fragmentation.

This is not inevitable, however. I do not accept the premise that deeply held and disparate religious, spiritual, and moral convictions must lead us into cultural warfare. I also do not believe that religious influences are always benign—or that America should nostalgically return to some earlier time in which Christian moral values seemed to be more infused in our culture. We need to look forward, viewing our diverse, deep convictions as both a challenge and a resource for our public life. *With God on All Sides* explores the opportunity that leaders and citizens face in what I am calling, in shorthand, a devout and diverse America.

Leading with Our Better Angels

We expect divisive rhetoric from the extreme voices in our politics: Pundit Ann Coulter says the United States would be a better place if Jews would "perfect" themselves into Christians, and she calls Islam a "car-burning cult." Author Sam Harris lambastes religious believers as irrational and bemoans religious moderates for giving cover to the extremists—even as he talks of "arming" secularists with his arguments.[6]

When talk of religious diversity reaches the political mainstream, the language is not nearly so pointed. But the subtler messages convey equally troubling undertones. Facing attacks from people who wanted to undermine his candidacy by linking him to Islam—and by implication—to radicalism, Barack Obama emphasized his Christian faith. One of his campaign flyers featured him speaking in front of a church pulpit with an illuminated cross behind him; the back of the flyer stated in large type: "Committed Christian." With the vehemence that he would have used against charges that he was a criminal, he denounced the false rumors that he was a Muslim. Instead, he could have used the occasion to say that bigotry or bias against a Muslim candidate would be un-American.[7]

Republican senator and presidential nominee John McCain, trying to gain ground with conservatives, called the United States a Christian nation and stated that a president should "carry on in the Judeo Christian principled tradition that has made this nation the greatest experiment in the history of mankind." He suggested that a Muslim would be less fit than a Christian to serve as president but later "clarified" his comments by explaining that he would vote for a Muslim if that person were the most qualified candidate.[8] McCain missed the opportunity to state in no uncertain terms that he stood with the constitutional guarantee that there is no religious test for office.

Leaders from both political parties argue that the United States is locked in a global "clash of civilizations" that pits the nation against the non-Western world. In a number of ways, the Bush administration suggested that God is on our side. The initial military response to the 9/11 attacks was named Operation Infinite Justice. Strong public objection—particularly concerning how this claim sounds to Muslims and others who believe that only God metes out infinite justice—convinced officials to change the name to Operation Enduring Freedom.[9] Bush asserted that this war was one of good versus evil, freedom versus terror. In his remarks at the National Cathedral after 9/11 he stated, "[O]ur responsibility to history is already clear: to answer these attacks and rid the world of evil."[10] The following week he declared before Congress, "Freedom and fear, justice and cruelty, have always been at war, and we know that God is not neutral between them."[11]

The war on terror has also raised the stakes in our domestic conflicts. Arguments that would have once been a matter of mere political disagreement have exploded into accusations of lack of patriotism or of support for fundamental American values. The war on terror has influenced arguments on issues ranging from immigration to disaster relief, from education to the economy.

Polarizing pronouncements based on an embattled America do more than describe reality—they help create it. Through their language, their public appearances, and their alliances, leaders shape the culture. A key question for our leaders is this: Will they offer an inclusive vision that is true to America's principles?

It is helpful to refer again to Lincoln. Just one month before the first incursion at Fort Sumter, the new president offered a constructive vision for the future in his first inaugural address. It was a vision he hoped would appeal to all Americans and help avoid civil war. He said, "[W]e are not enemies, but friends." Passion, he urged, should not loosen the bonds of citizenship. In language perhaps only Lincoln could deliver, he declared: "The mystic chords of memory, stretching from every battle-field, and patriot grave, to every living heart and hearthstone, all over this broad land, will yet swell the chorus of the Union, which again touched, as surely they will be, by the better angels of our nature."[12]

The nation could not hear that chorus over the approaching drumbeat of war. Today, however, we have an opportunity to choose a hopeful, forward-looking vision for our common life. Precisely because people are not angels, we need our leaders to appeal to the higher qualities within us. We can take the low road alongside those—across the ideological spectrum—who choose to vilify those who dress or behave or believe differently from the way they do. We can opt for a politics that uses fear as a bumper-sticker slogan to rally political support. Or we can look for—even build—the high road, as Lincoln calls us to do. Lincoln was a realist, willing to draw arms when he believed it necessary for the public good. At the same time, he also offered a model of leadership that preempts conflict by exercising humility and engaging our fellow citizens with respect.

In my own city of Richmond, Virginia, a statue of Abraham Lincoln and his twelve-year-old son Tad sits on the grounds of the American Civil War Center. They are seated on a bench engraved with the words from his second inaugural: "To bind up the Nation's wounds." Lincoln had come in peace to the former capital of the Confederacy immediately after the South's troops had abandoned it in April 1865. A journalist recorded Lincoln's visit in this way: "He walked through the streets as if he were only a private citizen, and not the head of a mighty nation. He came not as a conqueror, not with bitterness in his heart, but with kindness. He came as a friend, to alleviate sorrow and suffering—to rebuild what has been destroyed."[13] Today the monument, which overlooks Richmond's buzzing downtown, communicates the solemn, quiet message of a leader who reached out his hand in the spirit of reconciliation to reunite a divided nation.

A Time to Lead

Lincoln shared with Thomas Jefferson a firm belief in the freedom of conscience and a disdain for self-righteousness. Jefferson expressly criticized those dogmatic Christians who had lost sight of the morality taught by Jesus. Noted Harvard professor Benjamin Waterhouse once asked Jefferson for permission to publish a letter he had sent describing his religious beliefs. The former president responded: "No, my dear sir, not for the world. Into what a nest of hornets would it thrust my head!"[14] Although Jefferson could sometimes be too sweeping in his criticism of religious believers, he was surely correct to anticipate the sting from discussions about religion, especially in the context of politics. Perhaps we are all well advised by Jefferson to avoid making public claims about religion. Perhaps this book will stir the hornets.

Despite his refusal to jump into theological debate, however, Jefferson showed leadership genius in drafting the Virginia Statute for Religious Freedom. This document set into law the right of citizens to disagree peacefully about matters of religion, effectively guaranteeing religious freedom to all.

In the spirit of the Virginia Statute, passed into law in Richmond in 1786, this book sets aside interfaith debates over dogma and focuses on the proper role of religious expression in our public life. It sets forth a vision of political and civic leadership that we, a devout and diverse society, need in order to face common challenges.

The term *leadership* can refer solely to those in positions of formal authority—president, senator, governor, priest, rabbi, imam, chairperson, and so on. But the lines between citizens and leaders are often blurry. Only one of us is the American president, but many of us are presidents or chairpersons or captains of neighborhood associations, PTAs, and sports clubs. Moreover, citizens without any of those titles act as leaders whenever they initiate group action in their community. Experts in leadership report that the traits and behaviors of successful leaders tend also to be the traits and behaviors of engaged followers.

With God on All Sides urges leaders—in Washington, in our state capitals, and in our communities—to appeal to the better angels of our nature. From recent and ancient studies of leadership, we know that leaders help shape the vision of their people. We also know that it is regular citizens who enact that vision. This book explores the overlapping work of those leaders and citizens.

The work of leadership, falling on all of us, occurs in the ordinary places and common interactions. It brings together people from different positions, backgrounds, and affiliations to address public challenges. Leadership has a lot to do with a Spanish term, *convivencia*, which concerns how we manage (or do not manage) to live together in our daily activities. We do not have a good, direct translation into English, but the concept calls for showing respect to our neighbors when our paths cross and even working together to build connectors between our paths. This is much more than just tolerating one another or agreeing to "live and let live." It requires interacting with our fellow citizens—whether we share their view of the world or not—to understand their basic values and find ways to get along well.

Convivencia sounds like a nice word, you might say, but does it mean I have to listen to my neighbor preach to me? Would it not be better to steer clear of "sensitive" topics? Religious voices can spark the flames of passion, but they can also light a path toward solutions. In our own time of domestic and international trials, will our leaders be willing to shape a constructive message? Or will they provoke suspicion along lines of religion, ethnicity, and ideology? Will we as citizens work together, drawing on our deepest convictions, to build a respectful society? Or will we choose the moral equivalent of staying home in gated communities—separated not only by our burglar alarms but also by our faiths?

Many people of goodwill—left, right, and center—believe deeply that we can do better than our conflict-based politics. We know that "religion" itself neither produces nor resolves conflict—religious believers do. In addition, as in other aspects of human life, our actions arise out of the substance of particular beliefs and practices. Rather than view our religious diversity as a problem to be fixed—as we typically do—we can look to a devout and diverse citizenry as an abundant source of cultural and moral perspectives.

In the following pages I examine the ways in which religion in its varied forms has functioned in American public life throughout our history. I discuss approaches to public faith that have failed because they are either too narrow or too shallow. Finally, I offer a metaphor of "crossroads and connectors" to describe a more inclusive politics. We need religiously literate leaders and citizens who engage one another where their paths cross with equal regard, respectful curiosity, and humility.

2

"The Vision Thing"

Where there is no vision, the people perish.
—Proverbs 29:18

AS VICE PRESIDENT PREPARING FOR HIS OWN PRESIDENTIAL RUN, GEORGE H. W. Bush asked a friend to counsel him on campaign strategy. This advisor suggested that Bush take the time to reflect on his own ideas on where he would lead the country. "Oh, the vision thing," Bush retorted dismissively.[1] His comment only fueled the criticism that he lacked this essential quality.

Effective leaders have the ability to influence our collective vision. However, it is not enough to have a vision of leadership. That vision must be sufficient to meet the challenges facing society and compelling enough that citizens will embrace it.

Virginia Visions

I was driving home when a white sport utility vehicle caught my eye. How could I have missed it? It featured three large American flags—one across the rear window, another on the bumper, and a magnetic one on the tailgate. It was also adorned with these words in large red type: Offended by my flag? Call 1-800-Leave USA.

What could have motivated this SUV's owner? This was not quiet patriotism; it was an in-your-face statement. But was the intended message political, cultural, or both? Who were the targets—immigrants, antiwar activists, religious outsiders? I do not know. Nonetheless, it is clear this citizen saw an America in conflict. Who or what had shaped his vision?

In Virginia some leaders have helped to develop a vision of an embattled American culture. During his 2006 reelection campaign, former U.S. senator George Allen created his infamous "macaca moment." Locked in a close race with challenger Jim Webb, Allen was crisscrossing the state. At a campaign event in Breaks, Virginia, a small, remote Appalachian town, Allen unexpectedly saluted one of Webb's volunteers, S. R. Sidarth, with these words:

> This fellow over here, over here with the yellow shirt, Macaca, or whatever his name is, he's with my opponent. He's following us around everywhere. . . . We're going to places all over Virginia . . . it's good for [the Webb campaign] to see what it's like out here in the real world. So welcome, let's give a welcome to Macaca here! Welcome to America, and the real world of Virginia!

The word *macaca,* technically a genus of monkey, has come to function as a derogatory slang term widely used in various cultures. Although it is disputed whether Allen knew the precise meaning of macaca, it is clear from the context that Allen was mocking Sidarth, an Indian American, portraying him as an outsider to "the real world" of Virginia and the United States.

In fact, S. R. Sidarth is an American citizen and a Virginian, born and raised in Fairfax County. (Allen himself is from California.) Sidarth graduated with honors from Thomas Jefferson High School and went on to attend the University of Virginia. He is a practicing Hindu whose parents contributed to the founding of the Sri Siva Vishnu Temple in the greater Washington, D.C., area.[2] Clearly, S. R. Sidarth is as American as either George Allen or the owner of the flag-adorned SUV. But Allen's vision of America was too narrow to recognize it.

Congressman Virgil Goode began representing Virginia's Fifth District in the U.S. House of Representatives in January of 1997. Goode sought to speak for a segment of the nation that feels its traditional values are under siege. In 2007 he made public statements expressing his disdain for Mexican flags hanging in his district and his hope that all inhabitants of the United States would fly the Stars and Stripes.[3] After the elections of 2006 Goode also spoke out directly against the presence of Islam in American public life. Voters in Minnesota's Fifth District had elected Keith Ellison, an African American attorney who converted to Islam during his college years, to the U.S. House of Representatives. He was the first Muslim ever elected to Congress. Less noted in the national media was the fact that two Buddhists were also elected as representatives that same year. Indeed, with Jews, Catholics, Protestants from many denominations, Orthodox Christians, and Mormons, the 110th Congress was the most religiously diverse in history. It also included the first representative ever to declare himself an atheist and six other people with no declared religious affiliation.[4] The most noteworthy fact about this diversity was that it received only passing media attention. Most Americans took it in stride as part of a changing America. For some traditionalists, however, it set off alarm bells.

Representative Goode was one of the most vocal. He was particularly troubled by Ellison, who had stated his intention to participate in the ceremonial swearing-in with his hand on the Quran. Goode used this occasion to explicate his vision of American identity. In a letter to constituents he wrote the following:

> When I raise my hand to take the oath on Swearing In Day, I will have the Bible in my other hand. I do not subscribe to using the Koran in any way. The Muslim Representative from Minnesota was elected by the voters of that district and if American citizens don't wake up and adopt the Virgil Goode position on immigration there will likely be many more Muslims elected to office and demanding the use of the Koran. We need to stop illegal immigration totally and reduce legal immigration and end the diversity visas policy pushed hard by President Clinton and allowing many persons from the Middle East to come to this country. I fear that in the next century we will have many more Muslims in the United States if we do not adopt the strict immigration policies that I believe are necessary to preserve the values and beliefs traditional to the United States of America and to prevent our resources from being swamped.[5]

Goode embarks here on a series of incorrect inferences. To begin with, Ellison was born in Michigan, and he is not an immigrant but a descendant of slaves. Indeed, many U.S.-born citizens are Muslims. The first Muslims arrived in America as slaves in the 1600s, and practicing, organized Islamic congregations have existed in the United States for more than one hundred years.[6] Moreover, contrary to Goode's assumptions, most Muslims do not live in the Middle East. Finally, Goode's suggestion that Muslims do or would "swamp" U.S. resources is far fetched. In 2007 a major study by the Pew Research Center found that Muslim Americans' income closely mirrors that of all Americans.[7]

Fellow Virginia Republican John Warner, the state's senior U.S. senator, criticized Goode's letter in his characteristically understated manner. Warner publicly defended the right of members of Congress to "exercise the religion of their choice, including those of the Islamic faith utilizing the Quran."[8] Warner showed that respect and religious free exercise are not partisan issues; they are core American values.

For his part, Ellison responded to Goode's comments by telling CNN, "I don't know the fellow, and I'd rather just say that he has a lot to learn about Islam, and we all have a lot to learn."[9] Goode, however, refused to back down from his position. Instead, he continued to utilize his influence and access to the national media to try to sway the public toward his political agenda, based on an exclusivist vision of America.

As history would have it, Goode's district includes the homesteads of both Thomas Jefferson and James Madison—two of the country's greatest proponents of religious freedom. Indeed, Jefferson's grave marker at his home at Monticello excludes his service as U.S. president in favor of these three great works: the Declaration of Independence, the University of Virginia, and the Virginia Statute for Religious Freedom. Madison also played a vital role in the actual passage of the Virginia Statute and then helped push the freedom of religious expression (and religious nonestablishment) into the First Amendment. These two leaders shaped a vision of religious freedom into Virginia laws and influenced America's basic legal and moral framework.

So it is no small irony that Rep. Virgil Goode represents the area that gave us both Jefferson and Madison. A more fitting legacy to their work is that S. R. Sidarth excelled at Thomas Jefferson High School and at Jefferson's beloved University of Virginia and that Rep. Keith Ellison, over Goode's objections, was sworn into the U.S. House of Representative using a Quran once owned by Jefferson.

In contrast to the narrow visions of George Allen and Virgil Goode—and closer to the view of these founders—Americans witnessed extraordinary leadership in response to another Virginia community's unspeakable tragedy in 2007. Virginia Tech, located in the Appalachian town of Blacksburg, Virginia, is a truly diverse community of students, faculty, and staff. On April 16, 2007, a mentally troubled student killed thirty-two students and faculty before also killing himself. The victims hailed from at least seven countries. The Americans among the dead were of European, Lebanese, Chinese, and African descent. The families who mourned the victims were Christian, Jewish, Muslim, Hindu, and Buddhist.

Even before the bodies were identified, Virginia Tech officials and local, state, and national leaders responded to the grieving community. The day after the shooting, the university hosted a convocation that filled the basketball arena, with the crowd spilling over into other venues. President Bush and Virginia governor Tim Kaine spoke alongside a mixed group of school administrators, students, and faculty members. Bush, a Methodist, and Kaine, a Catholic, approached the tragedy from their own understandings of faith while clearly acknowledging the religious diversity of the Virginia Tech community—and, by extension, of Virginia and the United States. Representatives of Muslim, Buddhist, Jewish, and Christian communities contributed words of reflection and consolation. Adapting a familiar sports slogan, "We are Virginia Tech," African American poet and Virginia Tech professor Nikki Giovanni called the campus community together.[10] The entire service communicated a spirit of unity within a remarkably varied university.

The responsive leadership modeled at Virginia Tech was evident not only in the fitting remarks by the political, educational, and religious officials but also in the very presence of many high-profile figures, who quickly arrived in Blacksburg without grandstanding or getting in the way and played an important role. This group included the entirety of Virginia's U.S. congressional delegation.[11] Although it may seem obvious in hindsight that these leaders needed to be present, this was not a simple achievement; Kaine had been in Tokyo on a trade mission, Bush had been scheduled for a full day at the White House, and the Senate and House had an active agenda.

The most significant evidence of good leadership was displayed in the fact that in one day the organizers managed to cobble together an event reflecting the international, racial-ethnic, and religious diversity of Virginia Tech—and in microcosm the group that lost their lives. Together the convocation speakers confronted the tragedy by identifying the many sources of support—religious, moral, institutional, familial—that could help sustain the members of the university community during their grieving. Organizers could have opted for an institutional response that steered clear of religion to a significant degree, or they could have invited only those leaders from majority religious communities to speak for Virginia Tech. Yet campus officials chose a more inclusive route.

Governor Kaine declared April 20 a statewide day of mourning. On that day he joined an estimated twenty-five hundred people at an interfaith memorial service in Richmond, the state capital, hosted by Virginia Commonwealth University. The participants in that nationally televised service included political figures and leaders from a multitude of religious traditions: Christian, Jewish, Muslim, Hindu, and Sikh.[12] Kaine himself spoke of three aspects of the tragedy that "touched people around the globe," namely, the value of human life, the universality of grief, and the universality of hope. Grief, he said, makes us all the same:

> If you've heard those names read or if you've looked at the list of these students who were killed you'll see that they're Virginians, sure, but they're from other states, from other nations, students, teachers, the

young, the old, from all religions, speaking different languages from different cultures. But all grieving the loss of a child, the loss of a parent, the loss of a spouse, in every culture, in every part of the world, bring[ing] forth a similar response.[13]

Kaine framed the tragedy as one that affected a range of persons and communities, but he also said it could bring people together around the feelings of loss and the reminder of the preciousness of life itself.

Given that the shooter was a South Korean student, words or acts of so-called retribution against non-U.S. citizens could readily have occurred (as they did in many cases across the United States after the events of 9/11).[14] It is not possible, of course, to attribute the absence of a backlash to good leadership from university or political officials. Yet these leaders' immediate and inclusive efforts set forth a vision of a diverse community that could not be undermined by an act of unspeakable violence. In a university that had become an international and cultural crossroads, local, state, and national leaders provided the cues for everyone to draw together.

Challenges from Sea to Shining Sea

How did we get to a point where religious difference is seemingly reason for suspicion? Unfortunately, we find ourselves in a political climate in which the war on terrorism plays a defining role in our vision of American leadership. Muslim Americans feel subject to intense public scrutiny, such as when the media add "Islamic" as a qualifier before the term *terrorism* or when leaders single out Islam as violent. This suspicion affects Muslim Americans disproportionately, but it impacts many others, too. Sikhs, Hindus, Buddhists, Jews, and Christians have also experienced words or acts of hate intended either for Muslims or for religious outsiders in general.

Leaders and citizens from many backgrounds and from across the country must confront issues of religion and identity in public life. From Christmas trees in Seattle to driver's licenses in Florida, questions of how different faith commitments contribute to leadership challenges have become more and more common.

Since 9/11, airports have remained a particularly tense public space. Controversies surround airport security, especially checks of passengers who stand out because of their religious attire or ethnic or racial appearance. Do people with "foreign-sounding" names or non-Western dress receive excessive scrutiny? Is the Transportation Security Administration (TSA) profiling at security stations? Are female passengers being subjected to pat-downs by male security officers? The TSA has faced each of these questions and made efforts to address the criticisms.

As if the issue of security vs. passenger rights were not big enough, airports have also become highly symbolic. In December 2006, the Seattle-Tacoma airport became the central battleground for debates over a frequently contested public symbol: the Christmas tree. After an Orthodox Jewish rabbi requested that a menorah be placed in the airport to mark Chanukah, officials opted to remove the Christmas trees already on display rather than engaging in messy questions about religious displays in public. Then, after a public outcry and the rabbi's insistence that he had only requested "adding light to the holiday, not diminishing any light," the trees went back up. Is the Christmas tree a religious symbol—or rather, a cultural, commercial, or "pagan" one? Which different symbols would need to be included in a religious display to make it properly inclusive? Who would pay for them? Should public institutions acknowledge religion at all? These questions vex well-intentioned leaders across the country. The intensity of the surrounding debates indicates the importance of the vision of American society that our public symbols communicate.[15]

At the Minneapolis–St. Paul International Airport, religious sensibilities also sparked controversy. There, some Somali-born Muslims, who form the majority of the cab drivers serving the complex, understand their faith to dictate that they may not allow alcohol (even in closed containers) in their cabs. Rather than break this rule of their faith by transporting passengers with alcohol, these cabbies chose to pass up potential fares and return to the back of the taxi line. Passengers in turn complained of being refused rides.[16] The airport authority, under public pressure after a provisional compromise, imposed new sanctions that would suspend the taxi license of anyone refusing rides to passengers.[17] In one sense, this is a typical example of employees torn between the requirements of their faith and their job. On the other hand, isn't the availability of secure transportation from airports to private citizens' homes a matter of public interest? Because it is, this issue requires public officials to seek feasible solutions that measure the public good against individuals' religious views.

In Oklahoma, Governor Brad Henry had sought a proactive approach to promoting mutual understanding among citizens from different cultural and religious backgrounds. In 2004 he established the Governor's Ethnic American Advisory Council. This group formed the Muslim Community Outreach Program "to bridge the gap between local, state, and federal law enforcement agencies and the Muslim community to combat terrorism and criminal activity."[18] In 2007, as one of its outreach efforts, the council offered a Quran displaying Oklahoma's centennial logo to all state lawmakers. Earlier that year, state officials had received a centennial edition of the Bible—an action that seemed to have raised little or no controversy. This was not the case with the Quran, however. For his part, Governor Henry said he had happily accepted the Quran as an act of friendship. However, at least 24 of the 149 lawmakers rejected the Quran. In an outspoken refusal, Rep. Rex Duncan told the media: "Most Oklahomans do not endorse the idea of killing innocent women and children in the name of ideology."[19] Rep. Duncan could also have acknowledged that the Bible—like the Quran and numerous other sacred texts—contains passages that seem to condone violence against outsiders and innocents. The challenge for Oklahoma's leaders—many of whom are Christians—was whether they would accept this gift as an invitation to mutual understanding or, alternatively, reinforce public perceptions of Islam as prone to violence.

The case of Sultaana Freeman stands as another public leadership challenge raised by religious commitment. Freeman, a Muslim woman living in Florida, had her driver's license revoked by the state when she refused, on grounds of her religion, to pose for a photo without her full-face veil, or *niqab*. In June 2003 a Florida judge refused her petition, stating that the state had shown a "compelling interest" to require photos on its licenses for reasons of public security.[20] Does it matter that this person believes that, as a part of her deepest identity, she has a religious obligation to cover herself? How are issues of security and religious expression to be balanced in this case?

These vignettes identify a set of difficult questions that require innovative and thoughtful public leadership, which was largely lacking in these cases. They are only a few examples of the hundreds of challenges that arise in the encounters among diverse citizens in a multifaceted society. On the one hand, they concern everyday matters like taking a taxi. On the other hand, they raise the most fundamental questions of political and moral identity. Navigating this religious difference is central to effective leadership.

International Vistas

This book focuses on the United States, and yet the kinds of challenges we face as a nation are not unique. Throughout the book I refer to developments in other countries when they can shed light on leadership in the United States. After all, part of the reason that leadership in America is increasingly complex is because the United States is becoming more and more like the rest of the world. We can learn a great deal about the difficulties ahead—what to do and what not to do in response—by examining the ways in which other countries address them. And seeing how other countries view us can help clarify our own vision.

In his thoughtful book *God's Continent,* Philip Jenkins examines Christian encounters with Islam and secularism in Europe and suggests that Americans can learn from these experiences. Jenkins also notes a variety of ways in which the two contexts are interrelated and how religious changes in Europe could affect U.S. foreign policy, domestic policy, and culture. Although he takes seriously the concern of some Americans over the potential "Islamicization" or secularization of Europe (or both), he offers a balanced and dynamic picture of religious and cultural interchange.[21] Many of the issues Jenkins examines in Europe are relevant to the United States.

Cases such as the Florida driver's license brought the issue of head covering and the veil to public notice in the United States, but the debate has been raging throughout Europe and the Middle East for some time. Should it be permissible for women to wear the veil on the street or in public schools, parliament, courtrooms, and the like? Is it a matter of religious freedom? Does it pose a security risk? Is the covering a symbol of oppression from which the state should protect girls (if not women)? The then leader of Britain's House of Commons, Jack Straw, stepped into the thick of this controversy in October 2006 with his comments encouraging Muslim women to lift their *niqab,* thus uncovering their faces, when they meet with him. Then prime minister Tony Blair called the *niqab* "a mark of separation" but stopped short of endorsing Straw's call, whereas then chancellor Gordon Brown supported Straw by affirming the view that British public life would be improved if fewer women wore veils.[22] The French created a firestorm in 2003–2004 when they banned the *hijab,* or veil, and other religious head coverings from public schools. The Italian, Dutch, and Turkish parliaments have all debated the legality of covering one's hair or face in public. In every case, the discussion returns to the basic question of what national identity means.

Such deliberations inevitably took on a new tenor after 9/11. In this unfamiliar climate, covering one's face can provoke more distrust and discomfort than ever. What are the veil wearers' motives? What are they hiding? More to the point: Are they terrorists? Fear and security thus come face to face with religious identity and civil rights.

On 9/11 I was visiting Jordan, a Middle Eastern ally of the United States. Along with an American colleague, I had conducted a cross-cultural leadership seminar that morning under the auspices of the United Nations University Leadership Academy. In the afternoon we met with a women's cooperative organization in a rural village. I was impressed by the array of colors in our large tent, which was decorated with local textiles. The Jordanian women also wore varied combinations of attire, including the *niqab* and the *hijab.* I was heartened by the energetic pragmatism of these local leaders who had set about to improve their lives and those of their children. In the process they were navigating the tensions between Muslim identity and a Western-influenced global economy. Theirs was a practical vision of mixing cultures and of transforming traditions along the way.

The hopeful spirit was broken, of course, by the news that quickly arrived by cell phone. Terrorists had attacked in New York and Washington. Later I learned that CNN and other media outlets repeatedly aired controversial footage of a group of Palestinians rejoicing in the streets of East Jerusalem. Nothing could have been further from the response we experienced in Jordan, however, where the local citizens showed tremendous compassion toward me and my colleague and offered good wishes for America. A hotel clerk stopped me to ask whether I had family in Washington or New York. We soon learned that Jordan's King Abdullah II had publicly denounced the acts of terrorism and expressed solidarity with the United States. Jordanian police had already contended with a number of terrorist plots, including one planned for the previous day in Jordan's cultural jewel, the ancient city of Petra. This was a vision of compassion, not division.

In Spain, the most significant date in recent history is not September 11, 2001, but March 11, 2004, the day that trains in Madrid were bombed by a network of al Qaeda operatives. The nation's progress in quelling violence from the Basque separatist group ETA (Euskadi Ta Askatasuna, or "Basque Homeland and Freedom") was suddenly overshadowed by the specter of active al Qaeda cells. Although there was potential for a violent backlash against Muslim citizens and immigrants, Spain has thus far managed to avoid a politics driven by the fear of Islam—unlike responses in France, England, the Netherlands, and arguably the United States. The Spanish leadership efforts to navigate religious diversity in public life—successful and less than successful—can be instructive for the United States. Although we cannot, of course, simply import a "foreign" approach, we can expect to find ideas that might inform U.S. leadership.

Religious Identity in the United States

Tocqueville, the international observer who wrote the most famous analysis of American democracy, marveled at the vitality of religion in the United States. Moreover, he focused not just on individual beliefs and practices but also on institutions. In the nearly two centuries since, many European observers have likewise remarked on the degree of religious affiliation and practice in the United States. Tocqueville also reflected carefully on the public significance of religious individuals and communities for American democracy. That is our task as well.

A major study released in 2008 by the Pew Forum on Religion and Public Life gives a good perspective on the vibrancy and diversity of American religion. This U.S. Religious Landscape Survey, which is based on a sample of thirty-five thousand U.S. adults, shows a shifting religious terrain in which religious affiliation is not a fixed, lifelong label that people wear.[23] Yet neither is it simply a voluntary choice that religious "consumers" pick from a menu of spiritual options.

The Pew survey found that 44 percent of Americans have changed their religious affiliation during their lifetime.[24] For some, this has meant switching from Methodist to Baptist; for others, it has been a more extensive conversion—say, from Catholicism to Buddhism. For still others it has meant going from one of these categories to being religiously unaffiliated or, conversely, going from unaffiliated to embracing one of these faiths.

These data suggest we should think of religious identity as a combination of "voluntary" and "constitutive" commitments, in the language of political philosopher Michael Sandel. Do we choose our religion, or do we discover it, through self-reflection, to constitute part of our very selves?[25] For some people, religion is a matter of their fundamental nature: "I was born a Calvinist" or "I am a Jew." Some people joke about trying to "recover" from their religious identity, whereas others seek to retain their cultural identity while rejecting religious belief. All of these perspectives speak to the complexity of affiliation. Sandel's distinction between voluntary and constitutive community helps us to understand that our various affiliations are matters of our will, but many are also more than that. Indeed, for a variety of reasons, some people have more choice than others in determining their religious identity, and that, too, deserves attention.

The philosopher Immanuel Kant maintained that human beings are truly enlightened once they are liberated from all of those influences that obstruct the voluntary choice of *autonomous* (self-ruled) individuals. Any outside influences, including religious teachings or institutions, which he called *heteronomous* authority (rule by something other than oneself), were trappings that block people from being truly free.[26] Kant himself made room for "religion within the bounds of reason alone," but he was deeply suspicious of any commitments that could not be derived from reason.[27] Yet many—if not most—people uphold commitments that are partially constitutive of who they are. Kant wants us to ask: Are these affiliations consistent with their autonomy? But for these persons, distinguishing whether their beliefs and practices *derive from* reason, merely *fit with* reason (but derive from some other source like religious teaching), or actually *diverge from* reason would be nearly impossible. Commitments are not easily sorted out in this way.

The 2008 Pew survey also demonstrates America's remarkable religious diversity. Table 2.1 summarizes key results related to affiliation for all respondents over age eighteen. Encompassing almost four in five Americans, Christianity as a whole continues to be a strong majority. At the same time, it is very clear that the Christian tradition is characterized by diversity, fragmentation, and movement.

The findings of the Pew survey also suggest that diversity is more of a factor among younger adults. In each progressively younger age cohort, the proportion of Christians is slightly lower, and the respective proportions in "other religions" and "unaffiliated" are higher. In the eighteen-to-twenty-nine age group, Christians make up 68 percent, "other religions" reaches 6 percent, and the unaffiliated make up 25 percent.[28]

It is into this messy world of identity and moral commitments that leaders must venture, drawing citizens together to solve common problems. Would it not be easier to ask citizens to leave their religious identities behind when they enter the public square? It might. However, it would also be morally undesirable because it would require religious leaders and citizens to split themselves into public and private in ways that would be wrenching—if not impossible—to do. The tradition of divorcing public governance from private religion dates back as least as far as John Locke's 1689 essay *A Letter concerning Toleration,* and there

TABLE 2.1. Religious Affiliation of American Adults, 2008

Tradition/Affiliation			Percentage
Christian			78.4
Protestant		51.3	
Mainline churches	18.1		
Evangelical churches	26.3		
Historically black churches	6.9		
Catholic		23.9	
Mormon		1.7	
Other (Jehovah's Witness, Orthodox, etc.)		1.6	
Jewish			1.7
Buddhist			0.7
Muslim			0.6
Hindus			0.4
Other faiths/religions			1.3
Unaffiliated			16.1
Don't know/refused			0.8

Source: Pew Forum on Religion and Public Life· *U.S. Religious Landscape Survey. Report 1: Diverse and Dynamic* (Washington, D.C., February 2008), 5, 12.

is something to this school of thought.[29] However, Locke himself struggled with differentiating between public and private matters. Dividing religion and politics may sound good in theory, but it is difficult in practice.[30]

It would also make unavailable a host of moral and spiritual resources for addressing public problems. Admittedly, proponents of both slavery and abolition claimed to have God on their side. During the civil rights movement, supporters of the Ku Klux Klan and leaders of the Student Nonviolent Coordinating Committee read from the same Bible.[31] Opening up the public sphere to religious beliefs and practices will result in battles over God.

However, allowing religion in public life also brings many benefits, four of which are primary.[32] First, because religion is institutionally grounded, it brings a *historical memory* to contemporary debate on social issues. Naming the history of moral reasoning often (or usually) requires candid assessment and a sense of humility, if not remorse. Looking to history certainly does not mean longing for some purer or simpler era. Still, historical memory of moral and social debates give a sense of context that American public discourse often lacks. On issues such as immigration, the minimum wage, and just war, there are centuries of moral reflection in Catholic, Protestant (mainline, evangelical, and African American traditions), Jewish, Muslim, Hindu, and other sources. To disregard or set aside these resources would be tantamount to discarding much of the best moral thinking in the history of the human experience.

Next, religious traditions are *institutionally situated,* and this is, by and large, a further reason that they offer resources for framing our public life. For the roughly 40 percent of Americans who are active participants in religious communities, these institutions provide a sense of community, the good of experiencing membership.[33] Many Americans say they are "spiritual, but not religious." Even for these people, though, their understanding of faith comes from those institutions called church, mosque, temple, gurdwara, or synagogue. Alternatively, they form their own communities, whether through the workplace, a book club, or a neighborhood, to express their individuality— together. As Tocqueville explains, this kind of social participation also serves as a school of citizenship.[34] Moreover, institutions provide resources for social activism. The success of the famous Montgomery bus boycott, for example, is too readily credited to individuals such as Rosa Parks or Martin Luther King Jr. Less visible in popular accounts are the African American churches—notably, women's groups and ministers' alliances—that undergirded the movement.[35]

Religious communities produce, as a byproduct of their religious mission, what scholars call *social capital*.[36] Indeed, a major research initiative is analyzing the role of what is called *spiritual capital,* a subset of social capital.[37] Social capital is generally defined as the social trust, norms, and networks that are resources for economic and other transactions among individuals in a society. Observers argue that religion is a primary source of social capital in the contemporary United States. "Faith communities in which people worship together are arguably the single most important repository of social capital in America," political scientist Robert Putnam has found.[38] As American civic engagement declines in overall terms, religious affiliation takes on an increasingly important role.

Scholars of social capital emphasize the ways that religion can contribute to the growth of positive social ends and the reduction of negative ones. Not enough attention is paid to the ways in which religious practices vary. Putnam's distinction between *bridging* and *bonding* forms of social capital is helpful here. Bonding social capital deepens the local ties of identity within a particular group or enclave, while bridging capital is broader but not as deep and brings people together across lines of division and beyond categories such as race, religion, or class. Putnam refers to the potential of religious involvements to be bonding, bridging, or both. Racially separated churches reinforce deep—albeit segregated—bonds, while the religiously influenced civil rights movement promoted fundamental bridging across racial divides. Church-based study and fellowship groups tend to be bonding, while ecumenical and interreligious groups are bridging.[39]

Third, religious communities are *self-consciously and self-critically sustained*. That is, they regularly reflect on their own purposes, and they change in response to that reflection. Thus, when we read of those who switch affiliations within a religious "marketplace," we should remember that all of these traditions and subtraditions ("religious suppliers," in this market analogy) are also dynamic. The philosopher Alasdair McIntyre referred to a tradition as "an historically extended, socially embodied argument . . . an argument precisely in part about the goods which constitute that tradition."[40] Each institution must find ways to deal with internal conflicts and disagreements. These ongoing struggles over theology, ritual, and practice shape the ways in which the tradition as a whole (and institutions within it) will develop. This necessitates careful attention to seemingly mundane matters such as administration and organizational structure. It also requires institutions to be able to change in response to the times and the needs of its members. At times the fights within religious institutions are more brutal than in the secular society—witness recent arguments in the Episcopal Church in the United States over the ordination of practicing homosexuals. Yet in countless other, less sensationalized contexts, religious institutions find ways to tolerate significant internal diversity.

Finally, religious institutions are *symbolically rich*. They provide symbols, rituals, language, and stories that help shape the meaning of people's lives. These are powerful forces that can contribute to public ends. In the following pages I examine ways in which the cross, the Quran, the headscarf, the Christmas tree, the menorah, and a host of other symbols have set off firestorms of protest and been involved in significant disruptions, if not crises, of leadership. At the same time, religious symbols have been employed to powerful, constructive purposes. Martin Luther King Jr. led a march for voting rights from Selma to Montgomery, Alabama—an act that brought its own share of tension—while invoking the biblical imagery of the Exodus of Israelites out of bondage and toward the land of promise.

As sociologist Robert Bellah argued in a now classic essay published in 1967, U.S. presidents have sought to unify and mobilize Americans around what he called an American civil religion.[41] While this tradition is not Christian, it is deeply influenced by Christian symbols.[42] In this civil religion, U.S. history is narrated in religious terms: The early colonists and settlers were all pilgrims, and America is a city set upon a hill. Americans are seen as a kind of chosen people, whose destiny was to settle this new promised land. However, slavery was a kind of original sin, and redemption was necessary through the sacrifices of the Civil War. Prominent national holidays create a ritual calendar—besides Christmas, the country's "holy days" are Thanksgiving, Memorial Day, the Fourth of July, and so on. The speeches of the presidents and other top leaders are peppered with allusions that fit into this civil religion. Religious and civil-religious symbols are "often indicative of deep-seated values and commitments that are not made explicit in the course of everyday life."[43] As such, they help leaders shape a culture. They are powerful tools that can do either harm or good—to leaders and to the political community.

How leaders and citizens can most appropriately invoke religious symbols is indeed a critical component of "the vision thing." What vision of leadership can draw people together rather than dividing them along lines of difference? What vision will welcome the breadth of religious, spiritual, and moral diversity in the United States and the depth of symbol-laden expressions in public life?

3

From Tocqueville
to the War on Terror

America is "a nation with the soul of a church."
—G. K. Chesterton

Same Story, New Characters

IN 1951 THE MAINLINE PROTESTANT PERIODICAL THE *CHRISTIAN CENTURY* RAN AN editorial titled "Pluralism—National Menace." The editors were targeting a minority religion because it threatened to form a separate enclave within American society and, in the process, "to subvert the traditional American way of life." Published during a time of national anxiety, the editorial went on to suggest that "the plural society becomes particularly vulnerable to communist propaganda." The minority tradition in question was Roman Catholicism.[1]

More than five decades later we now face a different source of national and international anxiety—terrorism. Once again a religious minority group in the United States finds itself criticized as a threat to the peace and good order of our society. This time the group under fire is the Islamic community.[2]

According to the conventional wisdom, the post-9/11 period has been a terrible trial for Muslims in the United States. After all, the terrorists who attacked the World Trade Center and the Pentagon claimed to be acting as faithful Muslims—and in so doing, they in effect hijacked Islam itself. In the subsequent period, Muslims and people mistaken for Muslims have been the victims of various kinds of discrimination, harassment, and violence.

Islamic organizations have also received intense scrutiny from public authorities. A few charities have been shut down for their alleged support of persons or organizations linked to al Qaeda.[3] As a result of this surveillance and the personal complications that arise solely from being investigated for possible links to terror, many Muslims have reduced their contributions to charities, making these organizations' work even more difficult.[4]

Pundits and others with a public platform often ask why moderate Muslim leaders did not quickly and visibly reject terrorism committed in the name of Islam immediately after 9/11 or in the time since then. Leaders of Islamic institutions respond by expressing their frustration over the fact that they did immediately denounce acts of terrorism and that they have consistently done so.[5] The Muslim American community now faces the task of battling for the future of Islam.

Yet this is not the whole post-9/11 story. The ensuing years have allowed Americans from majority religions an opportunity to express their ignorance of and their desire to know more about their neighbors. Some Muslim citizens have reported that their fellow Americans are willing to ask them questions and to learn from them about Muslim beliefs and practices. Across the country, interreligious events such as open forums, worship services, picnics, and the like have multiplied since 2001.

The events of 9/11 and its aftermath simply turned up the volume on a perennial conversation—one that has been going on since colonial times—about the role of religion in the nation's public life. The discussion has merely taken on a new focus—and it has provided some new opportunities.

Consider, for example, the comments of Hesham Issawi, a Muslim and a Hollywood director, when he was asked whether the legacy of 9/11 is wholly bad:

> Well, for Arab[s] and Muslim[s], yeah, of course it is. But also it made people more aware. I mean, really, Americans start[ed] to ask questions, start[ed] to want to know. People are more curious after 9/11 about Muslims and Middle Eastern[ers], and especially about Islam. They ask a lot of questions. You know, who are the Muslims? Why [do] women wear scarves? How [do] they pray? All that stuff, yeah. And also for artists, you know, for—I mean as a storyteller, yeah, it did open the door to tell lots of stories.[6]

In addition, since 9/11 American Muslims and citizens from other traditions underrepresented in the nation's public life have had opportunities to embrace their identity publicly. The results have been mixed. The Council on American-Islamic Relations (CAIR) documented a rise in discrimination and harassment after 9/11. However, its study suggests that two opposing factors may have been at work. Although an actual increase in malevolent actions toward Muslims probably occurred, it was accompanied by a heightened sense of awareness on the part of Muslims (and perhaps even a sense of empowerment among the Muslim American community) to report these discriminatory acts.

This is not to say, of course, that the cloud of the war on terror has made life easier for Muslims in the United States. On the contrary. They have not been able to choose the terms of the conversation about faith and civic life, and much of that discussion has taken on an accusatory tone. Nonetheless, the atmosphere exists for a public reflection upon American and individual identity, for promoting tolerance and educating one another.

Not everyone welcomes such a conversation. In fact, much of the energy comes from observers who bemoan the loss of "Christian values" in our national life. Yet this is an adaptation of an ongoing lament. Before 9/11 some feared that America had become a godless society. After 9/11 the threat, in their view, came from competing gods.

As a point of comparison, consider Western Europe. There, as in the United States, the predominant discourse on religion concerns the increasing public role of Islam, but in Europe the decibel level is much higher. Some commentators have gone so far as to ask whether Islam will fill the void left by the loss of a so-called Christian ethos in Europe and result in the "Islamicization" of Europe.[7] Still, comments like those of Rep. Virgil Goode notwithstanding, the United States seems to lack the Europeans' fears that Islam will take over society as we know it if Americans do not act.[8] Thus, despite the ill effects of the war-on-terror rhetoric on the American Muslim community, an opportunity still exists in this nation to nudge the public's attention to religious diversity in positive directions.

Thus, in post-9/11 America, questions that have long been debated in our country have come back to the fore. What does it mean to be an American? Who are we as a people? How will we live together? At the same time, 9/11 added tension to that discussion, especially with regard to religious minorities. Yet we can take advantage of this moment by addressing religious identity and conflict in a direct way.

How did we get here? What has changed? What historic visions of America or past practices in public leadership can help us point the way forward?

Religion, America's First Political Institution

Nearly two centuries ago Tocqueville called religion the first of America's political institutions.[9] In his travels across the United States in 1831 and 1832 the

Frenchman observed a complex relationship between religion and democracy. As outside observers are often able to do, Tocqueville saw something that Americans had overlooked. His observations show up in contemporary debates, and, indeed, proponents of competing political positions often draw on Tocqueville's vision to justify their own.

I, too, might easily give in to the temptation to claim an understanding of Tocqueville perfectly in sync with my own arguments. But I do not claim that Tocqueville justifies a vision of an inclusive America. Rather, we must continue to explore his work critically. Although his work has some severe limitations as it relates to contemporary society, we can hold fast to his appreciation for an engaged citizenship.

Tocqueville published the two volumes of his masterwork, *Democracy in America*, in 1835 and 1840, about fifty years after the drafting and ratification of the Bill of Rights to the U.S. Constitution. The drafters, under the leadership of James Madison, had written into the First Amendment these twin principles: no legal establishment of any religion and religious freedom for all citizens.[10] The debates among the American founders are well documented—and, like the fight to own Tocqueville's legacy—they are hotly contested today.[11] Theologian Ronald Thiemann astutely argues that the founders took for granted that public virtue was the bedrock of the demands of citizenship. Yet, Thiemann continues, through the protections of the First Amendment and the rejection of any religious test for political office, the founders omitted the traditional source of such public virtue: a common, legally endorsed national religion. They simply assumed a culturally established "civic piety" based on American Protestantism.[12]

When Tocqueville visited the United States, he remarked on just how significant this civic piety had become. As a Roman Catholic, Tocqueville understood Catholicism's role in helping provide a moral foundation for public virtue. He viewed Christian faith, whether Protestant or Catholic, as the source of citizens' moral virtues and the motivation for civic duty. In this vein, Tocqueville had a particular fascination with religion's ability to serve as a buffer against the tides of disorder. He frequently expressed apprehension about the effects of equality resulting from democracy. Indeed, much of *Democracy in America* might be read as the internal struggle of a French aristocrat to understand how a democratic people could live in peace without a more hierarchical political structure.[13] What would prevent the American experiment from devolving into sheer chaos? As Tocqueville explained, it would be the order and moderation created by religious expression: "Despotism may be able to do without faith, but freedom cannot. . . . [W]hat can be done with a people master of itself if it is not subject to God?"[14]

Religion—in Tocqueville's case, Christian religion—creates in the hearts of citizens a moral law that functions where no formal law exists to prevent democracy from devolving into anarchy. It is in this context that Tocqueville describes Americans' religion "as the first of their political institutions, for although it did not give them the taste of liberty, it singularly facilitates their use thereof."[15]

George W. Bush frequently invoked Tocqueville in speeches to assert that his administration's faith-based initiative aligned with Tocqueville's vision of the importance of religion in American democracy:

> Tocqueville . . . really figured out America in a unique way when he said that Americans like to form association[s] in order to channel the individualistic inputs of our society to enable people to serve a cause greater than themselves. . . . Really, what we're doing is we're carrying on that philosophy today, a vision and philosophy . . . that gives us . . . responsibility for saving lives, a unique opportunity to empower people, encourage people, partner with people to save lives in America. And that's what we're here to talk about today.[16]

Nonetheless, it is a stretch to use Tocqueville to support government funding for faith-related services, which in essence contract some government services to faith-based organizations. The possible effects include not only government influence on religion but religious influence on government as well. As a way of avoiding these entanglements, Tocqueville makes the most fundamental component of his analysis his appreciation of the *indirect* effect of religion on the political system. He concurred with the common view of the Americans he met, all of whom believed that "the main reason for the quiet sway of religion over their country was the complete separation of church and state."[17]

The influence of religion was due precisely, Tocqueville observed, to the lack of official connection between religious and state institutions. Indeed, contrary to the European examples familiar to Tocqueville, the fact that clergy held no governmental positions and received no direct governmental support was stunning.[18] Religion is a fundamental political institution not because it is deeply entangled with politics but because it provides moral and civic formation for citizens. It is this indirect influence on the mores of Americans that makes religion significant for political life.

Tocqueville wondered whether creature comforts and the unbridled freedom of economic pursuit would be the downfall of American democracy. On this point, too, religion could play a vital public role by opposing the materialism of the American way of life. In more structured societies "the people finally get used to their poverty just as the rich do to their opulence," Tocqueville reasoned. "[W]hen distinctions of rank are blurred and privileges abolished, when patrimonies are divided up and education and freedom spread, the poor conceive an eager desire to acquire comfort, and the rich think of the danger of losing it."[19] The result, he noted, was anxiety for all classes. As an antidote, Tocqueville suggested that religion provides "the taste for the infinite and love of what is immortal."[20] Religion thus helps keep citizens from being consumed by materialism because they can place worldly things in perspective. If religion provides a safeguard against political anarchy, it also protects against the vanity of materialism.

What are the implications for political leaders?[21] On the question of civic piety, Tocqueville takes less for granted than the American founders did. In a five-page reflection, he calls on leaders to lift up religion, to highlight the sense of the "immortality of the soul," and to speak about the dangers of a materialist worldview.[22] He fears that, without religion, citizens will stray from morality. Thus, he urges political leaders not to tinker with people's basic beliefs lest—in moments of transition between beliefs—people be tempted by the "love of physical pleasures."[23] Tocqueville continues to emphasize the necessary independence of faith as a moral force, separate from but related to political affairs.

In this context, political leaders must promote civic piety in order for democracy to function. Furthermore, although he does not want political leaders to mistake themselves for clergy, Tocqueville does call politicians to model public virtue for the citizens they serve. For Tocqueville, it does not matter whether or not political leaders actually believe religious doctrine; they must act as if they do. Why? Because "only by conforming scrupulously to religious morality in great affairs" can they teach citizens to uphold morality in civic life.[24]

Thus, religion is a vital institution for democracy. Religious faith provides order by warding off the misguided view that we are nothing but physical matter. More than anything else, religion is a key source of public virtue. But whose religion is Tocqueville talking about? Is he domesticating Christian faith? Does his argument exclude other religions?

Tocqueville's Limited Vision

For all of his interesting and enduring observations about America, Tocqueville's vision was obscured by a number of factors. We have already noted that his aristocratic background led him to be skeptical of the benefits of equality. As much as he wanted to appreciate the American experiment, there is the sense that he found Americans to be simpletons, enjoying material comforts but not really understanding a finer culture (like France's). He was fascinated by American religious expression, but his analysis can read like that of a cultured anthropologist writing appreciatively—but condescendingly—about the tribe he is observing.

Tocqueville's Olympian view makes him speak of his subject as religion in general. He claims that religion is a part of human nature: "[M]ost religions are only general, simple, and practical means of teaching men that the soul is immortal."[25] In one passage, he goes on at length in what appears to be a universalist vein:

> There is an innumerable multitude of sects in the United States. They are all different in the worship they offer to the Creator, but all agree concerning the duties of men to one another. Each sect worships God in its own fashion, but all preach the same morality in the name of God. Though it is very important for man as an individual that his religion should be true, that is not the case for society. Society has nothing to fear or hope from another life; what is most important for it is not that all citizens should profess the true religion but that they should profess religion.[26]

Are we to take from these generic references that Tocqueville views all religions as functionally equivalent to one another? Certainly not. Tocqueville writes sweepingly about religion, but he is clearly referring to Christianity—a wide array of Protestantism along with Catholicism—when he writes about the breadth of American faith. The passage just cited continues in this way: "Moreover, all the sects in the United States belong to the great unity of Christendom, and Christian morality is everywhere the same."[27]

Tocqueville takes for granted that the diversity of religions in his civic/political analysis need not extend beyond Christianity. Other traditions (and even nonbelief) remain outside his main practical, political concern. "Christianity reigns without obstacles, by universal consent; consequently, as I have said elsewhere, everything in the moral field is certain and fixed."[28]

Tocqueville did not completely ignore Islam, however:

> Muhammed brought down from heaven and put into the Koran not religious doctrines only, but political maxims, criminal and civil laws, and scientific theories. The Gospels, on the other hand, deal only with the general relations between man and God and between man and man. Beyond that, they teach nothing and do not oblige people to believe anything. That alone, among a thousand reasons, is enough to show that Islam will not be able to hold its power long in ages of

enlightenment and democracy, while Christianity is destined to reign in such ages, as in all others.[29]

In four sentences Tocqueville discounts Islam's compatibility with democracy and reveals his view that Christianity supports democracy only because it stays afield from political matters.

This is a singularly important passage. It shows that Tocqueville's positive interpretation of religion as the first of America's political institutions depends upon seeing religion as a private matter, distinct from the political order. In this view, the relationship of democracy and Christianity works only because Christian leaders and Christian doctrines stay out of politics. In this sense, Tocqueville is expressing appreciation for a *domesticated* Christianity. Indeed, it is no coincidence that he praises Christian women in particular as those who shape the moral character of their families. "When the American [man] returns from the turmoil of politics to the bosom of the family, he immediately finds a perfect picture of order and peace."[30] In Tocqueville's account, in the home female models of Christian values relax the anxieties and turmoils that accompany public life.

From his perspective, Tocqueville could imagine neither Muslim, Jewish, Hindu, nor Buddhist citizens standing alongside Christians in public life; he also could not envision the Islamic faith supporting the politics of enlightened reason. Indeed, in his narrative, only European and American forms of Christianity were capable of sustaining democracy.

To his credit, Tocqueville did notice that the democratic polity and the "Anglo-Americans" who inhabited it were only one part of the American story.[31] Two minority communities inhabited American space—Native Americans and African Americans. Tocqueville recognized that each had been subjected to the tyranny of the "Anglo-Americans." His vision was expansive enough to see these undersides to the American experiment. The stories of two minority groups needed to be included in his account of America—even if he labeled his discussions "tangents" to the subject of democracy.[32] Certainly, Tocqueville accepted many of his hosts' stereotypes; he states that the African American slave "hardly notices his lot" and that the Native American prefers barbarity to civilization.[33] However, he also lambasted white Americans for their account of their so-called civilized treatment of Native American peoples, which in fact led to their oppression. And he foresaw that slavery would become incompatible with democracy.

So what does this discussion reveal about Tocqueville's vision of religion and public leadership? Most apparent is that his assumptions seriously limit its applicability to a society more complex and diverse than the America of his time. That is, while Tocqueville's account of religion in American public life appears at first to be quite wide (considering various sects to support democracy) and deep (viewing religion as important for political life), a closer examination exposes its limitations. It is only as wide as Christianity and only as deep as very generalized moral guidance.

This is not to deny that Tocqueville offers something of value for contemporary America, however. Even with his limitations, Tocqueville believed in an integral link between Christian religious conviction and American democracy. He believed that, in Thiemann's language, Christian values were a source of public virtues that would help hold the United States together in its early tumultuous period.

We should also appreciate Tocqueville's observations on the significance of religious commitment for America's voluntary associations. In Tocqueville's day and now in our own, many associations have religious affiliations. More than that, historian James Kloppenberg tells us, Tocqueville saw the key value of civic life—an "ethic of reciprocity"—as arising from the Christian tradition.[34]

Thus, conservative leaders who would today invoke Tocqueville are correct to state that Christian faith played a role in his vision of a flourishing democracy. Nonetheless, it is difficult to find in him any support for government sponsorship of faith-based activities. On the other hand, some liberals typically—and correctly—appreciate Tocqueville's account of civic activism but too often downplay the role of religious associations.

It is vital to connect Tocqueville's account of religion in the United States to his thoughtful discussion of majority and minority political influence. Tocqueville fears that the opinion of the majority may hold too much sway in the American system, dominating the political process and public conversation on any issue. The "tyranny of the majority" is an inherent danger in any democracy. Tocqueville defends the right of the majority's will but only within the bounds of justice.[35] He believes the possibility for tyranny is ever present in the American system even as he notes those factors that mitigate against such danger. A democracy that managed to ward off tyranny would remain open to deliberation and respectful of the rights of those in the minority. Yet it was not clear to Tocqueville that America could achieve that.

What does this potential for tyranny then demand of our political leaders? First, it means guarding against abuse of power by the majority by standing up for minority voices in the political order. It means refusing to enflame the passions of the majority against the minority through religious language or otherwise. It means creating a civic and political culture in which people are not ostracized for exercising unpopular or "sacrilegious" points of view. That kind of shunning of the minority, however, is exactly what Tocqueville saw in America.[36]

In this vein we can read Tocqueville's regard for the separation of church and state as an argument for protecting religious minorities (whether within or beyond the Christian tradition) from those in power who would impose religious beliefs or practices on them. As later chapters discuss, it is possible to embrace his perspective on institutional separation without accepting his fuller call to keep religion as a domestic (or domesticated) matter.

Can a variety of American religions indeed serve as a vital political institution? If the answer is to be yes, then they must together foster a culture of engaged citizenship, consistent with Tocqueville's vision of a flourishing political culture that protects minority viewpoints. But contrary to Tocqueville, a healthy democracy would fully incorporate myriad religious perspectives as sources of public virtue and respected voices in political debates. That would require more capacity to tolerate cacophony in the public sphere than Tocqueville's aristocratic ears could bear. How those multiple voices might hold together is an enduring question, one to which later American thinkers would respond.

Dueling Symphonies

The America Tocqueville visited had experienced only the beginning of the waves of immigration that, over the next century, would drastically change the nation's demographics. The decades before the Civil War brought Catholics and Jews to the United States to live alongside English and German Protestants in increasing numbers. At midcentury, Chinese and Japanese immigrants began arriving in California and the rest of the American West. They brought with them their own cultural and religious practices, including Buddhism. From the last two decades of the nineteenth century until World War I, millions more immigrants streamed into the United States, including Italian Catholics, eastern European Jews, and Sikhs, Muslims, and Hindus from the Indian subcontinent.[37]

The flood of immigration at the turn of the twentieth century led to a number of public responses. Beginning with the Chinese Exclusion Act of 1882, the government severely limited the number of Asians entering the United States. Southern and eastern European newcomers, who by the 1890s outnumbered immigrants from northern and western Europe, faced public backlashes. Catholics and Jews chose multiple strategies for engaging others within their own religious communities and for interacting with the wider American culture. Adherents of both traditions, however, were recipients of American nationalist criticism and discrimination.[38] The harsh treatment of these immigrant groups culminated in the Immigration Act of 1924, which reduced southern and eastern European inflow to a trickle—and excluded Asians altogether.

It is no wonder that new and competing visions for the United States had arisen during the early twentieth century. Was American identity being lost? Enriched? Transformed? How could everyone live together peaceably?

During that period two thinkers offered new visions for an America of immigrants. In effect, each was rejecting an isolationist or exclusionist view of the nation. Incredibly, both employed the same metaphor but to quite distinct ends. Each called America a symphony yet had in mind distinct musical and societal compositions. How would Americans with such different instruments and training learn to play music together? What (whose) music would they play? Israel Zangwill composed one score; Horace Kallen another.[39]

Zangwill is closely associated with the title image of his play *The Melting Pot*. A Jewish writer from London, Zangwill was, like Tocqueville, a foreign observer of American life who was intrigued by its ethnic, cultural, and religious diversity. *The Melting Pot* debuted in 1908 in Washington, D.C., to intense but short-lived public interest. Even President Theodore Roosevelt saw the play on opening night and enthusiastically praised its vision of America.

Zangwill's script communicated an idealistic vision of a strong, singular national identity: "America is God's Crucible, the great Melting-Pot where all the races of Europe are melting and re-forming!"[40] Zangwill hearkened back to images from colonial times and Ralph Waldo Emerson, but it was his play that secured the "melting pot" metaphor in the American public's imagination.[41]

The Melting Pot is first of all a love story between David Quixano and Vera Ruvendal. David is a Jewish immigrant from Russia who escaped the pogrom (rioting or violence against Jews) in his village. Vera is also a Russian immigrant, but, as a Christian, she had hated Jews in their common homeland. A gifted musician, David represents the hopeful immigrant who sees abundant opportunity in the United States. His dream is to write a musical masterpiece, which he calls his American symphony. Yet while David pours his heart into his "idealistic" score, his uncle, also an immigrant, must use his own musical skill simply to make a living.

David eventually achieves his dream, overcoming the hurdles all immigrants face in a new land. His passion and humanity, so brilliant in his American symphony, cause Vera to fall in love with him. In bringing the two together, the play is also a love story about America because there David and Vera can overcome the religious divisions that would elsewhere have kept them apart. This personal relationship across religious lines allows each character to be transformed. Vera overcomes her hatred of Jews.

David performs his American symphony on the Fourth of July—for a group of recent immigrants. And what does the masterpiece sound like? It is the song of "the real American," who, David says, "will be the fusion of all races, perhaps the coming superman. Ah, what a glorious Finale for my symphony—if I can only write it."[42]

President Roosevelt loved the play, leading Zangwill to dedicate the work to him when it was published in 1909. "We Americans are children of the crucible," the president said. "The crucible does not work unless it turns out those cast into it in one national mold."[43] Accordingly, the American symphony that Zangwill's lead character writes expresses a highly unified melody.

Sociologist Horace Kallen, an American Jew, countered with an alternative vision of national identity. In a 1915 essay in *The Nation*, Kallen acknowledged that the political unity that would result from a melting pot was indeed achievable. But at what cost? It would violate "the basic law of America itself, and the spirit of American institutions."[44] The Europeans had enforced political uniformity on their people but in so doing had oppressed minority groups across the continent. Kallen puts his point in musical terms, claiming that the unison so achieved would in fact be "the old Anglo-Saxon theme 'America.'" [45] Kallen preferred "a harmony, in which [the Anglo-Saxon] theme shall be dominant, perhaps among others but one among many, not the only one."[46]

Kallen's was a vision of "cultural pluralism." His American symphony would incorporate "the harmony and dissonances and discords" of the instruments played by diverse citizens. He pushes the symphony metaphor even further by suggesting that the players, having no musical score, would make up the tune as they went along.[47]

Cultural pluralism emphasizes the shared contribution—not just the toleration—of ethnic, cultural, and religious identities. Kallen argues that the melting down of immigrant identities is contrary to America's basic ideals. Rather than a melting pot, he argues, America should be a "nation of nationalities." Immigrants must be loyal to fundamental principles of American democracy. Within those constraints, however, immigrants should be welcome to express their cultural and linguistic identities, as well as their religious beliefs. These are the elements that would create in America "a multiplicity in unity, an orchestration of mankind."[48]

Notably, Kallen's cultural pluralism, like Zangwill's melting pot, focused on European immigrants. Asian immigrants, Native Americans, and African Americans are not players in either man's orchestra. Zangwill had defended himself against contemporary critics of his limited scope by noting—albeit with language that today reads as an unacceptable description of superior and inferior races—that David does refer to "black and yellow" in his melting pot.[49]

By the end of his career, Kallen had enlarged his own vision of American cultural pluralism to encompass various immigrants, as well as African Americans and Native Americans.[50]

When Kallen speaks of the American symphony, he emphasizes that all citizen-musicians can make their own musical sound without having to imitate the instruments of the predominant players. And so the musicians together determine the composition of the music. While Zangwill used this image to emphasize that immigrants can overcome differences to speak a common musical melody, Kallen's symphony highlights the harmonious music that results when diverse, yet aware, musicians improvise together.

Which vision of symphony is more appealing—the well-ordered, unified score or the more spontaneous, even cacophonous one? We still hear the dueling American symphonies in the background of contemporary debates. My own vision of an inclusive America has more in common with Kallen's vision than with Zangwill's. The more cacophonous the public sphere, the more citizens from diverse religious and moral backgrounds can share their symbols and stories to the benefit of our wider civic and political life. But that is getting ahead of the story.

Three Melting Pots or One World?

Fast-forward to the period after World War II. The Immigration and Naturalization Act of 1965 began another and more varied surge of immigrants entering the United States. What visions of America predominated in this period? What insights can we draw for leading a devout and diverse nation today?

The election of John F. Kennedy, a Roman Catholic, as U.S. president in 1960 was a watershed event. In 1928, stereotyping and bias may have contributed to the failure of Al Smith, a Catholic, to gain even 41 percent of the popular vote as the unsuccessful Democratic candidate for president. The anti-Catholic editorial that opened this chapter was published in a liberal-mainstream magazine only nine years before Kennedy's election. However, unlike those before him, John F. Kennedy was able to confront "the Catholic question" in politics and establish himself as a viable candidate—"despite" his faith. He famously told a Houston ministerial association: "I believe in an America where the separation of church and state is absolute—where no Catholic prelate would tell the President (should he be Catholic) how to act . . .—and where no man is denied public office merely because his religion differs from the President who might appoint him or the people who might elect him."[51] And he won.[52]

Kennedy succeeded in addressing his religious identity as the country was becoming increasingly aware of diversity. In 1955 Will Herberg had published his now classic work, *Protestant, Catholic, Jew.* The millions of immigrants who had come to this country over the previous century had radically changed America, and America had changed them. Nevertheless, Herberg rejected the idea that the identity of immigrants had melted away to reveal "American" citizens. Adapting the metaphor of the melting pot, he suggested that something less homogenizing but equally profound had happened. The United States had produced a "triple melting pot" grouped along the lines of Protestant, Catholic, and Jew. Each category served as a distinct melting pot that absorbed the immigrants from many ethnicities, nationalities, and religious traditions. Categories like Lutheran and Methodist, Orthodox and Reform, Irish-Catholic and Italian-Catholic certainly still had significance, but they were not as important as they had been in Europe or earlier in the United States, and their importance was still diminishing.

Herberg's image of the triple melting pot helps us understand the increasing acceptance of Catholics and Jews in public life. Earlier, critics had largely maintained that the original melting pot was essentially dominated by English or western European Protestantism. Now Catholics and Jews were undeniably a significant presence in and influence on U.S. public life. In this schema, Catholic and Jewish identity is compatible with American democratic life. "[B]eing a Protestant, a Catholic, or a Jew is understood as the specific way, and increasingly perhaps the only way, of being an American and locating oneself in American society," Herberg said.[53] The common commitment to American "civic piety," the ideal of the American way of life, was stronger than any religious differences among these groups.

As Herberg himself notes, the triple melting pot does not adequately encompass African American religions, however,[54] and it certainly does not reach the myriad traditions that were already present in the United States at that time and that would increase in significance after 1965. Herberg had this to say about individuals who were living outside the triple melting pot:

A convinced atheist, or an eccentric American who adopts Buddhism or Yoga, may identify himself to himself and find his stance in life in terms of his anti-religious ideology or exotic cult, although it is more than likely that a Yankee turned Buddhist would still be regarded as a "Protestant," albeit admittedly a queer one. But such people are few and far between in this country and are not even remotely significant in determining the American's understanding of himself.[55]

What are we to make of Herberg's sociological description of these minority religious and American identities? His book is surely a significant shift from an assimilationist account of the melting pot, in which religious identities are nearly lost or are transformed into a generic patriotic Protestantism. Herberg's analysis acknowledged and even helped shape the categories American Catholic and American Jew. Yet by defining what the triple melting pot includes, Herberg is also naming what it excludes.

Could the idea of multiple melting pots extend beyond the so-called Judeo-Christian bounds? One scholar notes the relevance of Herberg's approach, for instance, in describing how Hindus in the United States have downplayed regional distinctions, which are more fundamental in India, in order to construct a solid Hindu community in America.[56] This element of Herberg's work is valuable for viewing changes in contemporary society.

The more challenging question is whether Herberg's suggestion—that non-Christians and non-Jews are so "few and far between" in America that they are not significant for American identity—still stands. Even if he was more or less correct for America in the 1950s (no small assumption), his analysis is now outdated. The post-1965 wave of immigration did not change the fact that Christians remain a strong majority among those expressing a "religious preference" in the United States. The numbers of Muslims, Hindus, and Buddhists are considerable, but they remain small relative to the number of Christians. (Arriving at an accurate number of nonbelievers, atheists, and/or agnostics is arguably even more difficult.)

The numbers game is not the most important issue, however. Both the 1965–2001 and the post-9/11 periods have raised the public profile of religious minorities in American public life. Even the embattled visions of America tend to acknowledge the significance of minority religious traditions—albeit as a problem. The "exotics" and the "eccentrics" who did not fit under the Protestant, Catholic, or Jewish banner in 1950 command fuller attention today.

Ten years after the publication of Herberg's text, the Immigration Act of 1965 led to a rapid rise in immigration from around the world. Asian, Middle Eastern, Latin American, and African newcomers entered America alongside Europeans. Included among them were Hindus, Buddhists, Muslims, Jains, Sikhs, and Zoroastrians. And for the first time, Christians from the developing (or "two-thirds") world—many of whom had been converted by Christian missionaries from the United States—were coming to this nation as well. Hence substantial numbers of Latin American, Asian, and African immigrants were Protestants, including Evangelicals and Pentecostals, and Roman Catholics.

All of these factors together make immigrants who arrived in the past four decades a religiously wide-ranging group. A burgeoning academic and public literature chronicles this phenomenon and considers the impact of "world religions" in the United States.[57] Religion scholar Dwight Hopkins calls it "implosion," or a globalization at home.[58] The Pluralism Project at Harvard University dedicates itself to "mapping America's new religious diversity," and the project's director, Diana Eck, received the National Medal for the Humanities for her efforts to describe the changes to America's religious landscape.[59]

What did all of this newfound variety do to and for American public life? How have leaders helped us to make sense of it? Lyndon Johnson made diversity an important symbol of his presidency by signing the Immigration Act at the foot of the Statue of Liberty. He called the national quota system that had anchored U.S. immigration policy for forty-one years both unjust and "un-American in the highest sense." He offered his own idealistic vision of the United States as a microcosm of the world:

> Our beautiful America was built by a nation of strangers. From a hundred different places or more they have poured forth into an empty land, joining and blending in one mighty and irresistible tide. The land flourished because it was fed from so many sources—because it was nourished by so many cultures and traditions and peoples.[60]

This vision makes no mention of cultural conflicts or the need to be held together as one people. Johnson errs, certainly, by failing to state that the land was not actually "empty" before European settlers arrived. Slavery is also absent from his story. This is the rhetoric of America as the world, a peaceful nation built up by immigrants. From this idealistic land, Johnson envisions the following relationship with other nations: "We, because of what we are, feel safer and stronger in a world as varied as the people who make it up—a world where no country rules another and all countries can deal with the basic problems of human dignity and deal with those problems in its [sic] own way."[61]

The "America as the world" vision was also reflected in the second World's Parliament of Religions, held in Chicago in 1993. Convened one hundred years after the Chicago World's Fair and the first Parliament of Religions, the seven thousand delegates came from all over the world and an astounding array of religious traditions. As Eck emphasizes, however, the greater Chicago area alone already embodied the world's diversity. Indeed, it was a planning committee of local citizen-leaders from Chicago, representing the wide range of the "world's religions," who made the event happen.[62]

One central outcome of the 1993 parliament was the signing of a document titled "Towards a Global Ethic." Signed by two hundred leaders of different faiths, it called on all people to concern themselves with public issues such as nonviolence and respect for life, tolerance, gender equity, and economic justice.[63] The 1993 parliament and the quest for a global ethic displayed the dream of one world—a world that exists within the United States. This is a hopeful, albeit idealistic, vision.

The Cloud of Terror and Leadership beyond It

These "historic" visions inform ongoing public debate. They also provide resources we should recover to help us find our way in our conflicted times. Regardless of their limitations, the visions of Tocqueville, Zangwill, Kallen, Herberg, and Johnson all portray religious diversity as a key element of a healthy democracy.

In the best tradition of Tocqueville, Americans' religious beliefs and practices can together serve as a key political institution. Religious communities can foster a culture of engaged citizenship, and religious institutions and leaders can steer clear of direct influence in political matters. While training citizens in virtuous civic engagement, political leaders should avoid pandering to majoritarian religious groups and instead seek to protect religious minorities. In so doing they will encourage the presence of myriad religious voices in public life.

In the enduring duel between the two musical scores for the American symphony, we should above all be aware of the challenge of preserving ethnic, cultural, and religious identities while fostering a shared American identity. We cannot assume that religious commitment and citizenship go easily hand in hand. In more substantive terms, Kallen's caution about the losses associated with the melting pot seems particularly valuable in the era of the war on terror. In this period of tension over religion, ethnicity, and national origin, it is too easy to pressure people of minority backgrounds to give up their distinctive practices and deeply held convictions. America would be worse off if they did.

Herberg's analysis, especially as it contrasts with the fearful view of American Catholicism discussed at the beginning of the chapter, offers an exemplary hope for the incorporation of two minority religious communities (Judaism and Catholicism) into "the American way of life." To translate his analysis to a discussion of American Muslims or Hindus or humanists, however, requires a leap of imagination beyond Herberg's own vision.

The vision of America as the world evokes the hope of interreligious collaboration rather than the idea of religion as a source of evil or conflict. Not that the one-world advocates saw a peaceable or harmonious world; rather, they expressed optimism about religion's capacity to help overcome conflict. Today, in our society's unprecedented complexity, where our paths intersect daily with a remarkably varied set of people, we need a vision of leadership that is as realistic as it is hopeful. Yet it should also be every bit as forward looking as David Quixano's American symphony or Johnson's speech at the Statue of Liberty.

PART II

Exploring the Landscape

4

How Wide Is Our Lens?

Gradually it was disclosed to me that the line separating good and evil passes not through states, nor between classes, nor between political parties either, but right through every human heart, and through all human hearts.
—Aleksandr Solzshenitsyn

AMERICANS DISAGREE ON THE DEFINITION OF THE WAR AGAINST TERRORISM, ON THE severity of the threat, and on the nature of the enemy, but we all agree that our nerves are frayed. Newscasts blare vivid stories about plots to blow up American and international landmarks. Airport travel comes with orange (or yellow or red) terror-alert status signs. In the security line, we must strip down to our socks and place our most personal toiletries in clear Ziploc bags for all to see. And for citizens whose religious convictions lead them to wear a turban, a skullcap, or a veil, the level of anxiety and the potential for humiliation are even greater.

Security checks are frustrating for all. I once overheard a passenger say, as he returned his laptop to his briefcase and slipped on his shoes, "Damn these Muslims." His experience of post-9/11 security had silenced any better angel that might have helped him to accept Muslims as respectable fellow travelers. It had narrowed his field of vision.

Picture this man viewing the world through his own personal camera. Imagine that each of us has such a camera with its own lens. When we look through it, we see only part of the horizon surrounding us. A telephoto lens narrows the scope of our field of view, whereas a wide-angled lens broadens it. Analogously, how wide is the lens that we use to see our own national identity? Is it narrowly focused on one affiliation or tradition? Can it be zoomed out to encompass other identities and people from diverse backgrounds?

Amid tragedy, 9/11 created an occasion for such wide-angled solidarity not only among U.S. citizens and between political parties but also in the international community. The terrorist attacks killed citizens of some eighty countries. The dead included Christians, Jews, Muslims, Hindus, Sikhs, Buddhists, and people of no professed religion.[1] Words and acts of common grief and support were shared around the world. Europeans hung black flags of mourning over their parliament buildings. With much of the global community feeling as if it had been attacked, an opportunity arose to unite against terrorism. Seizing it, however, would have required leaders to embrace a wide vision.

The additional tragedy of 9/11 is that we have squandered much of the compassion offered by people and governments around the world. We have also, to a significant extent, lost the goodwill built up over time with moderate Muslim regimes in the Middle East, North Africa, and beyond. Even our relations with European allies have been strained by our government's response. In contrast to the international solidarity against terrorism that marked the turbulent days immediately following 9/11, American leaders have helped create and then taken on a vision of an "us-versus-them" world. In the current political climate, few, if any, well-articulated alternatives exist to this narrow approach to religious and cultural diversity. Republican and Democratic politicians alike criticized the Bush administration for particular aspects of the war on terror, but they often accepted its basic assumptions.[2]

Clashing Civilizations

On the fifth anniversary of the 9/11 terrorist attacks, President George W. Bush delivered a nationally televised address full of religious images, including reference to the Twenty-third Psalm and the image of Americans "united in prayer" with "confidence in our purpose, and faith in a loving God who made us free."[3] He seemed to suggest that God was on our side. Within that context, he restated his commitment to waging a war on terror. "This struggle has been called a clash of civilizations. In truth, it is a struggle for civilization. We are fighting to maintain the way of life enjoyed by free nations."[4]

When Harvard political scientist Samuel Huntington coined the term "clash of civilizations" in a 1993 essay, he was offering a new way to understand international affairs in the wake of the Cold War. Huntington viewed the West, the Islamic world, and the Confucian world as major civilization-based blocs that would shape the contours of the twenty-first century. "The fault lines between civilizations will be the battle lines of the future," he said.[5]

Bush had taken Huntington's thesis and made it American policy. He even upped the ante by equating civilization itself with the Western bloc. Was he thereby implying that the countries of the Islamic bloc are uncivilized? This is precisely how conservative newspaper editor and commentator Tony Blankley read Bush's remarks. In a congressional hearing later that week, Blankley sharply criticized Bush for his "presumptuous" suggestion that "a civilization that has been going on for a millennium and a half is not a civilization simply because it has vastly different approaches [from America's]."[6]

As a senator and during his 2008 run for the White House, John McCain sought to draw a distinction between a civilization-level conflict and a fight over ideas. In his "class day" speech at Columbia University in May of 2006, McCain described the struggle against al Qaeda in these terms:

> It is not a clash of civilizations. I believe, as I hope all Americans would believe, that no matter where people live, no matter their history or religious beliefs or the size of their GDP, all people share the desire to be free; to make by their own choices and industry better lives for themselves and their children. Human rights exist above the state and beyond history—they are God-given. They cannot be rescinded by one government any more than they can be granted by another. They inhabit the human heart, and from there, though they may be abridged, they can never be wrenched. This is a clash of ideals, a profound and terrible clash of ideals. It is a fight between right and wrong.[7]

Eighteen months later, McCain expanded his vision for reaching out to the Muslim world in an essay in *Foreign Affairs:*

> Defeating the terrorists who already threaten America is vital, but just as important is preventing a new generation of them from joining the fight. As president, I will employ every economic, diplomatic, political, legal, and ideological tool at our disposal to aid moderate Muslims—women's rights campaigners, labor leaders, lawyers, journalists, teachers, tolerant imams, and many others—who are resisting the well-financed campaign of extremism that is tearing Muslim societies apart.

In these statements McCain makes the key distinction between the terrorists of al Qaeda and the millions of moderate Muslims who should be America's allies. Although he does not state explicitly that some Americans are Muslims, too, his rejection of the civilization-based clash acknowledges that people can live with both identities. McCain rightly acknowledges that people from various regions and traditions can and do hold much in common, and thus a notion of clashing civilizations is flawed. At the same time, he states that the clash is one "between right and wrong," a phrase that retains much of the civilization clash's oppositional and confrontational vision. His remarks here resonate only a little with Lincoln's call for humility concerning the limits of what humans can know. Yet McCain's comments about common values leaves the door open for mutual engagement across religious and cultural divides. This would require, of course, an openness on all sides to learn and adapt from each other.

For his part, Bush noted that al Qaeda terrorists "are driven by a perverted vision of Islam." In other settings he stated that Islam is a religion of peace and that the United States seeks to stand with peaceable Muslims, both within and outside this nation. He deserves credit for his high-profile visit to the Islamic Center of Washington, D.C., in the days immediately following the 9/11 attacks.[8] Yet, his prominent reference to the clash of civilizations in a momentous address defaulted to a view of a monolithic, looming Islamic threat.

Others have been even looser in pointing a finger at Islam as a whole instead of at al Qaeda. During his bid for the 2008 Republican nomination for president, Rep. Tom Tancredo stated the following: "I believe that what we are fighting here [in the war on terror] is not just a small group of people who have hijacked a religion, but it is a civilization bent on destroying ours." He suggested that, in response to an al Qaeda attack in the United States, our president should consider bombing an Islamic holy site, even Mecca.[9]

Framing the war on terror as a clash of civilizations shifts the enemy, whether wittingly or unwittingly, from a group of radical terrorists to Islam itself. At a minimum it muddies the waters where the distinction is critical on military, political, and moral grounds.

In the days after 9/11, Bush invoked, on at least two public occasions, the language of a "crusade" against terror.[10] Crusade talk invokes earlier centuries of Christian-Muslim violence, not to mention the notion of a win-by-whatever-means mentality. Crusade, after all, is an approach to warfare that is opposed to just-war theory. To their credit, Bush's advisors acknowledged such references had been unintentional and unwise, and Bush avoided the term thereafter.

When our leaders choose to use the language of clashing civilizations, they add weight to the view, now taken for granted by too many, that Islam is principally a source of conflict or even violence and that it is inherently opposed to America and the West. In this view, religious adherents "on the other side" take their faith to the extreme—by being willing to commit acts of terror in the name of God. Unfortunately, U.S. leaders escalate the religious nature of the fight against terrorism by implying that God is on the side of the United States—and by suggesting that the line separating good and evil runs between Western civilization and the Islamic world.[11]

Enlisting God on the side of the West against Islam is not only presumptuous. It is also dangerous. Al Qaeda and its leaders want to create a worldwide battle between a global Muslim community (*ummah*) and an American-European-Israeli enemy. Invoking the image of a civilization clash—not to mention a crusade—to describe the war on terror plays right into al Qaeda's hands.

Clashes Closer to Home

"Fightin' words" are not reserved only for the international arena. Social issues have also maintained their high-pitched presence in public debate. In the early nineties sociologist James Davison Hunter coined the term "culture wars" to describe the fractious state of our political and civic culture. In the intervening years, key political-moral issues—abortion, capital punishment, gay rights, gun control, prayer in school, and so on—have not been settled. The ongoing culture wars pit traditionalists, among them religious conservatives, against progressives, who are sweepingly labeled secularists.[12]

New York Times columnist David Brooks painted the cultural divide as red America versus blue America.[13] This cultural partition does not correlate directly with political parties, though the "red" (Republican) and "blue" (Democrat) correspond with the electoral maps used to monitor elections. As former *Washington Post* reporter David Von Drehle succinctly asserts: "Politics in red-blue America is less the art of compromise than a clash of cultures."[14]

The culture wars narrative portrays religion as predominantly on the traditional, red side of the divide. More specifically, these frames place Christianity in the red, often grouping the terms *evangelical, conservative,* and *fundamentalist* together without attention to the complicated meanings of each of those terms. Religious-political groups like the Christian Right and, in earlier times, the Moral Majority belong here.

Ironically, on most social issues, immigrant Muslim citizens align with the traditionalist side,[15] but "red America," especially in post-9/11 times, has led a backlash against cultural pluralism and religious "outsiders" in favor of a "Christian nation" model. For their part, American Muslims expressed their dissatisfaction with Bush's first-term leadership by voting for John Kerry in strong numbers in 2004.[16]

Painting "blue America" or cultural and political progressives as secularists is also too simplistic. Progressives include many Protestant mainliners, white evangelicals, African Americans, Catholics, Jews, Muslims, and other religious "minorities," along with people who would call themselves spiritual but not religious. The recent ascension, for example, of a progressive evangelicalism, led by Rev. Jim Wallis of the Washington, D.C.–based Sojourners community, has been framed largely in terms of a religiously oriented political effort to counter those on the Religious Right. Yet the so-called Religious Left should be seen as wider than an evangelical Left or a Christian Left.

In reality, religious people and groups inhabit the Left, Right, and Center of American politics. Recent surveys have shown, on a related note, that while differences exist in Republicans' and Democrats' views on the role and importance of religious faith in politics, significant numbers in both parties believe that religion has a fundamental part to play. Amy Sullivan has traced the contemporary history of faith in presidential campaigning and governing, showing that the Democrats introduced faith into public view in a new way. Jimmy Carter, a Democrat self-identified as a born-again Christian, gave the famous (or infamous) *Playboy* interview in which he admitted, "I've committed adultery in my heart many times."[17] Later discourse attributed to conservatives the labels "Christian voters" and then "values voters," but this approach is too simplistic. Complicating the situation further is the fact that, at every point on the political spectrum, "religious citizens" include people from every tradition and subtradition. Seen differently, every religious group includes conservatives, moderates, and liberals. No wonder politicians, seeking to build up their support in all corners, have moved from sweeping generalizations to "microtargeting."

The twin images, the domestic culture wars and the international clash of civilizations, describe a bleak world reminiscent of Thomas Hobbes's "every man against every man." However, the world is far more complex than proponents of these theories would have you believe.

In moral terms, these models are inadequate because they exacerbate old divisions and create new tensions that make cultural-religious conflict a self-fulfilling prophecy. In the international context, current U.S. strategy is contributing to the ideological war that al Qaeda wants. In domestic terms, leaders help fuel a polarized public discourse that prevents us from forging practical ways to live together as equal citizens.

Just as important, the models of an embattled America create a narrow vision of who a "real" American is. No aspect of identity is more important on this issue than religion. Does religion divide and exclude? Or do religious commitments provide resources to help address our public challenges? The answer is more complicated than either question.

Are We a Christian Nation?

The normally articulate John Edwards found himself tongue tied when CNN correspondent Soledad O'Brien posed this question to him in a forum on faith featuring the leading Democratic presidential candidates in 2007:

O'BRIEN Do you think this is a Christian nation?

EDWARDS No, I think this is a nation—I mean I'm a Christian; there are lots of Christians in the United States of America. I mean, I have a deep and abiding love for my Lord, Jesus Christ, but that doesn't mean that those who come from the Jewish faith, those who come from the Muslim faith, those who come from—those who don't believe in the existence of God at all, that they don't—that they're not entitled to have their beliefs respected. They're absolutely entitled to have their beliefs respected. It is one of the basis [sic] for which our democracy was founded.[18]

Edwards knew the question is as divisive as they come. Those who would have answered "yes" will cite statements by American founders or the Supreme Court justices that call America a Christian nation. They typically fail to acknowledge, however, the rejection or qualification of the idea in the writings of founders such as Jefferson. Those who would say "no" appeal to the First Amendment to demonstrate that there is no official establishment of any religion. But they ignore the practices of official chaplains and public prayers that, even with a polite nod to diversity, have historically leaned Christian. The American "civil religion" can be invoked on either side of the question, as it clearly draws deeply on Christian theology without being Christian theology.[19] Thus, the question itself has become a flashpoint for warring factions, a litmus test in the culture wars.

In some cases, the clash of civilizations question relates directly to the Christian nation question. In 2003 Lieutenant General William Boykin, a U.S. deputy undersecretary of defense, came under significant criticism for making church appearances while dressed in military uniform. In his speeches he linked al Qaeda to Satan and said that Islamic terrorists were attacking the United States "because we're a Christian nation." He also referred to his role in the 1993 operations in Somalia against a Muslim warlord: "I knew that my God was a real God and his was an idol."[20] For Boykin, there was no distinction between his own Christian faith and that of America, and that faith was locked in global (or cosmic) battle with Islam.

Samuel Huntington also—albeit in less colorful language—ties religious identity to the clash of civilizations. After his widely read works on that topic, in 2004 Huntington published *Who Are We? The Challenges to America's National Identity*. Consistent with his international perspective, Huntington sees many potential threats to American identity, including immigration and the ideologies of multiculturalism and diversity. These challenges have arisen since 1965, but 9/11 increased the intensity of the threat to traditional American identity.

Huntington suggests that Christianity is part of the "core" of America's identity. To recapture it, he suggests, the nation must return to that core so as not to lose what makes it unique. Restoring Christian faith to public life, especially if it is transmuted into civil religion, will help achieve that end.

Is America, in Huntington's view, a Christian nation? Yes. A vast majority of Americans are Christians, he notes. He calls America "a predominantly Christian nation with a secular government."[21] The constitutional framers "prohibited an established national church in order to limit the power of government and to protect and strengthen religion," Huntington notes, overlooking the converse point about protecting government from institutional religious interference.[22] He emphasizes that, throughout the country's history, officials have called America a Christian nation and its population a Christian people.[23]

Have recent immigrants changed the situation? For Huntington, the answer to this question should follow the numbers. When he reads the demographics, he can claim that any increased religious diversity due to immigration is overshadowed by the boost to the Christian community by immigrants from Latin America, Asia, and the Arab world. In sharp retort, then, to scholars who have highlighted religious diversity in the United States, he concludes the following from these demographic patterns: "The increases in the membership of some non-Christian religions have not, to put it mildly, had any significant effect on America's Christian identity."[24]

What place do non-Christians have in Huntington's America? Surely they are to be tolerated, and surely Huntington would reject any form of overt discrimination against them. Yet he believes they should also recognize that America is a Christian nation. As he views it, "Given [a] general tolerance for religious diversity, non-Christian faiths have little alternative but to recognize and accept America as a Christian society. They are tiny minorities among a people overwhelmingly devoted to the Christian God and His Son."[25] He goes on to suggest that American civil religion, which "provides a religious blessing to what Americans feel they have in common," is compatible with American Christians of all kinds and other monotheists and deists. "It is not compatible,

however, with being atheist."[26] What this incompatibility means for U.S. atheists (or agnostic or secular humanists, etc.) is not clear. Huntington likewise
does not specify what the religious minorities' "acceptance" that America is a
Christian nation should mean in their everyday life.

Huntington's argument is essentially this: America is a Christian nation
because a strong majority of its people are Christians. The numbers have not
changed beyond the margins, so America is still Christian. Notwithstanding
the jump in judgment from individual religious affiliation to society-level
identity, this is a *descriptive* assertion. Clearly Huntington's book also has a
normative or *prescriptive* purpose. Huntington is not just describing society.
He is also suggesting that if America wants to remain strong and have a clear
identity—and why would it not?—then Americans should reclaim its core
values. This means rejecting the "cosmopolitan" vision, as Huntington labels
it, in which all peoples share their values in common; it also means rejecting
a vision that he calls "imperialist," which asserts U.S. supremacy over the
world. The alternative he favors, which he calls the "national" approach to
identity, requires Americans to "recognize and accept what distinguishes
America from other societies."[27] This includes cultivating its identity as a
Christian nation.

If we accept Huntington's line of reasoning, which assumes that the political, cultural, and moral significance of religious diversity is wholly determined
by demographic figures, then he is correct. No one disputes that Christians
make up an overwhelming majority of Americans. The generally accepted figure is about four-fifths of the population.[28]

Huntington cites Tocqueville with approval, but he seems to overlook
Tocqueville's warning that the tyranny of the majority is democracy's greatest
potential weakness. In asserting certain fundamental American values, Huntington in effect downplays others, including equality, freedom, and mutual
respect.[29] Upholding these values, as Tocqueville saw clearly, meant protecting
minorities from undue influence from the majority.

Because Huntington is quite general in his call to reclaim America as a
Christian nation, it would be easy for Christian leaders to see in his work a
justification—even if Huntington did not agree—for divisive demagoguery
drawing on their strength in numbers.

Take, for example, David Barton, who also believes that the United States
is a Christian nation. Named by *Time* in 2005 as one of the twenty-five most
influential evangelicals in America, Barton speaks across the country about
the loss of the country's Christian values.[30] Drawing on selective quotation
of the founders, he claims that America was essentially shaped by a group
of evangelical leaders who wanted to infuse the American government with

Christian values. "Was America ever a Christian nation? Well, according to the eyewitnesses—yes." Barton also looks at the present numbers to back up his claim: "[I]f 88% call themselves Christians, I would say, yeah, you probably have a fairly good basis to call it a Christian nation."[31]

We might discount Barton's view as simply less nuanced than Huntington's, but Barton's current political influence is clear. He has taken the language of a Christian nation out of abstract debates and into the policy arena. As vice chair of the Texas Republican party in 2004, he managed to insert into the official Republican platform the claim that "America is a Christian nation." The platform further stated that "We pledge to exert our influence toward a return to the original intent of the First Amendment and dispel the myth of the separation of church and state."[32] These are themes that Barton has raised through his Wallbuilders ministry.

Barton's influence extends beyond Texas. He was a regular participant in the late D. James Kennedy's annual Reclaiming America for Christ conferences in Fort Lauderdale, Florida, which regularly drew some eight hundred people. The Republican National Committee hired Barton to support George W. Bush's 2004 presidential campaign; Barton gave speeches to evangelical audiences across the country over the course of a year, urging them to support the Republican party.

If Huntington does not specify what political difference it makes for America to be a Christian nation, Barton leaves little doubt. Throwing Tocqueville's caution to the wind, he claims a Christian justification for prayer and Bible teaching in public schools, public displays of the Ten Commandments, legislation against abortion, and prohibition of gay marriage.[33] Moreover, he calls on ministers to preach and teach politics that reflect what he calls the "biblical point of view" and even maintains that churches can preserve their tax-exempt status while pastors endorse candidates "as long as they make it clear it's their own personal opinion and not an official church endorsement."[34] He unabashedly calls for Christians to support the Republican Party as an act of faithfulness.

It is important to note that the term *Christian nation* means different things to different people. Not all believe as Barton does that it has a direct political meaning. Sociologist of religion Christian Smith notes, based on empirical studies, that American evangelicals use the term *Christian America* in at least six ways. Some of these are directly political, while others connect more generally to a call for the nation to uphold moral values and principles:

[T]he belief that America was once a Christian nation does not necessarily mean a commitment to making it a "Christian" nation today, whatever that might mean. Some evangelicals do make this connection explicitly. But many discuss America's Christian heritage as a simple fact of history that they are not particularly interested in or optimistic about reclaiming.[35]

This discussion suggests that, when we ask whether America is a Christian nation, we should really ask, which Christian nation do we mean? For some people, calling the country Christian is a way of acknowledging the undeniable, significant, and varied roles Christian ideas and practices have had throughout U.S. history. For others it serves as a buzzword for a specific political agenda. In this latter sense it is a particularly narrow lens through which to view America.

Religious Minorities: Caught in the Cultural Crossfire?

For many Americans, the clash of civilizations and the culture wars remain distant from their everyday reality. Certainly, tighter security lines at airports are an annoyance. Nonetheless, it is otherwise possible to leave the topic of terrorism to CNN, Fox News, and the politicians — at least as long as the conflict stays off U.S. soil. Moreover, as sociologist of religion Alan Wolfe has argued, the culture wars make good fodder for the media's talking heads, but, for average Americans, we are, to cite Wolfe's book, *One Nation, After All*.[36] In other words, polarizing debates on hot-button issues do not accurately describe the beliefs of most Americans.

Yet for Americans whose own identity is part of the battle — whether they are minority groups based on race, national origin, sexual orientation, or religion — the situation is typically much more complicated. For example, millions of Muslim Americans face a reality in which a significant number of their fellow citizens view all Muslims with suspicion. More than any other religious group, Muslim citizens are ill affected by rhetoric of civilization clashes and culture wars. The notion of the West versus Islam calls into question their own overlapping identity. The separate-civilizations argument too easily suggests that it is impossible to be a faithful Muslim and a loyal American.[37] The rhetoric our public leaders use when talking about the war on terror, such as the careless use of "we" and "they," arguably exacerbates this suspicion.

Viewing America as a Christian nation raises the question, as we have seen, of what role people of other religious or moral backgrounds can enjoy in society. The answers vary, of course, based on one's particular vision of the Christian nation. From his perspective, David Barton suggests that Muslims in America, especially public leaders, bear the burden of proof to show how they can be peaceable contributors. It may not seem right, he says, but Muslims "share the same faith" as al Qaeda terrorists, and thus they must prove fellow Americans wrong in their assumptions about Islam.[38]

Even though we might discount the interpretation of a commentator-activist like David Barton, we are still left with the question of how Muslims, in Huntington's words, should properly recognize and accept the fact that they are living in a Christian nation. What would this mean for everyday life? Since 9/11, Muslim Americans have been forced to decide how much of their Muslim identity to express in public life. Some women, for instance, have chosen to wear the *hijab* (headscarf) out of pride for their tradition, whereas others have stopped doing so—thus denying what they understand to be a religious obligation—out of fear of discrimination. More than half of Muslims surveyed in a 2007 Pew Research Center poll reported being worried that women wearing the *hijab* would be treated poorly.[39]

It is important to state that seeing Muslims through the narrowing lenses of either a clash of civilizations or the notion of a Christian nation contrasts sharply with careful studies of the Muslim experience in the United States. The most rigorous survey to date, conducted in 2007 by the Pew Research Center, led to a report titled *Muslim Americans: Middle Class and Mostly Mainstream*. Noting the difficulties of accurately determining a population figure for Muslim Americans, the survey estimated that 0.6 percent of American adults, or 1.4 million adults, are Muslims.[40] Although they do not provide an estimate of the total, including children, they cite another Pew study with comparable results (1.5 million adult Muslim Americans), which estimates there are also 850,000 Muslim American children under 18. The study also cites other studies that give estimates ranging from about 1 million to 6 or 7 million Muslim Americans.[41]

The Pew researchers described Muslim Americans, of whom two-thirds are immigrants, as people who share most experiences and social opinions with other Americans. They are roughly as content in America as the mainstream, are slightly less civically engaged, and earn close to the overall median salary. Even the data on religious practice show roughly parallel patterns between Muslims and Christians in the country.[42]

On security and terrorism, Muslim Americans are more critical than Americans overall about the U.S. strategy in the war on terror. At the time of the survey, 75 percent of Muslim Americans disapproved of the decision to invade Iraq, whereas the comparable figure for the U.S. population overall was 47 percent.[43] The overwhelming majority reject terrorism.[44]

Yet this is not the image that comes through in the narrow visions we have examined in this chapter. Unfortunately, it is also not the typical impression of Muslim Americans that our media and many of our politicians convey. In light of the war on terrorism, Muslim Americans are viewed with suspicion— particularly in the embattled visions of America that we have been exploring. Citizens of other faith traditions, too, can be and have been left out of narrow visions of America. For their part, Jewish Americans are marginalized in distinct ways. Although Muslims have had a presence in the United States since the earliest slaves arrived in America, Jews were a much greater part of the nineteenth- and early twentieth-century waves of immigration. In the nineteenth century, Jews arriving from Western and then Eastern Europe were treated—as were Catholic immigrants—as outsiders. It was not until 2000 that a Jewish politician appeared on a campaign ticket of a major political party: Joseph Lieberman ran as Al Gore's running mate for the Democrats. Lieberman found himself criticized by the Anti-Defamation League, the ACLU, and Americans United for the Separation of Church and State for talking about the faith practices he would bring to public life.

In an apparent embrace of Jews into the common values of American public morality, politicians have in recent decades attempted to modify the image of a Christian nation through reference to the so-called Judeo-Christian heritage. This nod to commonality, in fact, allows Christians to employ symbols and images from their own tradition and to assume that Jews will go along.[45] But this should not cause us to lose sight of the "supercessionist" perspective that many Christians hold, presuming that Judaism has not changed since biblical times and that it was merely a precursor to Christianity.

For instance, when leaders talk about the Ten Commandments as something Christians and Jews have in common, the version of the commandments that is typically displayed in public is the Protestant, Christian one.[46] Talk of the Judeo-Christian tradition tends to suggest that Jews are welcomed as equals within the American mainstream while it overlooks the marginalization that they continue to face.

In fact, for some people who embrace the Christian nation vision, the addition of "Judeo-" to "Christian" is problematic. Kirk Fordice, former governor of Mississippi, spoke to the press at a 1992 meeting of Republican governors and referred to the country as a Christian nation. The governors' meeting had been intended to display the Republican party's inclusiveness. Governor Carroll A. Campbell Jr. of South Carolina then stepped to the microphone to expand Fordice's term to encompass the "Judeo-Christian heritage," explaining to reporters that he "just wanted to add the 'Judeo' part." Fordice's reply: "If I wanted to do that I would have done it."[47] The Republican national leaders went into damage-control mode, issuing a statement (without mentioning Fordice by name) that denounced "any statements that demean Americans on the basis of religious beliefs" and applauded religious diversity. Jewish groups also issued strong condemnations of Fordice's remarks.[48]

Muslims would seemingly be excluded from the boundaries of the Judeo-Christian tradition. Not so, argued the supervisors of Chesterfield County, Virginia. In their view, Muslims are indeed part of the Judeo-Christian tradition, at least for the purposes of determining who is eligible to pray before public county meetings. The point at issue in Chesterfield County, Virginia, was whether a Wiccan priestess, Cynthia Simpson, would be allowed to open a county supervisors' meeting with a prayer. The county had a longstanding practice of inviting local clergy to open the meetings. Nonetheless, the supervisors refused to invite Simpson to do an invocation. Why? Simpson wanted to know, and, receiving no adequate reply, she sued the county in 2003 for religious discrimination.

In its legal arguments, the Chesterfield County supervisors argued that American civil religion was based in the Judeo-Christian tradition.[49] Most invited clergy were Christians, but a few rabbis had been included as well. The county had one potential problem with this argument: It had also allowed an imam from the Islamic Center of Virginia to participate in the leading of prayers. The supervisors asserted that this practice was consistent with their position. Their legal case argued that Islam arose out of the Judeo-Christian tradition, noting the religions' shared Abrahamic roots and some common sacred texts. In this case, the defense argued that Islam is Judeo-Christian. There was no comment, of course, concerning how the Islamic tradition was thus invisibly subsumed in the term *Judeo-Christian*.

In this case the Judeo-Christian tradition was curiously defined, but it still had the effect of excluding a person from a minority tradition—Wicca—from public participation. Indeed, any notion of a Christian, Judeo-Christian, or Judeo-Christian-Muslim nation does not reach as wide as the religious, spiritual, or moral beliefs of all citizens. In the post-9/11 era, Muslims, Hindus, Sikhs, and Buddhists (alongside some minority Jews and Christians whose appearance made them look outside the mainstream) have suffered discrimination for their identity. Incidents against atheists and agnostics are also included in the FBI's religiously motivated hate crimes statistics. Like adherents of non-Christian religions, however, citizens without professed religious beliefs are excluded from the vision of a Christian nation.

Choosing a Wider Lens

The problem with leadership visions that focus on civilizational clashes and culture wars is that they define who is included in terms of who is not. In the view of the United States as a Christian nation, citizens who are Christians start in a more favored position than those who are not. The previous discussion of the Judeo-Christian tradition and the difficulties of defining who is in and who is out gives some idea of the complexities of defining American civic life with respect to religious values.

This is the wrong direction from which to be tackling the American "vision thing." Who is included and who is excluded? This is really a normative question— who *should* be in and who *should* be out? Contrary to what a respected scholar such as Samuel Huntington or a polemical figure such as David Barton or a politician appreciative of either man says, calling America a Christian nation cannot simply be a descriptive fact. Moreover, even as a mere description, it is a flawed way of reading U.S. history.[50]

Further, seeing America as a Christian nation turns the country into a battlefield. Some people like what it stands for; others do not. For many people, even those who affirm the term, its meaning is unclear. Whose religion fits and whose does not? Governors Kirk Fordice and Carroll Campbell gave different answers. The Chesterfield County board of supervisors gave yet another one. In all cases, however, the response is not merely a description of what America is; it is a vision for what America should be.

Advocates of a Christian America might say that I have missed the point. Citizens can call America a Christian nation with the best of intentions. To speak of the ways in which Christian citizens have drawn on their faith to contribute to the development of American society seems relevant and valuable. Yet, both intentions and effects matter. One effect of this language is that it suggests to religious minorities that they are not fully American.

The clash of civilizations is likewise a divisive vision of leadership that closely relates to a unified cultural vision of a Christian West. The relationship of Huntington's books on the civilization clash and on American identity makes that connection clear. For American Muslims (or for that matter Confucians or Hindus in the United States), the clash of civilizations cuts through one's own identity.

Critics might say that Huntington and political leaders who invoke him are merely describing the tensions that individuals and societies face in a world marked by division. Nonetheless, this framing of both world politics and identity politics is no mere description, especially when the president employed it to bolster support for national military and antiterrorism policies. Leaders should indeed try to get their citizens to act in certain ways and toward particular ends, but the visions we have examined in this chapter are unacceptably narrow.

How should we widen our perspective? First, we need leaders who do not divide the world according to one aspect of identity. Religious affiliation is a vital part of life for many people, but it is not the only thing. We must avoid the temptation to label people only—or primarily—by some particular faith. We need an understanding of citizen identity that captures various aspects of one's commitments, interests, and attributes. No one fits in a simple box.

Second, we should recognize that America's "first freedom"—grounded in the First Amendment's religion clauses—protects and includes all persons as full citizens regardless of religious affiliation or lack thereof. Reflecting on the Virginia Statute for Religious Freedom and its enduring significance, Jefferson expressly rejected a Christian vision of America. He noted that an amendment to the statute to include a reference to Jesus Christ had been soundly rejected. According to Jefferson, Virginia leaders "meant to comprehend, within the mantle of its protection, the Jew and the Gentile, the Christian and the Mohometan, the Hindoo, and Infidel of every denomination."[51] That inclusive protection is even more relevant today than it was in 1786.

Third and finally, all citizens deserve to stand for themselves. We must remember that no one Muslim speaks for all Muslims, and no single Christian speaks for all Christians. It is easy to lump people together and then divide them into teams, civilizations, or colors (whether black vs. white or red vs. blue). Rather than succumb to this temptation to take sides, we must choose a more inclusive approach based on equal regard for each person.

5

How Deep Is the Water?

So we secularists have come to believe that the best society would be one in which political action conducted in the name of religious belief is treated as a ladder up which our ancestors climbed, but one that now should be thrown away.

—Richard Rorty

WHY ALL OF THE TALK OF CULTURE WARS AND CIVILIZATION CLASHES? CAN'T WE all just get along? Why must some people drag their God into the public sphere? With all of the feelings stirred up by religion, it is no wonder that many Americans would like to exclude faith from public life.

Others would choose, rather than banishing faith altogether, to remove its "peculiar trappings"—beliefs, rituals, attire, and so on. The more generic, the better. The sentiment behind this—seeking common ground and thus avoiding the problems of religious particularity—is noble, but politely overlooking our differences is not a real alternative.

Think of exploring a lake or a river. From the surface, we can observe significant details. Where there are waves, the water is moving. Whitewater suggests rocks near the surface—and potential danger. Clear water gives us the opportunity to see a few feet or further beneath the surface. But even under the best of circumstances, our own vision at surface level does not allow us to see far into the water. A depth finder would enable us to learn how deep the waters are. An even fuller view, of course, would result from putting on scuba gear and jumping in. Staying at the surface of human interactions does not allow us to discover our own and others' profound religious traditions. To follow this metaphor through, however, it is true that it is a lot safer to keep out of the water—at least in the short term. Over time, given the presence of water all around us, it is prudent both to learn to swim and to identify the perils and opportunities of being underwater. In terms of analyzing religion's role in public life, staying at the surface overlooks the depth of resources that faith might have for our public life.

American Secularism

An array of recent books, essays, and editorials has called for religion's excommunication from public life. These have been driven, in part, by a backlash against the Christian Right. George W. Bush's unabashed discussion of his faith gave Christian conservatives an invitation to speak more openly and publicly about their own faith. Bush's references to his Christian faith journey are much discussed and debated. In 1999 Bush famously answered a question in a presidential debate on who his favorite political philosopher was: "Christ, because he changed my heart." As we have seen, Bush injected biblical references into many major addresses in ways that suggested the Christian narrative was equally familiar to all Americans. He used Christian language to articulate a dualistic worldview of good and evil, identifying America on the good side and calling America's opponents and anyone who assisted them evil. At the close of his speech marking the first anniversary of 9/11, Bush made this reference to the Gospel of John: "The light shines in the darkness. And the darkness will not overcome it."[1] In place of the faith in Jesus Christ named in the gospel, Bush's use of this passage suggested "the ideal of America" as the messianic hope of the world. That is, in the Gospel of John, the "light" refers to Jesus; Bush is substituting America for Jesus. Bush's faith gave him a sense of certainty and a distaste for ambiguity.[2]

Criticism of Bush's use of his personal faith in public office came from many voices, including fellow Christians such as disillusioned White House insider David Kuo and moderate Republican John Danforth, a former U.S. senator and an Episcopalian priest. These two figures still see a vital role for faith in public life, but they believe that Bush and the Christian Right have used faith in the wrong ways.[3]

Other critics offer a more radical response to what they call a fundamentalist takeover of America: They cry out for a secular society. Sam Harris's two books, *The End of Faith* and *Letter to a Christian Nation,* are meant to stir people to denounce religion in public life. Harris rightly takes to task the Christian Right's assumption that it holds an exclusive place in American politics. He enjoys exposing the hypocrisy of Christians who talk about compassion but then demean and threaten non-Christians.[4] Unfortunately, he condemns all believers with the same broad brush: "As we have seen, there is something that most Americans share with Osama bin Laden, the nineteen hijackers [of 9/11], and much of the Muslim world. We, too, cherish the idea that certain fantastic propositions can be believed without evidence."[5] He calls religious beliefs "both impossibly quaint and suicidally stupid," rooted in "absurdity."[6]

Inflammatory epistles like Harris's inject additional vitriol into our public life. Proponents of secularism can be as hypocritical as the Christians who talk compassion and then speak damnation. Harris calls for a more reasonable public sphere, but he volleys insult and condemnation.

Harris's cause has been helped by a group of authors criticizing the nature of religious faith and making a case for atheism in the contemporary moment. Perhaps most notable are Richard Dawkins and Christopher Hitchens, authors of their respective bestsellers *The God Delusion* and *God Is Not Great: How Religion Poisons Everything.*[7] Each writes in a tone of moral and intellectual superiority over anyone who might maintain a faith in anything beyond the scope of human rationality.

It is not just doctrinaire atheists who embrace a position of complete separation of religion and the state. The "strict separationist" reading of the First Amendment and Supreme Court jurisprudence offers an important and reasonable perspective, especially on the need to protect all Americans from the establishment of religion. Groups such as Americans United for the Separation of Church and State have spoken up when powerful religious groups try to impose their reading of morality on all Americans.

Yet even articulate leaders such as Rev. Barry W. Lynn, executive director of Americans United, easily revert to "fightin' words." Lynn's book *Piety and Politics: The Right-wing Assault on Religious Freedom* is more of a passionate call for than a reasoned explanation of secularism. Lynn, an ordained minister in the United Church of Christ, paints himself as the whipping boy of Pat Robertson and the late Jerry Falwell. More colorfully, Lynn casts himself as the shepherd boy David, thrown onto the made-for-TV battlefield against the Goliaths of the Christian Right. This trope may catch the reader's attention, but it also raises the level of public animosity.

Even more troubling, perhaps, Lynn's disillusionment with the Christian Right leads him to stray from his organization's core mission: to protect the government from religious influence. Rather, Lynn expresses his doubts about religion's role in politics in general. He does not dispute the right of conservatives and "moderate-to-liberal Christians" to fight over Christian insights for pressing social questions. However, he discounts the appropriateness of such discussions for policymaking debates.[8] He does not consider the possibility that they might be conducted respectfully and constructively. This is an unfortunate case of "mission creep," shifting from opposition to the official establishment of religion to a wider rejection of religion in the public sphere.

Going Spiritual

What is an appropriate alternative, then, to a form of secularism that would shun religious expression from public life? Secularists are right in one regard: Many forms of religion—and some expressions of atheism—seek to divide people rather than to uphold mutual respect. Can we accept this point without banishing religious and moral commitments from our politics?

A word has emerged in our contemporary vocabulary that promises to save us from our dilemma. Behind this word is a movement of sorts, but it is one that, somewhat ironically, claims to reject institutional affiliation. The word is "spirituality." The movement's mantra is "I'm spiritual but not religious."

For people who are spiritual but not religious, human life is more than rational deliberation, and it is more than instrumental calculation. Humans quest for something beyond themselves. For these Americans, churches, synagogues, and other institutions seem too focused on their bureaucratic structures or dogmatic positions to support seekers and doubters as they pursue questions of ultimate purpose.

Religion scholars such as Robert Fuller and Wade Clark Roof have demonstrated that these spiritual people are quite a disparate group.[9] For some, spirituality is a general name to capture a quest for meaning in their life. They might reject anything with overt reference to religion, God, or transcendence. For others, spiritual-but-not-religious means an avid curiosity, a desire to seek truths from a variety of religious traditions. An interest in Asian traditions brings an exotic feel to their journey. Some people embrace their spirituality as individuals; others find or establish communities for their shared alternative practices.

Arguably, spirituality is attractive precisely because the word is so flexible as to encompass almost any search for meaning.[10] In general, it describes those activities that preserve the prerogative of spiritual seekers to pick and choose their own combination of beliefs and practices. Religion, especially organized religion, thus becomes the object of critique because proponents of spirituality define it as dogmatically rigid and intolerant of dissent or even thoughtful reflection and questioning.

Unfortunately, many religious institutions do stifle independent thought. Nonetheless, the label of rigid dogmatism does not, of course, adhere to all religious perspectives or organizations. There is a certain irony in this point. Seekers defining an open and inclusive spirituality typically exclude religion because they see religion as exclusionary.

Welcoming spirituality but rejecting specific religious expressions from our politics merely avoids the toughest questions. If only it were so easy. Talk spirituality, but don't mention Jesus. Practice yoga, but don't connect it to any religious teaching. Meditate or pray, but don't let it get in the way of our politics. It is not that simple. Who can really draw the line between what is spiritual and what is religious? Who has the power to decide? And what do we tell people whose deepest obligations are determined to be (divisively) religious, not (acceptably) spiritual? We cannot ask them to dump their deepest commitments in the hope that it will create harmony.

The spiritual-but-not-religious approach may work for some individuals but is not a real solution for public interaction or public leadership. It does not answer what to do with religious adherents who accept, for example, the obligation to wear religious attire. It does not help those who find themselves in a moral quandary between their faith commitments and a particular public policy. It is admirable to try to find common ground among people of diverse backgrounds, but to declare that we are all spiritual and hope that this declaration suffices is a simplistic approach to a complicated reality. Like it or not, if we are to respect the identity of fellow citizens, we must acknowledge their religious commitments in all their specificity.

Getting Religion

While it is easy to name politicians who embrace the vision of a Christian America discussed in the previous chapter, it is rarer to find a serious American politician who would argue for a secular politics. A 2007 survey by the Pew Research Center for the People and the Press found that 69 percent of Americans either completely or mostly agreed that "it is important for the president to have strong religious beliefs."[11] Politicians have recently responded to this fact, but they have not always been so open.

In her book *The Party Faithful*, Amy Sullivan rightly notes that Jimmy Carter was the first president of the recent era to talk frequently and openly about his faith in Jesus Christ.[12] In the wake of Carter's electoral plunge and Ronald Reagan's active courting of Christian conservatives in 1980, Democrats began to shy away from talking about their faith, creating what Sullivan terms "the God gap" between Republicans and Democrats. Typifying the Democratic leadership in this era, Howard Dean expressed a cavalier attitude about faith, asserting that a church's refusal to permit a local bike path led him to quit his religion.[13] He later referred to the Old Testament book of Job, mistakenly calling it his favorite book in the New Testament.

During his 2000 presidential campaign Al Gore once stated that he liked to ask, when facing a tough decision, "What would Jesus do?" Gore had completed a year of study at Vanderbilt Divinity School. However, he tended to downplay his faith; his religious commitments are now more evident in his environmental leadership than they were on the campaign trail in 2000.

The Democratic candidate who "got religion" through a sort of political conversion experience was John Kerry, but it came too late for his campaign. In contrast, Bush continued to appear comfortable speaking about his faith. During the 2004 campaign, a series of Catholic bishops declared that Kerry, a Catholic with pro-choice convictions, should no longer receive communion in the Roman Catholic Church. Kerry had been reticent to talk about personal faith in the context of a political campaign, but in the wake of the bishops' statements he tried to shift course to alleviate mounting political pressure. By that time Kerry's talk about faith appeared to be no more than a defensive and opportunistic move made out of political desperation.[14]

In the 2008 presidential race candidates of both parties appeared to understand, from the earliest primary campaigning, that faith was part of the personal story that any viable candidate would need to communicate. For some candidates on both sides, this seemed natural. John Edwards, Mike Huckabee, and Hillary Clinton had clear histories of involvement in their respective faith traditions. Mitt Romney and Barack Obama, according to one poll, were considered to have the strongest faith.[15] Each was seen as coming from a minority tradition. Romney, as a Mormon, spoke for "family values" but was still viewed as a religious outsider, especially by conservative Christians, an important part of the Republican base. Obama, an African American in the Protestant mainline United Church of Christ, faced criticism for a faith journey influenced by a sometimes-controversial African American minister, Jeremiah Wright. In addition, Obama's father was Muslim, and Obama had been educated in a Catholic school and in a public school in Indonesia. Obama faced vague but persistent accusations that he had been educated in a Muslim *madrassa* (religious school) and that he had been under the influence of "radical Islam." Major news outlets, however, showed these accusations to be false. Nonetheless, their very existence—alongside provocative comments about race and other issues made by Jeremiah Wright—raised the question of whether Barack Obama was "mainstream enough" to be president.[16] This led Obama, in March 2008, to deliver a speech on race—and, to a significant extent, on religion—that sought to make the forging of unity from diversity

the defining theme of his campaign. Being identified with minority traditions created steep challenges for both Romney and Obama, who needed to
relate their own commitments to a common conversation about American
values.

For some other candidates, discussing faith was also a difficult task. After
John McCain had expressed disdain for leaders of the Christian Right in his
2000 presidential bid, calling Pat Robertson and Jerry Falwell "agents of intolerance," he found himself trying to build new bridges by talking about Christian faith. He even declared to a Beliefnet interviewer that he believed America
had been founded as a Christian nation and that a Christian president would
best be able to embody those values.[7] Yet even after he became the presump-
tive Republican nominee for president, he struggled to forge significant or
even sufficient support from Christian conservatives. His surprising selection
of running mate Sarah Palin, a Christian conservative, was partially a means to
energize a Republican religious base.

For a host of Catholic pro-choice candidates—Rudy Giuliani, Christopher Dodd, Bill Richardson, Joe Biden, and Dennis Kucinich—talking faith
quickly raised media questions about their conflicts with official church teaching against abortion. In the Republican primaries this issue proved to be a
stumbling block for Giuliani, who articulated a number of explanations for his
position.[8] However, he was able to deflect this criticism only by changing the
subject back to his lead issue—leadership against terrorism. His campaign fell
flat nonetheless.

Among the Democrats, Bill Richardson seemed particularly awkward in
talking about his role as a progressive Catholic politician. In an interview on
CNN, Paula Zahn asked Richardson about his position on abortion. This was
his response: "I am comfortable with that decision." After lauding efforts to
reduce abortions, he described the question as a personal matter between "a
woman and her God." He continued: "I respect the leadership of the pope
and my archbishop, who disagrees with me. But I think he is tolerant of my
view, as long as I continue to—to advance policies of social justice as a human
being." When Zahn asked about gay marriage, Richardson again said he was
"comfortable." Zahn followed up: "The pope is not comfortable with that position, Governor Richardson." Richardson replied, "Well, I know that. And I—I
respect the pope very much. And I'm sorry we're in conflict in some of these
issues."[9]

Richardson failed to name the struggle that many faithful and thoughtful
Catholics surely face in their own moral evaluation of topics like abortion and
sexuality. For them, it is a question of conflicting values related to authority and
community, faith and individual conscience. Even pro-choice Catholics do not

regard the pope as just another neighbor or public figure who deserves basic respect. This is a matter beyond emotional "comfort"; it is a question of fundamental convictions.

Even when politicians speak of faith, they sometimes depend on individualist assumptions about morality that fail to capture the complexity of religious commitment. Whether or not it is true, it can appear that some politicians have "gotten religion" for political ends. In the 2008 campaign, the field of candidates rejected secularism, but many embraced a "personal faith, public values" split that kept religion largely a matter of personal preference and without any binding authority. However, this approach leaves unacknowledged the actual conflicts that leaders and citizens face.

Academic Support

The view that religion should be kept out of public life has a solid academic pedigree. Indeed, the "domestication" of religion, in this sense, is a legacy of the sixteenth-century wars of religion and the rise of Enlightenment thinking. How could persons and groups of various Protestant and Catholic identities live together without killing each other? This question framed religion's role in public life as essentially negative: At least minimize religion's role in promoting violence.

Political liberalism put forth a conception of free, autonomous citizens who entered into the public, political sphere as individuals acting from reason. As I mention in chapter 2, Kant famously described religion as a *heteronomous* influence whose authority violated self-rule, or *autonomy*. If people were to be truly enlightened, they would need to renounce the outside authority of religion over their moral judgment.[20]

Jean-Jacques Rousseau's account of "civil religion" embraced a similarly suspicious view of religion. The quest for a unifying but shallow civic faith could be used to cultivate the allegiance of citizens to their state. This civil religion would have very few tenets—a belief in some deity and in immortality of the soul based on reward and punishment. Other religious beliefs were to be tolerated as long as they did not conflict with the state. Rousseau did not trust Christians, who would not make good soldiers because they might not fear death enough to fight hard for their nation. Loyalty to the state was the goal; religion must not get in the way of that.[21]

Recent scholarship in legal and political theory has started from the assumptions of political liberalism, the understanding that society is composed of free individuals who consent to govern and be governed but remain free to pursue their individual ends. Citizenship is the fundamental aspect of identity. Religion is a potential problem because it might challenge a citizen's loyalty to the state. Religious belief starts as a private matter; the question becomes how much, if any, of that private identity to welcome into the public sphere. For traditional political liberals, the answer is essentially none. Religion remains a private matter.

The most influential voice in this discussion has been the late philosopher John Rawls. In *Political Liberalism,* Rawls took a stringent line on the duty of fellow citizens and our leaders to communicate to one another in language that all could understand.[22] Rawls's prioritizing of the values of civility and mutual respect was certainly well placed. He interpreted these values to mean that, in practice, citizens and leaders should limit themselves to communicate only in the language of what he called "public reason."

Its application, however, was too limiting. Rawls recommended that we communicate to each other in public policy debate by "public reason." The language of public reason includes "non-sectarian" arguments based on principles held in common by all citizens. Yet, determining what political, moral, or scientific values are noncontroversial is itself a matter of debate.[23] Even if we could concur, however, on what public reason entailed, this limiting of public speech would produce a very shallow moral discussion.

Rawls himself acknowledged the shortcomings of his approach. In his aptly titled "The Idea of Public Reason Revisited," Rawls accommodated some of his critics' objections.[24] He allowed for appropriate roles for religious speech in political debate under certain circumstances. Christian arguments against slavery and for civil rights have played important roles in U.S. history, he recognized. Still, Rawls maintained, those who invoke religious speech should connect or translate their ideas to fundamental political values. He also foresaw a time when public reason itself would be "complete" or sufficient for conducting our moral and policy deliberations. When this came to pass, religion would not be needed for a well-ordered democratic life.[25]

Even in Rawls's revised perspective, the constraints on religion are overly burdensome. His presumption is that our default language is secular, based on something called public reason, which all citizens can recognize. Rawls places the burden on religious citizens to translate their deepest convictions into a public Esperanto, or common international language, so that they can be understood. In this least-common-denominator approach, citizens must leave many moral and religious resources in the private sphere. Public reason unnecessarily limits the depth of moral deliberation.

The Problem of Practices

Despite these criticisms, Rawls's revised position is arguably the most articulate statement on religion's role in public life within contemporary political philosophy. The real problem with even Rawls's nuanced account, however, is that it views religion essentially as a set of beliefs that are converted into arguments for policy.

How we talk to one another as we lead and are led and as we work together to enact just policies is fundamentally important. But the religion-as-belief argument neglects the plethora of practical, everyday questions of religious practice in public life.

It is one thing to discuss whether appeals to the question, What would Jesus would do?, are valid and helpful in policy debates. What is justice according to a Jewish or a Buddhist text—and can we discuss that in public? It is a related but different question to ask whether the people making those arguments can practice their religious commitments in public life. Can employees in corporate, nonprofit, and government jobs wear their religious garb without repercussions? Will the Senate be in session during Jewish high holy days? Will the city council host a luncheon during Ramadan, when Muslims are instructed not to eat from sunup to sundown? These questions are ones of practice.

Before Joseph Lieberman was named to the Democratic ticket as vice-presidential candidate in 2000, he faced public questions about how he would handle his observation, as an Orthodox Jew, of stringent Sabbath obligations not to work. The conservative *Weekly Standard* questioned his fitness for office because of his strict Sabbath rules. Lieberman had faced similar questions during his two prior Senate elections, but the executive responsibilities of the vice president (who is also a "heartbeat away" from the presidency) added urgency to the issue. He faced a similar line of questioning in his presidential campaign in 2004. Lieberman's answer was nuanced and thoughtful: He would do his best to uphold his religious obligations and avoid any strictly political activities but not hesitate to do what was necessary to govern.

It is important to acknowledge that issues of everyday practices—attire, food, holidays, and other matters of schedule and calendar—affect minority individuals and communities more than majority ones. That is to say, for the most part, our public and workplace calendars are set to accommodate Christian practices. The workweek was built around keeping the Christian day of rest (whether seen as Sunday for most Christians or Saturday for "sabbatarian" Christians) on the weekend. Of course, many economically vulnerable people (of whatever background) had to work whenever they needed to in order to make ends meet. At present, Americans are working longer hours, and many people still face economic pressures to work through the weekend. Nonetheless, in overall terms, the Islamic call for Friday midday communal prayers poses more of a challenge for Muslims than Saturday or Sunday worship does for Jews or Christians.

The Jewish Sabbath (from Friday until Saturday evening) falls on the weekend. In annual-calendar terms, however, the Jewish high holy days arrive in September or October, just as American political, business, and educational activity is running at full tilt after summer vacations. American Christians, in contrast, can enjoy Christmas at the beginning of a traditionally "slow week" for public life. Admittedly, Christian holy week (often coinciding with Passover) is a less definitive force on the American calendar, though many schools and some other institutions close or slow down. It often determines educational institutions' spring break.

Frequently, well-intentioned public leaders seek to accommodate America's diverse religious and cultural traditions. This usually happens in December at "Christmas time." (It's actually Christian Advent, but that is a topic for another day.) The intended result is a multicultural festival to celebrate diversity. The actual result is more complicated: First, minority communities ramp up the significance of minor holidays (like Chanukah) or create festivals (like Kwanzaa) so as to have a voice. Those who celebrate the winter solstice receive little public attention, even as they hear the public messages of more predominant groups. And some Christians get defensive about how their holiday has been "relativized" or even trivialized by so-called political correctness. Many people—Christians, Jews, and others—lament the way that the religious symbolism of their holidays has been used to fuel commercialism.

In terms of attire, minority groups must seek accommodation precisely because their practices are seen as different. In Jordan, for instance, to wear *hijab* (headscarf) does not require an accommodation, but in most American public settings, it does. Most (but not all) Christians and Jews wear Western dress. Many Buddhists, Muslims, and Hindus do as well. However, requests for accommodation of a veil, turban, skullcap, robe, and so on come disproportionately from those outside of the majority.

It is easier for members in privileged or mainstream positions to think that strict secularism might be an adequate alternative to all of these complicated questions of what is allowed, what is not, and what exceptions should be made. Those of us in the majority tradition of Christianity have already been accommodated to a significant degree. Thus, "shallow" visions of public life are more compatible with majority traditions that have helped shape it. In contrast, for members of traditions that differ from the predominant or "mainstream" practices, shallowness—like narrowness—limits their religious expression.

French Lessons

Whose religious practices should be welcome, and what should be left out? Who has the power to decide? These are fundamental questions for any diverse society. France has been a case in point. That nation's ban on the headscarf and other "ostentatious" religious symbols in public schools drew American criticism from the Left, Right, and Center, from politicians and religious leaders alike.

In March of 2004 French president Jacques Chirac signed into law a statute making it unacceptable for students in state-funded schools to wear any overtly religious symbols. Specifically targeting the *hijab,* the law also applied to things like the yarmulke and the turban, as well as religious jewelry bigger than small pendants. Since 2004, dozens of students have been expelled from French public schools and private schools funded by the government as a result of the law.

The ban was framed within the context of France's policy, established in 1905, of *laicité,* loosely translated as secularism or the separation of religion and the state. This policy was shaped in the context of French Republicanism, a tradition influenced by Rousseau's caution about religious commitment.[26] Even more directly relevant to the French were issues of Muslim immigration, particularly from France's former colonies like Algeria. In recent decades it had become increasingly common for French Muslims to wear "conspicuous" symbols like the headscarf in public life. As indicated by the 2005 riots of Muslim youths in the outskirts of Paris, tensions concerning the integration of Muslims and other French residents remain high.

Muslims now number an estimated 5–8 million people in a country of 61 million. The success of Jean Marie Le Pen and his ultraconservative National Front party in the presidential election of 2002—he placed second in the initial voting, surpassing the Left's established candidate—revealed a great deal of anti-immigrant sentiment in France.

In this context, public and political pressure mounted to formalize into law a strict interpretation of *laicité* in government-sponsored schools. In 2003 President Chirac appointed a high-profile commission to study the issue and make recommendations. He moved quickly to propose the ban against conspicuous religious symbols. The measure passed easily through the legislature and had the support of all of the major parties and a strong majority of French citizens. A majority of Muslims, however, opposed the law.

Public discourse around the issue focused on the role of Islam in public life vis-à-vis French identity. A leading analyst of the case, social anthropologist John R. Bowen, notes that one belief received near consensus: The headscarf ban would protect Muslim girls from a religious dictate that made them appear subservient and hence violated their dignity.[27]

A United Nations office on religious expression found that the law "protect[ed] the autonomy of minors who may be pressured or forced to wear a headscarf or other religious symbols." Yet, the UN report continued, the state's headscarf ban could also violate the autonomy of "minors who have freely chosen to wear a religious symbol to school as a part of their religious belief."[28]

Although targeted at Muslims, the law forbids all overt symbols—although, significantly, it allows for small symbols on necklaces, for instance, such as a cross, a star of David, or Fatima's hands. The Jewish yarmulke and the Sikh turban were also outlawed. In fact, Sikh students have already been expelled from schools as a result of this ban.

Leaders of the Sikh community chose an interesting strategy to oppose the ban and to seek exception from the law once it was passed. They argued that the turban is not a religious symbol after all. Rather, it was a *cultural* or an *ethnic* symbol and therefore should not be considered within the purview of the prohibition. Thus, instead of remaining in solidarity with Muslims and other religious adherents caught in the ban's snare, Sikh leaders chose to go it alone and appeal—unsuccessfully—their own community's case.[29]

Observers in the United States found this law to be an outrage. (This is not to say, of course, that there were not at least a few staunch critics of Islam who were willing to look past the restriction on religious expression in order to stop the so-called spread of Islam in the West.) The Bush administration expressed dismay over the law; the State Department's annual report on France and religious freedom has cited the concern of religious minorities about the law's effect on their religious liberty; and the U.S. Commission on International Religious Freedom stated strong disapproval of the ban, which "threatens the religious freedom of many in France, especially Muslim women and girls, Jews, and Sikhs."[30]

The strong U.S. public response to the headscarf ban reveals a common baseline for dealing with religious symbols in American civic life. Americans may not agree about the fine lines of the appropriateness of religious expression by our citizens and our leaders, but when a law runs counter to our fundamental convictions about the freedom of religious expression, we oppose it.

Leaving the Shallow Waters

The secular and spiritual approaches to public life offer alternative visions in light of the very real problem of the potential divisiveness of religious expression. Besides the challenge of variety itself, we cannot and should not be fully value neutral with regard to various worldviews. In the end, we must be willing to agree, as a society, about what general guidelines will shape our legal and moral environment. More to the point, we must together determine what worldviews—such as ones that would call for indiscriminate violence against innocent people—are unacceptable for public life.

It should not matter whether adherents of violent ideas say they are motivated by religious, philosophical, moral, or political ideas. Under secularism, religious ideas as a whole are banished from civic and political debate, but purely political ideas are not—all in the name of promoting harmony. Scientists speak of two kinds of errors—alpha errors and beta errors. In this case, the alpha error would be banishing perfectly peaceable religious ideas, with their constructive resources for solving public problems. The beta error would be tolerating those nonreligious ideas that incite violence. Secularism appears to allow both types of errors—excluding peaceable moral resources on the grounds they are religious and assuming that viewpoints are peaceable because they are not religious. We need a better formula than "religion out, politics in."

We should also acknowledge that secularism itself is based upon a particular set of values. Consider again the French case. The *laïcité* of twentieth-century and contemporary France is justified on the grounds of the core French values—*liberté, égalité,* and *fraternité.* The French certainly do not exclude values from public life—just religious ones. The French way might not be able to eliminate the beta error of political speech that inspires violence. The very effort to crack down on the religious attire of Muslims, many of whom are immigrants, was an outgrowth, at least in part, of the success of the ultrarightist Le Pen and his National Front, whose vision bolsters anti-immigrant sentiment. French secularism constrained the liberties of religious schoolchildren, but it seemed responsive toward the severe anti-immigrant sentiment of Le Pen's ultrarightists. Even if the French can quell political appeals that incite hatred and violence, however, the alpha error of excluding religious perspectives from public life remains.

Spiritual-but-not-religious is also a deeply value-laden approach. Like the secular way, the spiritual values themselves are laudable: inclusivity, equality, autonomy. Yet these ideals are too readily applied to achieve an easy universalism. Everyone has a higher power, it seems, and we simply need to embrace that fact in order to get along. As long as one's spiritual expression does not demand anything from us that affects our behavior, there is no problem. In many ways in this spiritual approach, the same alpha error persists. Specific religious practices are left out because they are portrayed as dogmatic or rigid. This approach excludes religious critiques of injustice from conservatives and liberals alike because they are seen as divisive. Even John Rawls, in his call to craft a politics in which public reason is our common language, realized that it would be a pity to lose the contribution of religious language to establishing basic justice in our society.

We must listen to the voices of secularists and the spiritual-but-not-religious people who fear the power of religion to fuel hate and curtail freedom. Yet, we need a way to welcome those deep religious commitments of diverse citizens who wish to contribute to a better public life.

In his famous "Letter from Birmingham City Jail," Dr. Martin Luther King Jr. addressed white moderate clergy who questioned his fight for civil rights. Though the argument of King's letter is certainly context specific, his overarching vision is timeless. King refused to accept a domesticated view of religion that kept hidden the calls for social change needed to correct injustice. He rejected the idea that religiously motivated citizens should be discounted as radicals:

> But though I was initially disappointed at being categorized as an extremist, as I continued to think about the matter I gradually gained a measure of satisfaction from the label. Was not Jesus an extremist for love: "Love your enemies, bless them that curse you, do good to them that hate you, and pray for them which despitefully use you, and persecute you." Was not Amos an extremist for justice: "Let justice roll down like waters and righteousness like an ever-flowing stream."...And Abraham Lincoln: "This nation cannot survive half slave and half free." And Thomas Jefferson: "We hold these truths to be self-evident, that all men are created equal..." So the question is not whether we will be extremists, but what kind of extremists we will be.[31]

From the perspective of leadership, we must create a moral environment in which we welcome people to express their deepest convictions. These may be religious, spiritual, moral, and political views—and for some people and in some circumstances, these may be extreme. The great power of the First

Amendment is the fundamental importance of such expression. We also presume a basic legal framework to protect all Americans from violence and infringement on their rights.

Within those legal parameters we need a civic culture in which fellow citizens recognize the difference between, in King's words, extremists of love and extremists of hate. We need leaders and citizens who are willing and able to work together to cultivate such a culture.

6

Crossing Paths

When anyone of them prayed in Hebrew, he was unable adequately to express his needs or recount the praises of God, without mixing Hebrew with other languages.

—Maimonides

Mixing Metaphors, Mixing People

COMPETING VISIONS OF AMERICAN IDENTITY SWIRL AROUND OUR POLITICS. IDEAS like the Christian nation, the clash of civilizations, blue-versus-red America, and the culture wars keep us thinking narrowly about American public life. Visions of a secular society and generic spirituality appeal to a broader but shallower America. The notions of cultural pluralism and the melting pot emphasize, respectively, the many identities of Americans and the one, unified nation that should arise if diverse citizens come together. And an American symphony sounds quite different depending on whether the composer is the melting-pot visionary Israel Zangwill or the cultural pluralist Horace Kallen.

The fundamental issue, in the end, is not the mixing of metaphors but the mixing of people: people of diverse experiences and complex identities; people who cannot easily be labeled by a single tradition, attribute, or affiliation; people whose commitments shape their choice to dress, act, or serve differently than others do; people who have the capacity to do good as well as ill—to themselves, loved ones, fellow citizens, and outsiders.

The competing and mixed metaphors result from our struggle, then, to find language adequate to the task of understanding the complexities of American identity in a devout and diverse nation. How can we create a more inclusive America? What kind of leadership is needed in an increasingly varied country? These questions are by no means new, as I have shown via the ideas of Jefferson and Tocqueville, Zangwill and Kallen, Herberg and Johnson, Huntington and Eck. Yet the realities of a post-9/11 globalizing world have raised the stakes of identity politics, and our changed context demands that we think in new ways about our leadership.

Into the mix of battle cries, melting pots, and musical scores I want to add a few ideas. We should engage each other not in a politics of fear but of *convivencia*. We should view the American terrain with a wide-angled lens to include the array of people that inhabit it. And we should recognize the depth of religious and moral expressions. Only then can we appeal, as Lincoln said, to each other's better angels, not to our worst instincts.

Americans are living "on common ground," to use the title of an important reference work about religious pluralism in America.[1] Despite the shared landscape, however, different individuals and communities are following their respective religious pathways. For most Americans, this is a figurative journey, though there are also those from a variety of spiritual traditions who embark on literal pilgrimages. Whether symbolic or geographic, do those paths remain largely divergent—or even protected against interlopers? What happens when the paths inevitably cross?

Spanish Lessons

On the main highway south from Madrid to the Mediterranean coast, drivers see evidence of a changing Spain. The road signs to Almería, a coastal province, and to Algeciras, a gateway city to Africa, are written in both Spanish and Arabic. This is just one of the many indicators of the influx of immigrants from *el Magreb,* as the Spanish call it, or northern Africa. Estimates place this predominantly Arab population in Spain at between five hundred thousand and one million people. The rate of immigration into Spain, dominated by people from Arab countries (alongside Latin Americans), has increased fourfold since 1998.[2] The number of Islamic communities registered with Spain's Ministry of Justice has similarly vaulted upward over the past decade, from 74 to 406.[3]

Like their American counterparts, Spaniards are engaged in a vibrant, sometimes noisy public discussion over their national identity, especially as it relates to religious and cultural differences. After the death of dictator Francisco Franco in 1975, Spaniards opted for a democratic federalism that granted a great deal of authority to the aptly named "autonomous regions." Spaniards in regions like Galicia and Catalonia are accustomed to seeing street signs in two languages—Castilian Spanish and the regional language. Nonetheless, the appearance of signs in Arabic indicates a new reality, a different degree of cross-cultural experience—with echoes not from the post-Franco democratic transition but rather from medieval, Moorish Spain.

Notably, the Basque region in Spain has experienced the debate over identity through the lens of a violent struggle by a minority group of Basque separatists who continue to support the terrorist group ETA. Indeed, all discussions of cultural diversity in Spain are significantly colored by the enduring problem of ETA violence.

It is not surprising that the ETA was blamed when, just prior to the 2004 Spanish national election, terrorists bombed trains in and near Madrid's historic Atocha rail station, killing 191 people. The Popular Party (PP), then in power under Prime Minister José María Aznar, attempted to blame the ETA for these bombings. Why? The PP, which had cooperated with the Bush administration on Iraq, did not want to be seen by the electorate as having provoked an al Qaeda attack on the Spanish people. The attempted deflection of blame to the ETA was a stunning political failure, and the leftist coalition led by the Socialist party (PSOE) regained national power. As Spaniards consistently name terrorism as one of the top two national issues—along with the economy—they are sweeping together the ETA and al Qaeda as threats to their security.[4]

Spain is a gateway for Muslim Arabs from north Africa into the European Union. It is the most geographically convenient entrance point (at the straits of Gibraltar, Morocco and Spain are fewer than ten miles apart). Just as important, the millennium-old history of Muslims in Iberia endures in the spirit of "al Andalus," or medieval Islamic Spain, which makes the country a relatively familiar and welcoming place for Muslims.

The Islamic community in Spain calls the southern city of Granada "the Islamic capital of Europe."[5] In 1492 the Moors were expelled from their Granada stronghold by Isabel and Ferdinand, but the cultural contributions remain an integral part of al Andalus, particularly in the southern region of Andalusia. The new Mosque of Granada sits in the middle of the city's old Moorish quarter, the Albaicín, and it offers a striking view of the Alhambra, the great architectural and cultural emblem of Moorish Spain. Now Muslims are flocking to Granada, many buying or renting property in the Albaicín. Indeed, the Mediterranean coast and the capital, Madrid, have developed significant Islamic populations.

At the national and the local levels, the Muslim communities are extremely diverse, even fragmented. As one example, the mid-sized city of Granada contains five or six different Muslim communities characterized by mixed levels of communication and cooperation. In addition to immigrants from north Africa, Granada is home to a distinct Muslim community composed largely of Senegalese and others from sub-Saharan Africa. Yet another is made up of Palestinians.[6] At the national level, there are at least two major organizations, which confederated in 1992 only in order to negotiate an accord with the national government.

Headlines in Spain devote a great deal of attention to issues of immigration, both along the Mediterranean coast and in the Canary Islands, a Spanish autonomous region off the west coast of Africa. Debate about Muslims pervades the national immigration conversation. In addition, the March 11, 2004, Madrid bombings receive news coverage roughly parallel to the enduring references to September 11, 2001, in the United States. Indeed, while Americans use "9/11" as shorthand for those events, Spaniards refer to "11-M." The perpetrators of the attacks (some of whom committed suicide; others were convicted by a special tribunal) are either Muslims from north African countries or Arab immigrants who had resided in Spain. Even after the 2008 national elections, which kept the Socialists in power, accusations about Spain's vulnerability to both al Qaeda and ETA terrorism continue to fly between the two major national political parties.

Given the high-profile attention these issues have received, observers might expect more anti-immigrant or anti-Islamic violence to have occurred in Spain since the Madrid bombings. Although incidents of vandalism and hate against mosques and individuals have taken place, Spain has not experienced the type of widespread violence that, say, France experienced among Muslim and other immigrant youths across the country in 2005. Similarly, Spain has not endured the type of emergency tensions that occurred in the Netherlands in late 2004, when an extremist who called himself a Muslim murdered filmmaker Theo Van Gogh—an incident that led to a backlash of violence against Muslims, including the burning of a Muslim elementary school.

What factors have helped enable Spain thus far to avoid substantial violence against or from the Islamic community? Scholars and political leaders point to the Spaniards' self-understanding as a culture of mutual tolerance. As one professor at the University of Granada, also a native of the city, views it, Spain is a land through which many peoples have passed: Phoenicians, Carthaginians, Greeks, Moors, the French, and so on. Spain is a cultural mixture.[7] The intercultural confrontations have often been bloody, but the cultural contributions live on. Modern-day Spanish identity is widely dependent, in particular, on Moorish influences.

However, the more recent, twentieth-century struggles also contribute to the present-day spirit or ethos of tolerance. As various scholars and leaders express it, Spaniards endured five decades of dictatorship following a tragic civil war. The transition after Franco could easily have been a violent one, but thanks to the leadership and unexpected democratic leanings of King Juan Carlos, as well as the calmness of the people, Spain secured a democratic state through its 1978 constitution.

That constitution guarantees, in article XV, religious freedom for all citizens. It declares Spain's official position of disestablishment from the Catholic Church. Yet, unlike the laicist (or secular) tradition of France, the article also allows for appropriate "cooperation with the Catholic Church and the other confessions." Spain's constitutional guarantee of religious freedom is a fundamental part of its modern-day democracy. A series of government accords signed in 1992 with the Jewish, Protestant, and Muslim communities attempted to extend the vision of appropriate cooperation to these groups.

As another Spanish academic says of the civil war and the Franco era, "We know where polarization and violent confrontation can lead us."[8] The Spaniards bent over backward to accommodate individuals and regions in the creation of its modern-day democracy. While there is significant public anxiety about immigration and a visible degree of anti-Islamic rhetoric in political life, Spain also exhibits a remarkable degree of tolerance toward the Muslim communities. Whether this situation will change (if immigrant numbers increase and if the economy tightens), remains to be seen. For now, the Spanish cultural reality of mutual tolerance offers at least some lessons for America.

Imagining Convivencia

Spaniards employ an evocative word for cross-cultural encounter and engagement: convivencia. Although it has no direct translation into English, literally interpreted it means the "state of living together." The word's narrow, technical meaning relates to medieval Spain's interactions among Muslim, Christian, and Jewish communities under the Moorish rule of al Andalus. Convivencia remains important in the ongoing scholarship on the cross-cultural and interreligious interactions that characterized the different ruling periods during eight centuries of Moorish rule. Scholars vigorously debate the degree of tolerance afforded by the various Muslim caliphates toward *dhimmis,* or non-Muslim subjects, whom the rulers protected. Although many scholars argue that significant coexistence and interaction occurred, they also debate the degree and duration of that convivencia.[9]

The term also has a second usage, one that relates not to medieval times but to the present. It refers to the current reality of diverse people living, working, and going to school together. Convivencia in this sense is about the mundane encounters that Spanish residents experience with their neighbors. Where do people eat, what do they eat, and at what times of the day? In public schools, do Protestant, Muslim, and Jewish students receive education about their faith when the Catholic children hear lessons about Catholicism? Are children (whether from majority Catholic or minority faiths) able to pray during the school day?

Consider the burying of the dead. Death is perhaps a peculiar example of everyday life, but individuals and communities struggle over how to treat appropriately the bodies of loved ones who have died. In cities and small towns, Muslims have appealed to the national government's 1992 accord with the Islamic community in their struggle to secure local Islamic cemeteries. For instance, in 2007 the town of Órgiva, in the mountains of Andalusia, secured such a burial ground for members of its 100-member Muslim community. As one local Muslim leader said, "All of us have to die, some sooner and some later, and we wish to be buried here [in Órgiva] . . . and, logically, to be buried in a site that conforms to our religion."[10]

To take yet another example related to the human body, restaurants significantly shape the everyday environment in which we live. In major cities across Spain, a steadily growing number of *teterías* (tea houses) and kebab shops reflects the increasing diversity of residents. Moorish dishes have long shaped Spanish cuisine, but recent decades have witnessed a more direct shift in eating habits toward largely immigrant-run establishments featuring *halal* meats and Moroccan teas.

Or consider a more visible and controversial question: Will the local *ayuntamiento* (city hall) permit a mosque to be built in town? The zoning questions and permit processes for new religious buildings, especially for minority communities, have parallels in Spain and the United States. Will citizens welcome the sound of the Islamic call to worship five times a day by the local *muezzin* from the minaret? Can this become a part of the "urban soundscape," like church bells and motorcycle engines? In this way Muslims can become a visible and an audible presence in the landscape of cities and towns.

Convivencia helps deal with these kinds of issues, those that concern the various activities of embodied living (and dying) in a civic community. Who are my neighbors, and how do they affect my daily life? Will people of different backgrounds merely live apart? Or will they interact with each other in ways that offer chances for mutual learning—and mutual changes in attitudes and behaviors? These are not abstract, interfaith dialogues; they are decisions about everyday matters that leaders and citizens have to figure out in practical terms.

Convivencia is sometimes translated as "coexistence." (It has also been translated as "cohabitation," a better literal interpretation but one that has other implications in English.) However, existence has a passive connotation, suggesting merely a detached acknowledgment of others' presence. Convivencia has the more active meaning of mutual encounter, if not reciprocal engagement. People who have to eat, work, shop, and ride the bus together must develop norms and routines of interaction that are more than simply acknowledging each others' existence.

Like many of the other terms that we use to describe our diverse public life—such as pluralism, melting pot, or Christian nation—the word *convivencia* can be either descriptive or normative. On one hand, it can merely name the reality that different people live and interact with one another. In this descriptive sense, no value judgment is made about whether such living together is a good or a bad thing. On the other hand, convivencia can also suggest how diverse people *should* live together. From this normative perspective, the word expresses a valuing of active interactions among people from many backgrounds.

This normative meaning of convivencia adds to our vision of leadership. Spanish public discussion employs convivencia in this aspirational sense. For example, in Madrid, the Foundation for Pluralism and Convivencia is a quasi-governmental organization that supports minority religious communities and promotes public understanding. This foundation was established in 2004 as a joint effort of the national Ministry of Justice and leaders of the country's religious communities. This organization's name communicates a vision of what it aims to accomplish in Spanish civil society.[11]

The foundation's director, Dr. José María Contreras, explains that both pluralism and convivencia are visions of what Spain seeks to achieve. They are consistent with the spirit of mutual tolerance that helped to achieve the post-Franco transition to democracy. Nonetheless, the ideals are not yet fully realized, especially vis-à-vis minority religious communities.[12]

Contreras sees the notion of convivencia as a "second step" in the process of developing a better civil society in Spain. Spaniards, he maintains, are willing to speak a great deal about the "integration" of minorities into civic life. Although this is better than exclusion, integration in this sense means the assimilation of minorities into the predominant culture.[13] Such integration, in the Spanish context, would not question the cultural (and financial) privilege accorded to the Catholic Church. Convivencia, living together on equal terms as neighbors, Contreras maintains, is a further step toward the reality of full citizenship for people of religious minority backgrounds and toward a more just society.[14]

It is helpful to put this in more concrete terms. Suppose an apartment building in Valencia has residents who are Catholic, Jewish, atheist, Protestant, and Muslim. Residents regularly pass one another in the hallways. The first step in living together successfully is to develop a basic live-and-let-live attitude toward one another. They might say a polite hello or simply walk silently past one another. This situation is already remarkable because people of different backgrounds are living together peaceably and without fanfare or rancor. We could easily imagine a different scenario, in which a few residents develop a deep suspicion of some of their neighbors; they might glare at one another in the hallway—or worse. So the basic level of coexistence—or what Contreras describes as integration—achieves no earth-shattering ends but does establish some minimal conditions of mutual respect. The next step—of convivencia in its fuller sense—involves more neighborly encounters and relationships among the residents. They might ask each other about their holidays, their attire, or their beliefs. They might share drinks or meals or activities together. They might work together on projects to improve their building or their neighborhood. And in the process, they might change and be changed.

Sociologist Cecilia Hita Alonso emphasizes the importance of the mixing of peoples through everyday encounters. Indeed, although Hita Alonso is a supporter of Spain's political Left, she criticizes the notion of "multiculturalism," as this idea tends to assume that cultures are fixed entities that do not change. In contrast, convivencia suggests that individuals do not necessarily prioritize any one aspect of identity (e.g., religious, cultural, political), and these dimensions surely overlap. Especially in European discussions, Hita Alonso maintains, multiculturalism encompasses defending the rights of each group to exist and to hold fast to an identity alongside other groups with their respective and respected identities. In this reading of multiculturalism, various ethnic, national, and religious enclaves live alongside one another but remain culturally apart. Such multiculturalism does not include the fuller dimensions of mixing across groups, of learning from each other, and of transforming people and groups.[15]

How far could a vision of protecting distinctive religious or cultural communities go? Consider India, which is one of the most religiously diverse and complicated nations in the world. The historical and political factors that led to Indian independence and the partition with Pakistan in 1947 created a legacy of religious "communalism" in India.[16] The country's enduring tensions between Hindus and Muslims in particular sustain the division along these lines. In India, as religion scholar William J. Everett states, "'Religion' does not really attach to an individual but to a 'community' which embraces economic, familial, social, and cultural aspects of life."[17] Policies address the welfare of communities, not individuals. For example, India has separate civil codes (governing noncriminal questions such as domestic-family and property issues) for distinct religious communities. As one result of these multiple civil law systems, Hindu and Christian men may have only one legal wife, whereas Muslim men are legally permitted to have as many as four wives. India's constitution states as a goal that "the state shall endeavor to secure for its citizens a uniform civil code throughout the territory of India."[18] However, more than five decades later that goal of the same civil law for all Indian citizens remains unrealized.

The Indian reality of communalism was surprisingly absent from public discourse in Britain when Rowan Williams, archbishop of Canterbury, suggested in 2008 that the United Kingdom consider making public space for what he called "plural jurisdiction." Specifically, he asserted that if Britain were serious about welcoming people of all religious backgrounds, then its universal secular law would need to find ways to accommodate religious law in some contexts. Anticipating a certain degree of criticism, the archbishop was clear in stating that "If any kind of plural jurisdiction is recognised, it would presumably have to be under the rubric that no 'supplementary' jurisdiction [i.e., based on religious law] could have the power to deny access to the rights granted to other citizens or to punish its members for claiming those rights."[19] The universal legal system would thus provide a minimum guarantee for all people, and religious law would open "additional choices" only for fully consenting religious citizens. He noted that the option to refer cases to Jewish law or Anglican ecclesiastical law has long been operative in the current system. However, in many Britons' eyes he had raised the spectre of Shariah law as a *parallel* legal system—as exists in India's multiple civil legal codes.

Archbishop Williams had tried to emphasize the supplemental, consent-based, constrained elements of his suggestion in a sixty-two-hundred-word address. Yet as one of Britain's most visible figures and one of the highest-profile leaders in Christianity anywhere, he should have seen the negative reaction coming. Williams was criticized by figures throughout the church and by former archbishop of Canterbury George Carey and Prime Minister Gordon Brown for his self-confessed "clumsily" delivered words. Indeed, it briefly appeared that his position was in jeopardy, but the Anglican Church's general synod strongly supported him, as did Carey and Brown.[20] Still, the visceral reaction to the suggestion of "plural jurisdiction" gives a clear signal of how strongly Britons reject any notion of communal autonomy that might trump a uniform legal system. There is little reason to believe American citizens would respond more positively.

Communalism, even when not extending to the law, is morally undesirable because it cannot generate the social cohesion necessary to hold a diverse population together. Yet, as philosopher Kwame Anthony Appiah suggests, advocates of cultural autonomy are right to raise concerns about the kind of mutual encounter that I have been describing as convivencia. Individuals from (and advocates for) minority communities have reason to fear that their identity will be washed away or at least diluted in open encounter with larger or more powerful communities. In many cases, no level playing field of cross-cultural encounter exists in which the ideas and practices of various religious and cultural groups have equal influence on each other. Marginalized communities, then, sometimes seek to remain apart so as to preserve their sense of identity.

Appiah uses the provocative term *contamination* to describe the loss of cultural identity. For minority groups, contamination happens because they lack the power to hold on to their collective identity. For their part, majority communities also fear that their own identity might be "contaminated" by the blood and genes (or the practices and beliefs) of minority groups. These views of cultural preservation are predicated on the view that cultures are pure. This viewpoint can also involve the belief that cultures do not change. Both ideas are wrong.

All of this leads Appiah to turn the pejorative term *contamination* into a desirable thing. He labels it a "counterideal" to purity. In his important book *Cosmopolitanism,* Appiah calls for the mutual interaction of individuals from various cultural backgrounds in order to build up, over time, a sense of world community. Indeed, his excerpted cover essay in the *New York Times Magazine* ran with the title "The Case for Contamination."[21] It is in the contamination, the path crossing, and the everyday interactions of diverse people—what I am calling crossroads and connectors—that we find hope for a more respectful and peaceable society.

Appiah makes the crucial point that we will not become a more harmonious world by arguing over values. Working through the challenges of our diverse identities is not principally a matter of public discourse or of rational deliberation. As I suggest in the previous chapter, Rawls's public reason may be the best account we have of how to conduct civil discourse, but that alone will not help us to get along with our neighbors. Rather, Appiah argues that we need to "get used to one another." Interaction will breed understanding. Fellow residents of an apartment complex do not need to have formal interfaith dialogue or even stage a political debate; instead, they need to keep living together with a willingness to engage one another. Only this could lead to genuine coalitions to work for more significant social transformation.

Appiah believes this mutual daily engagement and exposure will allow us to get used to one another—and social changes will follow. Robert Putnam, however, has argued that this is very taxing work. Returning to the image of the apartment complex, the more diverse a building becomes, the more likely the residents will shut themselves away in their own apartment. They will actively seek to avoid crossing paths with anyone. Putnam presents data from multiple studies that suggest that the more heterogeneous a neighborhood or locality, the less likely are citizens to engage one another. Not only are people in diverse areas less connected—compared to those in homogeneous areas—to neighbors who are different from them, but they are also less involved with people who are similar to them: "Diversity seems to trigger not in-group/out-group division, but anomie or social isolation. In colloquial language, people living in ethnically diverse settings appear to 'hunker down'—that is, to pull in like a turtle."[22] Putnam argues, then, that in the near term, diversity hurts solidarity and social capital.

However, he continues: "In the medium to long run, on the other hand, successful immigrant societies create new forms of social solidarity and dampen the effects of diversity by constructing new, more encompassing identities. Thus, the central challenge for modern, diversifying societies is to create a new, broader sense of 'we.'"[23] Thus, regularly crossing paths with one another—convivencia—is difficult work, but it is essential, Appiah and Putnam concur, because the world is coming to an apartment building near you. Convivencia is in that sense cosmopolitan, even as it is as local and everyday as it can be.[24]

Choosing a Vision

It is now possible to see and compare six competing visions for leadership in a devout and diverse America (see table 6.1). Each of these approaches provides a distinctive account of the religious, civic, and political landscape. Each suggests how American leaders should frame their work in general and, more specifically, how they should handle religious diversity. Each of these visions is connected to central moral and political values. Of course, each one is a generalization that groups together a range of thoughts and actions under a general heading.[25] Any particular leader would, in practice, not fit perfectly into any one category. And the categories, each meant to shed light on different aspects of leadership and society, can overlap, but this overview should clarify similarities and differences in the visions.

TABLE 6.1. Leadership in a Devout and Diverse America: Six Visions

Vision	Overall Approach *Approach to Diversity*	Moral Value *Political Value*
Clash of civilizations	We are right; they are wrong.	truth
	We protect ourselves from outsiders.	*security*
Christian nation	We lead and follow by God's will.	salvation
	We correct social evil in God's name.	*national purity*
Secularism	We keep all religion private.	autonomy
	We guard the public square from zealots.	*reasonableness*
Spirituality	We all believe basically the same thing.	universalism
	We declare our commonality.	*harmony*
Communalism	"We" are a set of distinct communities.	communal autonomy
	We protect groups from one another.	*communal purity*
Crossroads and connectors	We promote interaction and linkages.	commitment
	We draw on moral resources from all.	*convivencia*

The first vision, the clash of civilizations, focuses on American identity vis-à-vis the rest of the world. It defines American identity in terms of its conflicts with outsiders. It values security over all other political values and upholds the view that right is on our side. Opponents are wrong or even evil. The clash of civilizations, I have suggested, is the predominant post-9/11 vision of American leadership. It views the world in us-versus-them terms, and leaders perpetuate it by playing on citizens' fears. It rightly acknowledges the threat of terrorism in the United States and elsewhere, but it too readily fails to distinguish between terrorists and other persons in non-Western "blocs," especially in the so-called Muslim world. Worse, it may help to create the bloc-based clash that its proponents say already exists. This vision leaves little room for people or groups who straddle civilization-based identities, such as Muslim Americans.[26]

The vision of America as a Christian nation can complement the civilization-clash vision. It appeals to a historical account of America founded on Christian values. In the domestic context, proponents of this vision easily move from the descriptive reality that roughly four in five Americans identify with Christianity to the normative perspective that the nation *should* embody Christian values. Leaders who hold to this vision invoke Christian texts and symbols in public life; they submit that the existence of fellow citizens from minority traditions should not deny the majority a special status in public life. Believers from those underrepresented traditions are welcome in the country as long as they understand America's special relationship with Christianity. Proponents of the vision tend to overlook the possible negative effects that a de facto Christian culture can have on those from other backgrounds.

Secularism is a strong response to the Christian nation model. If Christian symbols decorate the public sphere in a Christian nation, secularists, in contrast, would have no problem removing religious symbols altogether from public life. The motivation for this position can be a high moral one—to ensure that all people are able to interact on a free and equal basis. In order to accomplish this, secularism equally and consistently says no to symbols from any religious tradition. Advocates of secularism discount the difficulty of asking religious people to separate their faith-based practices from their public lives.

Proponents of the spirituality vision seek a moderate path. If Christian language is too particular, excluding non-Christian moral and religious expressions, and secularism is too sweeping, excluding all religious expression, this middle position welcomes any spiritual expression—as long as it is generic. Behind this vision is the assumption of a universally shared spiritual dimension to the human personality so that, when the particular trappings of religion are removed, a common spirituality shines through. Yet, this discounts deeply held convictions that are particular and cannot be wished away.

Communalism starts from the standpoint of religious diversity. Proponents of this vision are typically looking out for outsider threats to a group's collective identity. They pay much less attention to diversity *within* these tradition-defined groups. To the extent that a national "we" exists, it is in strong tension with these communal identities. At its fullest expression, communalism requires separate legal codes to accommodate religious communities' diverse practices.

The vision of America as a place of crossroads and connectors welcomes the public presence of religious expression from a broad range of traditions and perspectives. A crossroads is a place where two or more paths come together. A connector joins two otherwise separate paths.

The crossroads metaphor, like the other images we have considered, has both descriptive and normative meanings. Given the number of people and the need to coordinate society, people's paths intersect. Because of the convergence of various routes, crossroads are promising places to locate restaurants, roadside markets, and inns, but what kind of intersections will we design? Who will build them? Will they be built in ways that can handle the traffic flow while retaining a "human feel" for social interaction? Will they be places of convivencia?

"Crossroads" has a rich tradition in religious studies as a site, sometimes seen as sacred, where key life decisions are made and where people's destinies are determined. Often it carries the sense of being a dangerous place. Perhaps as a result, these intersections are also the sites of certain gods—some of whom are protectors, others of whom have more ambiguous roles.[27] In the study of leadership, the concept of the crossroads has been used to suggest moments of opportunity and also the need for multiple perspectives to work together to solve challenging problems.[28] Each of these lineages captures something helpful for our purposes. Certainly, America is at a crossroads in terms of how we will live together as diverse citizens and what role religion will play in public life. An understandable response to such moments is fear, for when unfamiliar peoples and worldviews intersect, the possibility of danger arises.

The stakes are thus high at these points of encounter—and thus it is no wonder that, in one tradition, one can make a deal with a god at a crossroads and consequently either get lucky or encounter evil.[29] If we fail to pick up the right food or supplies, there may not be another chance to do so for many miles. If we take the wrong path, we will need to backtrack, find another crossroads, or cut a new path. If we provoke the wrong traveler, we can get ourselves killed. On the other hand, at the crossroads we can nourish ourselves and rest. We can pick up directions and advice from others—both travelers and locals. And we can meet people coming from all corners.

Since intersections do not just happen, designing them is a matter of leadership. To be sure, roads come together at natural points, but then they must be designed or redesigned if they are to be sites that encourage human interaction. Cities often take shape at transportation crossroads. Take, for instance, Indianapolis, the capital of Indiana. Because of the state's network of roads, railroads, and waterways, its official motto is "the crossroads of America." Three decades ago, Indianapolis was experiencing urban decay due to rust belt economics and white flight to its suburbs. The downtown area was losing its retailers, offices, and pedestrian traffic.

In response, a group of public, civic, and business leaders worked together to design a revitalization plan. City leaders, including Republican mayors William Hudnut and Stephen Goldsmith, based their strategy on strengths of Indianapolis, including the White River and historic canals, its attractive Monument Circle, and a culture of athletics, both professional and amateur. Because of intentional and coordinated leadership—including collaboration by government, business, and nonprofit entities—Indianapolis developed an urban state park, a new convention center, and sports arenas for three professional teams. It opened a large downtown mall and welcomed the headquarters of the National Collegiate Athletics Association (NCAA). Significant projects—some in historic areas—have increased the number of people living in or near downtown. Social and economic challenges remain for the city, and the development process produced both winners and losers, but Indianapolis transformed its center, once again, into a crossroads.[30]

Analogously, political and civic leaders can help the United States develop a public culture of crossroads. Indeed, a positive relationship actually exists between public urban spaces that facilitate citizen interaction and civic engagement.[31] Beyond the built environment, leaders help shape the ground rules for public life. In actual crossroads, the flow of traffic is managed by road layouts, street signs, and traffic lights. In the figurative crossroads of society, the flow of diverse people is managed by laws, norms, and customs. In the former, urban planners and civil engineers design systems that move traffic; in the latter, politicians and policymakers create a structure that helps create social harmony.

In neither case, however, are these elements of design enough. Whether driving a car or attending a public meeting, individual citizens must be willing and able to abide by the rules. Red lights mean nothing if drivers do not stop at them. Laws against discrimination mean little if citizens disregard them. In each case a harmonious system requires that citizens show a basic respect for others—and trust that their fellow citizens will do the same.

The very idea of a crossroads suggests that a point of overlap already exists between or among people's different paths. Connectors, on the other hand, are new roads built to join otherwise disconnected or divergent paths. Unlike crossroads, connectors must be built from scratch and occur only when someone from one or both pathways—or some outside party—takes the initiative. Building connectors may require more work than crossroads—especially if the ground between the paths is rough or overgrown. On the other hand, it may be easier to build something new than to redesign an existing intersection already used by many people who will be inconvenienced by the construction.

Connector also has senses in electronics, mathematics, and other fields. For instance, in his book *The Tipping Point*, Malcolm Gladwell uses the term *connector* to describe those people with the unique capacity to bring diverse individuals together—particularly as conduits for quickly spreading new ideas.[32] In my schema, I suggest that if connectors are to be built, say, between dissimilar religious groups, third-party connectors may be significant, but leaders within those groups also need to play key roles in forging the linkages. In terms of people, then, connectors can be politicians or other public figures who bring unlike groups together, or they can be leaders from within those religious, cultural, or civic communities.

Crossroads and connectors are thus two apt metaphors for linking unique paths on common ground. At these points of interaction fellow citizens can expand their perspectives or team up with others on political or civic questions. Through their interactions, some might even change their moral or religious directions. Crossroads are active, cacophonous, and sometimes tense because people believe deeply in their causes and their objectives. Leadership "at the crossroads" requires leaders to shape a place in which people from various backgrounds stand on roughly equal footing as they engage each other. The aim is not to deny conflicts when paths cross; on the contrary, it is to create a place where devout and diverse people can address their conflicts honestly, respectfully, and constructively.[33]

"Never Budge in the Least!"

How do leaders communicate this vision of crossroads and connectors? How do they promote convivencia? Howard Gardner, the wide-ranging Harvard scholar, suggests that leaders succeed when they relate their vision in stories that appeal broadly to the public. In Gardner's cognitive account of leadership, humans are moved by narratives that mesh with their own lives. Specifically, he asserts that those stories that can reach the mind of a five-year-old are most likely to be effective: "Those who address a more broad-based institution . . . a large and heterogeneous group like the inhabitants of a nation must at least begin by assuming that most of their audience members have a well-stocked five-year-old mind."[34] Gardner notes that the successful leaders he features have managed to put their message precisely in these terms—in simple, clear, compelling narratives.

Yet in almost all cases, they have *stretched* the standard or expected story in ways that offer a more inclusive vision. Martin Luther King Jr. appealed to Christian symbols and American values to argue his lead story, which Gardner simplifies as follows: "We must be color blind." Jean Monnet, pioneer of the European Community, argued that steps toward economic and political union would weave peace into a European story: "Europe must become one society, with close links to America." And Mohandas K. Gandhi drew on religious and humanist traditions to declare that "We in India are equal in status and worth to all other human beings."[35]

If Gardner is correct, then the notion of inclusive leadership amid religious diversity in the United States can draw on the proud tradition of religious freedom in America. The First Amendment and its guarantee of the free exercise of religion is broadly known. Indeed, assuming that leaders draw on this familiar story, the task of leadership of the devout and diverse is a case of *innovative* leadership in Gardner's terms. That is, American leaders have the task of "tak[ing] a story that has been latent in the population . . . and bring[ing] new attention or a fresh twist to that story."[36]

The American story of religious freedom, however, has its limitations. According to a recent survey by the First Amendment Center, the portion of Americans who believe that the rights of religious freedom extend to all Americans, regardless of their beliefs, stood at just 56 percent. The year before 9/11, that figure was 72 percent.[37] If civic and political leaders are to have success in communicating an inclusive vision, they will need to address these public perceptions of the limits of religious freedom. They will also need to move beyond the somewhat abstract nature of religious freedom to appeal to tangible, visual narratives. The basic story is familiar, if abstract; the task is to apply it more universally.

Running into people at the crossroads appeals to the five-year-old mind. Children understand intersecting roads, stop signs, and vehicles of all kinds that must give right of way to others. A Dr. Seuss tale introduces us to the "North-Going Zax" and the "South-Going Zax," whose paths collide. They refuse to yield: "Never budge in the least! Not an inch to the west! Not an inch to the east!"[38] At the story's end, an array of highways and byways surrounds the two—who are still facing off. "In a couple of years, the new highway came through/And they built it right over those two stubborn Zax/And left them there, standing un-budged in their tracks."[39] Even young children grasp the senselessness of Zax who refuse to give an inch to their fellow travelers.

Transforming Our Leadership

Something more than business as usual is required if we are to avoid these standoffs in our politics. Political scientist James MacGregor Burns developed the concept of *transforming leadership* in an effort to get both scholars and leaders to think differently about how to achieve beneficial social change.[40] Burns argues that leadership is fundamentally a moral process, a relationship among human beings who deserve to be full participants, whether they are formally leaders or followers. In Burns's normative analysis of leadership, those who merely exploit followers for their own gain and show no regard for the needs or interests of others are not leaders at all. They are merely power wielders.[41] This claim can distract us with some fascinating questions, but for our purposes, Burns is making an important point about what leadership *should* look like.

In other words, for a process to be morally good leadership and not just manipulation by the powerful, leaders and followers must come together as moral equals who all participate freely. This applies to what Burns calls transactional leadership, as well as transforming leadership. In the former, engagement may be little more than a market-based exchange whereby different parties come together to trade valued goods for the benefit of each. As Burns puts it, this form of transaction allows people with different needs to make mutually beneficial exchanges.

Transactional leadership corresponds to the coexistence model of society. Diverse citizens interact with one another—on the street, in stores, at work—in ways that resemble the free market in operation. This requires freedom of choice, basic fairness, and other norms of peaceful interaction but does not require any significant investment in shifting from being strangers to being real neighbors.[42]

Contrast the transactional model with what Burns calls transforming leadership. In this kind of leadership, leaders and followers engage one another in a mutual interaction toward some shared goals. They might enter the relationship with very distinct backgrounds and divergent, even competing, interests. But through the process of repeated interactions, their respective interests and purposes begin to overlap. This process takes time for the building up of trust among the parties.

Burns emphasizes that transforming leadership requires a high level of personal investment, or risk taking, to connect our needs and wants with those of our fellow citizens. This is a lofty vision of mutual engagement through which, Burns asserts, "leaders and followers raise one another to higher levels of motivation and morality."[43] In the process, followers and leaders develop a sense of common purpose toward which they strive together.

Enduring social and political transformation requires all of the parties to take risks. Burns, like Gardner, gives the example of Gandhi and the Indian resistance to British rule in India. In that struggle, Gandhi's followers were not bystanders who assented to high-profile leaders with status and privilege; rather, Gandhi strived to lessen the distance between himself and the people and to urge the followers to act. There were risks and sacrifices that all had to endure.[44]

Too many leaders fail to achieve greatness because they do not fully invest themselves when bold leadership is required. For instance, in the sharply titled book *Dead Center*, Burns and coauthor Georgia Sorenson fault President Bill Clinton for settling for transactional dealings with Congress and the American people when the United States needed a transforming vision and follow-through to achieve it.[45] Burns and Sorenson are talking about a transactional center that was marked, in their interpretation of the Clinton presidency, by missed opportunities and the president's unwillingness to take the necessary risks to change our politics.

Crossroads can, in fact, be places for mere transactions. People get what they want and move on through. As Burns notes, however, even these transactions need to be undertaken with mutual respect and regard for laws and social norms—or else we have nothing but the machinations of power. At their best, however, crossroads become transforming places. People are willing to linger there to engage and learn from others. Leaders take the initiative to create the public spaces—political, cultural, aesthetic, environmental—in which various parties can participate. Thus, leaders certainly play a key role in shaping the culture toward respect for the wide diversity and deep faith of citizens. The true work of leadership, however, also takes place through the mutual efforts of leaders and average citizens. Risk-taking citizens who dare to engage neighbors who look different from the way they themselves do deserve our praise as surely as does the risk-taking politician who shows up to defend an unpopular group.

In the end, transforming leadership turns followers into leaders, as both are active agents in a process of social or political change. As Gardner might state, through the influence of leaders, citizens will also live out the story of American religious freedom in their respect for citizens very different from themselves. Burns's and Gardner's conceptions may sound more idealistic than Appiah's "getting used to one another" or the Spaniards' idea of convivencia. Yet, each view infuses a sense of moral purpose into the encounters that occur every day at crossroads across America.

PART III

Building Crossroads
and Connectors

7

Shaping the Culture

[L]eaders fashion stories: principally stories of identity. It is important that a leader be a good storyteller, but equally crucial that the leader embody that story in his or her life.

—Howard Gardner

The Power to Frame

GENE NICHOL, FORMER PRESIDENT OF THE COLLEGE OF WILLIAM AND MARY, probably wishes he had spent a little more time learning about the land mines on his university's cultural map. It would have saved him from making national headlines over something that may have at first appeared to be a simple move toward inclusiveness. Nichol, leading the institution that U.S. presidents Thomas Jefferson, James Monroe, and John Tyler had attended, found himself scrambling to guide his campus community out of a culture war over an eighteen-inch cross. Ultimately, in a place where tradition and symbolism matter a great deal, Nichol was forced out of the William and Mary presidency in no small part due to the power of religious symbolism.

For his part, Keith Ellison entered the U.S. House of Representatives with much more publicity than anyone would have expected—or Ellison would have wanted. We have already seen that, as the first Muslim congressman in American history, Ellison was the subject of criticism before he took office in 2007. When he indicated that he would be sworn into office with his hand on the

Quran, his religious and cultural opponents mobilized against him.[1] Ellison turned to Thomas Jefferson for a powerful symbolic response.

To take another example, early in his tenure as U.S. president, Bill Clinton found himself highly criticized by Christian conservatives for failing to bring them to the table. Later Clinton's personal indiscretions opened him up to charges of religious and moral hypocrisy. He had failed to comprehend—or lacked the will to act on his comprehension—that many Americans closely associate personal morality with religious faith, especially in the case of our public leaders. Yet despite this lapse of judgment that dominated the headlines, Clinton achieved enduring protections for religious freedom.

These leaders learned the hard way that our cultural assumptions, though often invisible, are fundamentally important. Culture encompasses a people's habits, attitudes, and assumptions, and newcomers learn from citizens how they should think and act.[2] For many citizens, religious symbols are interwoven in American culture. Notwithstanding the First Amendment's clear statement against any official religion, few politicians have dared to question the many trappings in our public life that are religious in general or Christian in particular. Our currency states "In God We Trust," which became the national motto in 1956 and appeared on paper currency the following year. The Pledge of Allegiance added "under God" in 1954. Presidents now increasingly end their significant addresses with "God bless America," a custom that Richard Nixon began.[3] Whether you call it civil religion, public theology, or the remnants of Christendom, it is part of American culture.

Effective leaders are able to read clearly the culture in which they find themselves. Even if they must learn its contours and trouble spots through trial and error, good leaders draw their own maps of the cultural topography. However, as important as it is to *read* the culture, leaders must not accept it as an unchangeable landscape. Rather, great leaders are also able to *shape* their culture.[4] Indeed, this is a fundamental element of good leadership, and here I mean "good" in the sense not only of effectiveness but of morality as well.[5] Good public leaders bring a moral vision for their society and then summon their skills, leverage their influence, and tell clear stories to alter the cultural map in ways that move their followers toward that vision.

In this chapter we explore the dilemmas that the three aforementioned leaders—Nichol, Ellison, and Clinton—faced when they stepped into what Jefferson called a "nest of hornets." Good leadership, in such cases, requires facing the dilemmas that religious symbols can create and then transforming them into opportunities to broaden and deepen American public culture. None of the cases has an unambiguous result. Each one, however, sheds light on what leaders should and should not do to shape that culture.

"The Cross Problem"

After Harvard, the College of William and Mary is the second oldest university in the nation. It is unrivaled in its sense of history. Some call it the alma mater of the nation. At William and Mary, heritage and tradition are words of high praise. The school was founded under a royal charter granted by King William III and Queen Mary II in 1693, and it was affiliated with the Anglican Church.

The central, defining building of the college, completed in 1699, now bears the name of its famous British architect, Sir Christopher Wren. Alumni of William and Mary delight in declaring that it is the oldest college building still in use in the United States. When Queen Elizabeth II visited the university—in both 1957 and 2007—she appeared each time on the balcony of the Wren Building.

The most symbolic part of the building is Wren Chapel. In its early days, the chapel, as an Anglican worship space, displayed the Apostle's Creed, the Lord's Prayer, and the Ten Commandments on its front wall. A major renovation of the building and chapel in the 1930s removed these displays. In 1940 the historic Bruton Parish Church of Colonial Williamsburg, which had long been affiliated with the college, donated an eighteen-inch brass cross for display in Wren Chapel.[6]

William and Mary began receiving public support as a Virginia university in 1906. As a state-funded institution, the college is responsible for upholding the guarantees of the First Amendment—specifically, protecting religious freedom while disallowing religious establishment.[7] Consequently, college leaders have to navigate the complicated religious, cultural, and legal waters of its historic Anglican affiliation alongside its role as a state-sponsored university.

Gene Nichol became president of William and Mary in 2005. During the 1980s he had served for three years on the Law School faculty at William and Mary, which allowed him to claim insider status at the university, even though he was not an alumnus. A graduate of the University of Texas Law School and a constitutional scholar, Nichol arrived well aware of the legal challenges related to the display of religious symbols in publicly funded institutions. He was also renowned for advancing the rights of minority or marginalized persons within their communities.

It is not surprising that when Nichol learned that some people of minority religious backgrounds had expressed discomfort with and objection to the display of a Christian cross in Wren Chapel, he decided to change the practice. Prior to his policy change in October 2006, the cross had normally been on display; however, it could be removed at the request of groups using the space for worship or other activity at which the cross would not play a fitting part.

For instance, some couples who were being married in the chapel chose to have the cross removed for the ceremony. Organizers of musical concerts or non-Christian religious services could also opt to remove the cross for their events. At Nichol's direction, the policy was changed; now the cross would customarily be placed in the chapel's sacristy (a storage area for religious objects), but at the request of individuals or groups, it could be displayed during events or times of Christian prayer.

Nichol's policy change occurred in the wake of a collegewide debate over a new National Collegiate Athletic Association (NCAA) policy regarding Native American mascots at universities. This controversy had provoked sensitivities about tradition and inclusiveness on campus and among the alumni. The heated arguments at William and Mary centered around the team name, "the Tribe," and the associated green and gold logo with two feathers. In May 2006 an NCAA commission had denied the college's request to keep the feathers as part of its logo, stating that the symbol created a hostile environment for Native Americans. The college was allowed to keep the name "the Tribe," apparently because of the term's positive connotations of a strong community. Nichol and his administration had fought the NCAA's decision to ban the feathers from the school logo, but after the NCAA ruling on William and Mary's appeal, he called on the college to drop the battle and to focus, rather, on its "core mission." Some alumni and longtime supporters of the school had urged Nichol to keep fighting what they derisively called an NCAA campaign of "political correctness." Needless to say, this issue had mobilized the defenders of tradition at this tradition-laden school.

Just months after the logo battle, Nichol's administration instituted the cross policy without any prior notice to the William and Mary community. Then an assistant director at the college e-mailed university tour guides to instruct them on how to mention that the cross policy had been changed. The president, facing simmering student outrage, issued a brief, if not terse, campuswide e-mail on October 27: "Let me be clear. I have not banished the cross from Wren Chapel." He went on to note that religious people of all faiths used the chapel and that the university also utilizes the space for "events that are secular in nature." In the e-mail, Nichol hit the notes of dignity, inclusion, and retention of the historic values in a special community—values to which he would return as the crisis grew. But the e-mail of only nine sentences seemed to lack an appreciation for the depth of his critics' ire at what they would call the rejection of the school's Christian heritage.[8]

Word of the policy change quickly reached the student body, faculty and staff, alumni, and media outlets. Opponents of Nichol's decision began a campaign to restore the cross—and even to oust Nichol. A website, www.savethewrencross.org, was created. Eventually more than ten thousand signatures accumulated on a petition calling for a reversal in the cross policy. Outside parties, particularly conservative opponents of the new cross policy, pointed to Nichol's decision as an example of liberal thought police prohibiting Christianity on campus. The William and Mary case quickly became a leading front in the culture wars. One of the most outspoken opponents of the decision was alumnus Vince Haley, an employee of Newt Gingrich at the American Enterprise Institute.[9] The nationally recognized conservative pundit Dinesh D'Souza came to campus to debate a professor in the chapel.

Critics of Nichol and his decision were surely correct that problems with the former policy concerning the cross had provoked "no groundswell of public opinion."[10] However, this did not substantiate, in Nichol's view, the critics' conclusion that the policy "wasn't broke; it didn't need fixing."[11] For Nichol, the issue was a moral one about inclusion in the community. Nichol articulated his position in this way:

> And though we haven't meant to do so, the display of a Christian cross—the most potent symbol of my own religion—in the heart of our most important building sends an unmistakable message that the Chapel belongs more fully to some of us than to others. That there are, at the College, insiders and outsiders. Those for whom our most revered place is meant to be keenly welcoming, and those for whom presence is only tolerated. That distinction, I believe, to be contrary to the best values of the College.[12]

Given Nichol's legal background, it is reasonable to surmise that he saw the policy change as a straightforward administrative matter intended to comply with William and Mary's status as a publicly funded university. For Nichol this case was about guaranteeing the moral equality of all William and Mary students and building an inclusive community among the diverse student body. Nichol knew the cross was a significant symbol. He strived as a leader to symbolize inclusion and mutual respect. He believed he had acted for the common good.

Nichol miscalculated the power of symbolism, however. In Howard Gardner's terms, Nichol was not prepared for the simple story that opponents would be able to tell—that he had taken their college's cherished symbol and locked it away. He grossly underestimated the public outcry from people who saw the issue not as a legal one but, through the lens of tradition, as a cultural attack. Their moral perspective was thus in conflict with his.

Here, in vivid color (green and gold) was the test for this leader at a public institution facing a religiously and culturally diverse community. He encountered significant support for his policy move—especially from the faculty and student government—but he faced a highly motivated opposition. He had broached the issue of a prominent Christian symbol in order to shape a more level cultural playing field at a publicly supported university. But he had not done enough to frame his actions within a compelling story of inclusion, American values, the First Amendment, or the like. Could Nichol, his governing board of visitors, and the college find a solution—perhaps through a compromise that would bring the parties together? Or would this conflict turn into a battle to be "won" at whatever cost to the William and Mary community?

Nichol and his board had the clear sense, by December 2006, that some further response would be needed. His next move did not settle the matter, but it did contain some elements that would later help with the crisis. In a three-page, eighteen-paragraph e-mail to the William and Mary faculty, staff, and students, Nichol sought to communicate his understanding that this issue went to the heart of the identity of William and Mary and that it now threatened to divide the William and Mary "family." He introduced two alterations to the October 2006 policy: He declared that the cross would regularly be displayed on Sundays, and he announced plans to commission a plaque "to commemorate the Chapel's origins as an Anglican place of worship and a symbol of the Christian beginnings of the College."[13]

Perhaps more important than either of these action items was Nichol's identification of a few important elements that might help reframe the debate. First, Nichol sought to establish his own status as an insider who understood and deeply appreciated the specific elements of the culture that made William and Mary special. In his letter he included cultural references ranging "[f]rom the Yule Log, to the carolers and singers who have brought greetings to our house, to the later-night enthusiasts of the Sunken Garden." He closed his letter, "Go Tribe. Hark upon the Gale."[14] To outsiders (including me), some of these references are lost. We do not know exactly what he is talking about. But that is precisely the point: Insiders understood him.

Even more significant, Nichol acknowledged his own mistakes—what he called "my own missteps." He regretted acting hastily and without consulting more people. He was sorry for the "inelegant way" the new cross policy had been communicated to the community and the fact that he had missed that early opportunity to frame the action. He admitted he had failed to see either the need or the opportunity for public debate and education about religious, moral, and cultural diversity.

Six weeks after the original cross decision, Nichol also sought to identify elements of common ground—rather than dismiss critics or further polarize constituents. He asserted that "no member of the extended William and Mary family believes that any of our students should be cast as outsiders—however unintentionally—because of religious preference." He thus suggested that the debate was over the correct methods of achieving the value of mutual respect, not over the value itself. He also noted that all of the parties stood together in wanting to advance "the cause of the College" with "its singular history" and "promising role in the future of the nation and the world."[15]

Finally, in his call for a plaque to acknowledge the Anglican roots of the Wren Chapel, Nichol was introducing language for valuing both an inclusive, welcoming culture and respect for a storied Christian history. This pairing would create the space for a resolution.

In the new year, as tensions continued to simmer, Nichol appointed the William and Mary Committee on Religion in a Public University, assigning it a two-point mission: in the short term, to recommend a way forward on the cross question, and in the longer term, to reflect on wider issues facing William and Mary and other public universities in a religiously diverse society. Critics charged Nichol with stacking the committee,[16] but he in fact included members with a range of opinions and appointed cochairs who stood on the opposing sides of the cross issue.

The appointed committee acted quickly. It met first in late February of 2007 and again on March 5. In keeping with Virginia law and tradition, their meetings were announced and open to the public, but after public discussion appeared to conclude on March 5, the press and public left. The committee reconvened and proceeded to seek a substantive resolution to the cross policy that would be acceptable to all of the parties.

The committee did make a policy recommendation, which it forwarded to President Nichol later that evening. Nichol welcomed the proposal and received board approval to announce it as the new William and Mary cross policy the very next day:

> The Wren Chapel cross shall be returned for permanent display in the Chapel in a glass case. The case shall be located in a prominent, readily visible place, accompanied by a plaque explaining the College's Anglican roots and its historic connection to Bruton Parish Church. The Wren sacristy shall be available to house sacred objects of any religious tradition for use in worship and devotion by members of the College community.[17]

In addition, the college announcement clarified, the cross could be taken out of the case for use in Christian worship services.

According to several published accounts, the members of the committee had all recognized the damage that the ongoing controversy was causing and could continue to cause in the William and Mary community. Agreeing unanimously on the urgent need to act responsibly as a united front, the committee members found a resolution that gave the various constituents the substance of what they wanted.

All of the parties could claim victory or at least save face. President Nichol and the board of visitors issued a joint statement praising the committee's decision and "deeply welcomed" quick action.[18] The leaders of the group that had sought the return of the cross issued a laudatory statement on its website and expressed gratitude to the committee members for their "tremendously good faith" and for having "the best interests of William and Mary uppermost in their minds."[19]

The success of this resolution included a number of elements of trans-forming leadership. Nichol had been willing to engage with his opponents by acknowledging his own errors in the process—if not in the substance— of his decision. He continued to reach out to his opponents throughout the conflict and sought to build common ground with them. For their part, the opponents—at least the leaders who emerged from within the William and Mary community—expressed their position forcefully but without abandoning hope in the process Nichol and the board of visitors had instituted in order to resolve the crisis. The diverse group of committee members charged with find-ing a resolution worked together quietly to forge a compromise.

In substantive terms, the compromise worked because the committee had managed to determine which values were most fundamental to each side. For-tunately, and contrary to simplistic accounts in the media, the two parties were not in direct opposition. Nichol valued an equally enthusiastic William and Mary welcome to students of all religious and moral traditions, but he also wanted to honor the institution's rich history, including its Anglican affilia-tion. Opponents sought to hold on to William and Mary's history (which they were convinced was under attack from various angles), but their leaders never questioned that students from various backgrounds should all be welcome at the school or in the chapel. Thus, the key to effective leadership in this example was to split the historic honoring from the current welcoming and then to try to accomplish both.

The glass case that now surrounds the cross communicates the message that the cross is a treasured item, part of William and Mary's storied history. The cross thus serves a historic role. As a symbol of Christian practice, it also plays a contemporary role on the occasions when it is removed from the case and employed on the communion table as a part of worship or other religious activity.

Students from secular and non-Christian religious traditions might still object to the cross's visible presence, the glass case notwithstanding. Does not the cross still stand over the space, reminding all who are present that the chapel is "really" a Christian sanctuary? It would not be surprising if some observers understood the arrangement in this way. Still, it is undeniable that people who were Christian and Christian symbols, including the cross, played a major role historically in shaping the institution of William and Mary—and the society beyond its campus. The leadership challenge is not to deny that history of Christian influence but rather to acknowledge it, as well as the contemporary value of welcoming people of all backgrounds into the community. The policy is a reasonable blending of these values.

This resolution, however, turned out to be the beginning of Nichol's downfall as president. It appeared that Nichol and thoughtful people from a variety of perspectives had found common ground on an issue that threatened to rupture the tight-knit William and Mary community. But on February 10, 2008, the rector of the William and Mary board informed Nichol that his contract would not be renewed for a second presidential term. Two days later Nichol issued a lengthy e-mail to the William and Mary community, in which he explained that he was resigning, effective immediately. A number of questions had been raised about Nichol's leadership—but none was more significant than the cross policy.[20] As Nichol wrote:

> First, as is widely known, I altered the way a Christian cross was displayed in a public facility, on a public university campus, in a chapel used regularly for secular college events—both voluntary and mandatory—in order to help Jewish, Muslim, Hindu, and other religious minorities feel more meaningfully included as members of our broad community. The decision was likely required by any effective notion of separation of church and state. And it was certainly motivated by the desire to extend the College's welcome more generously to all. We are charged, as state actors, to respect and accommodate all religions, and to endorse none. The decision did no more.[21]

Nichol appealed, albeit too late to save his own position, to Jefferson: "I have also hoped that this noble College might one day claim not only Thomas Jefferson's pedigree, but his political philosophy as well. It was Jefferson who argued for a 'wall of separation between church and state'—putting all religious sects 'on an equal footing.'"[22]

We are left to wonder what would have happened if Nichol had thought to make his case for the cross policy change in terms of a story about Jefferson's legacy. That story, as we have already seen, has broad appeal in Williamsburg and throughout the Commonwealth of Virginia. At the very least, that move would have given him a better chance of success.

Even with an appeal to Jefferson, however, Nichol may not have been able to effect this change without alienating key constituents. Some influential board members and alumni benefactors might have been outraged at Nichol's decision no matter how he had introduced it. We will never know. Nichol would be the first to admit that his unpublicized policy change and a brief e-mail to the student body were by no means sufficient to shape the narrative justifying this significant symbolic change at William and Mary. Even though, as I have argued, the substance of his position was right and the choices he made to repair his "clumsily" framed action were effective, his blundered introduction of the policy made it ultimately impossible to hold together William and Mary's constituencies.

Jefferson's Quran

I have already noted the case of Keith Ellison, the first Muslim member elected to the U.S. Congress. Before taking office in January of 2007, Ellison decided to follow the unofficial tradition of being sworn in to Congress with his hand on a holy book. This was for the private ceremony following the official swearing-in, which is done as a group, without any texts. For most politicians entering political office, the book used for the individual swearing-in has been the Christian Bible, but Ellison's decision to use a different text has precedent. Instead of a religious text, John Quincy Adams took his presidential oath of office in 1825 with his hand on a law book that contained the U.S. Constitution. In more recent times, Congresswoman Debbie Wasserman Schulz was sworn in two years before Ellison using a Tanakh, or Hebrew Bible, as former New York City mayor Ed Koch had done when he joined Congress in 1969.[23] A handful of other Jewish lawmakers have also been cited as precedents for using an alternative text.

This issue was propelled into the national spotlight by culture warriors on the conservative side, most notably commentator Dennis Prager and Congressman Virgil Goode. Prager, who is Jewish, and a host of other critics of Ellison took the position that the Bible is the book that undergirds American morality. The Christian holy book is, in Prager's words, the "Bible of this country." After all, he writes, throughout "all of American history, Jews elected to public office have taken their oath on the Bible, even though they do not believe in the New Testament."[24] If officials were going to expand the list of "acceptable" texts, he asked, how could we avoid going down a slippery slope that could ultimately allow the use of Hitler's *Mein Kampf*? Interestingly, the issue split conservatives. Many defended the rights associated with America's tradition of religious freedom. They correctly observed that the Constitution bars any religious test for office and that no written stipulation exists for the use or prohibition of religious texts in an oath of office. Other conservatives, in contrast, downplayed talk of religious freedom and spoke of the "Christian nation."

This issue concerned symbolism of the highest order. It touched the nerve of national identity. Prager and his colleagues wanted to use this occasion to fuel fears that the United States was sliding toward moral relativism or toward the "Islamicization of America." He embraced language of "The Culture Wars" (capital letters his) and sought to fight on this terrain against the Quran. The cultural Left replied with calls for Prager's removal from the taxpayer-funded U.S. Holocaust Memorial council. Here both politics and religion fueled passions. Importantly, issues of race also contributed. Ellison, an African American, had earlier in his career praised Nation of Islam leader Louis Farrakhan, and conservative critics were quick to point this out.

Faced with this criticism before he even entered office, Ellison needed a solution that would appeal to a broad swath of Americans. He could have further stoked the conflict; Ellison has found his fair share of controversy both before and since. But in a brilliant stroke of leadership that showed a sensitivity to the symbolism at stake, Ellison elected to be sworn in using a Quran once owned by Thomas Jefferson.

Jefferson's Quran was located in the Library of Congress, part of the rare book and special collections division, acquired in 1815 among the volumes Jefferson sold to the library when its collections were being rebuilt after the British burned it during the War of 1812.[25] At the height of the controversy, Ellison's staff had requested use of this specific Quran.[26] The library granted Ellison special permission for its use, as it has done for other books used for ceremonial leadership occasions in the past. On inauguration day in 2007 Jefferson's book was transported across the street to the Capitol (accompanied by an armed guard, given the controversy) for the ceremony.

Jefferson had purchased this Quran in 1765 as part of his exploration of legal systems and natural law. According to Kevin J. Hayes, Jefferson viewed the Quran as both a legal and a religious text—though ultimately he chose to classify it under "religion" in his expansive library at Monticello.[27] Hayes presents evidence that Jefferson showed an appreciation and curiosity for the Quran and even opted later in life to learn Arabic. Nonetheless, Islam remained foreign from Jefferson's everyday experience. His most direct political encounter with Muslims would concern the threat of the Barbary pirates, who were threatening U.S. commercial and military vessels from the north African coast of the Mediterranean. Yet David Barton, an advocate of seeing America as a Christian nation, is incorrect in stating the following: "Why did Jefferson own a Koran? A simple answer is: To learn the beliefs of the enemies he was fight-ing."[28] Jefferson purchased the Quran in 1765; his involvement with the Barbary pirates took place twenty years later. Jefferson's greatest problem with Islam in general had to do with claims of the text's unquestioned authority—the same problem he had with many Christian views of the Bible.[29] Jefferson criticized those from any tradition who upheld an absolutist view toward their religious texts. He owned a Quran because he was intellectually curious and saw legal, political, and moral resources in a variety of religious traditions.

As we have already seen, Jefferson greatly valued freedom of conscience. He sought to preserve the broad reach of Virginia's Statute of Religious Free-dom against a proposed amendment that would insert language about Jesus Christ. Hayes writes: "[T]he Virginia legislators might not have had Maho-metans [Jefferson's term] in mind when they debated the bill, but Jefferson did when he wrote it."[30]

Keith Ellison accepted the sage advice (he reports that he received an anonymous letter informing him of this book) to appeal to Thomas Jefferson. In an interview on the eve of his swearing-in, Ellison framed his decision around Jefferson's vision: "It demonstrates that from the very beginning of our country, we had people who were visionary, who were religiously toler-ant, who believed that knowledge and wisdom could be gleaned from any number of sources, including the Quran."[31] As many leaders have done, Elli-son referred to the legacy of one of the American founders to communicate a vision of mutual tolerance. In a single act, he shifted the time frame from the twenty-first century and the rhetoric of Islamicization to a historic one in which religious freedom is a bedrock value of the nation. This act, then, shifted the focus from competing religious values to commonly held political ones. This decision subtly altered the public debate from one about compet-ing, fixed identities among Americans—Christians, Jews, Muslims, atheists, and so on—to a narrative of *mutual learning* through the mention of Jeffer-son's desire to acquire "knowledge and wisdom" from perspectives very differ-ent from his own.

In the end, the actual ceremony on January 4, 2007, received less press coverage than the preceding weeks of heated debate. Many newspapers ran a photograph of Nancy Pelosi, the first woman Speaker of the House, swearing in Keith Ellison, an African American Muslim, with his hand upon Jefferson's Quran. This was a symbolically powerful image with various meanings. Few commentators made any reference to the fact that Ellison, a descendant of slaves, was praising the inclusive vision of Jefferson, a slave owner. The fact that the Quran had belonged to Jefferson made the image traditionally Ameri-can, even as the other elements—Pelosi as the first woman Speaker, Ellison as a religious and racial minority, and the Quran itself—stretched our imagination of what the United States looks like. By appealing to Jefferson, Ellison succeeded in framing this expansion of the American imagination as simply the latest chapter in the American story.

Leveling the Playing Field

Bill Clinton entered the White House in 1992 as the second Southern Baptist Democratic president in two decades. Educated by nuns in elementary school and later a graduate of Georgetown University, a Jesuit, Roman Catholic institution, Clinton was well versed in Catholic practice and social teaching. As president, he reached out to religious people who held a wide range of theological and political perspectives.

Progressive Christians in particular had helped Clinton reach the White House, while Christian conservatives had sought to label him immoral for his reported affair with Gennifer Flowers. Despite this criticism, Clinton knew that he could reach out to fellow Christians across political and racial lines, particularly in African American churches. His ability and desire to connect with religious believers of all stripes, however, is arguably not just political but also an intrinsic part of his personality. His former aides describe him as voraciously curious about varied expressions of religious belief and practice. Clinton actively sought to create a level playing field in American public life for people of all backgrounds.

Toward that end, Clinton dedicated a 1993 White House prayer breakfast speech to bringing people together across denominational and racial-ethnic lines. He described a public culture hostile to religious faith. Citing Yale law professor Stephen Carter's book, *The Culture of Disbelief*, which he had read that summer, Clinton stated that "the environment in which we operate is entirely too secular. The fact that we have freedom of religion doesn't mean we need to try to have freedom from religion."[32]

As a former professor of constitutional law, Clinton believed that the First Amendment did not require the excommunication of religion from public life. He saw, rather, that the American system was intended to create a society in which all Americans could live together without preferential attention to any one religious belief or organization. He shared with Christian conservatives a sense that American society allowed too little room for religious expression. Clinton stated his support for—and worked with—religious and political leaders across the spectrum on the Religious Freedom Restoration Act, which was passed and signed into law in 1993.

Although Clinton and the conservatives agreed on much regarding what they saw as the problem of excessive secularism, they differed on the terms of what a reconsecrated public life would look like. Clinton envisioned a public square in which we "find strength in our diversity."[33] By contrast, after the 1994 Republican congressional victories, Newt Gingrich and other conservatives preferred a Christian nation approach and pushed for a constitutional amendment to allow school prayer.[34]

The public schools had become the leading battleground in the culture wars, and school prayer was a cause célèbre for the Right. In response, the Left pushed church-state separation. In the face of the Republicans' more radical approach—altering the Constitution—Clinton stepped forward and offered a position on religion in schools that would appeal to many Americans. In 1995 Clinton issued a Memorandum on Religious Expression in Public Schools. Never one to miss a symbolic opportunity, Clinton delivered his speech announcing the memorandum at James Madison High School in Vienna, Virginia. Madison had provided the political savvy and perseverance to pass the Jefferson-authored Virginia Statute for Religious Freedom, and he also took the lead in the drafting the First Amendment and the entire Bill of Rights. Clinton invoked both Jefferson and Madison in his speech, which was largely framed to find common ground in the First Amendment.

In that speech, which was longer than the official memorandum itself, Clinton was offering a vision for a diverse America that could share a commitment to mutual respect. Harkening back to his childhood in Arkansas, he recalled how his town had two synagogues and a Greek Orthodox church and how more recently a mosque had been built in his part of the state. Later in his speech Clinton returned to his personal narrative, recounting that in junior high school he and his classmates had started every day with a Bible reading:

> And I can tell you that all of us who were in there doing it never gave a second thought most of the time to the fact that we didn't have blacks in our schools and that there were Jews in the classroom who were probably deeply offended by half the stuff we were saying or doing—or maybe made to feel inferior. . . . I'm not sure the Catholics were always comfortable with what we did either. . . . This is part of my personal life experience.[35]

Clinton used his own story to reframe the discussion of school prayer. First, he painted a picture of the diverse America of his childhood, an America that had become even more so. Second, he noted that religion did not always make people more just or morally right—Bible reading and racial discrimination went hand in hand during his youth. Finally, cultural privilege can affect the manner in which minority students (and citizens) see themselves and their place in society.

Clinton offered a series of practical guidelines that aimed to allow students' private expression of religion while they were at school. In the memorandum, Clinton declared: "As our courts have reaffirmed . . . nothing in the First Amendment converts our public schools into religion-free zones, or requires all religious expression to be left behind at the schoolhouse door."[36] This was the narrative that framed his whole effort. The memo covered an array of topics, such as what types of student prayer meetings were allowed, when one could be excused from class for religious reasons, and what was permissible religious attire. The memo also clarified that teachers could teach about religion but not teach students to be religious. Teachers could also teach civic values and moral codes.

This act of leadership explained many issues about religion in public schools and received broad support from religious organizations and civil liberties groups. Indeed, a coalition of such organizations had helped draft the memorandum. It also managed to pull the rug out from under the proposed school prayer amendment. The amendment's chief sponsor in the U.S. House, Rep. Ernest Istook of Oklahoma, criticized the president and his memorandum: "He's trying to re-create himself once again. . . . He's saying let's focus on what religious liberties we have left rather than what we have lost."[37] Nonetheless, in overall terms, the speech and the memorandum were a tremendous success. Education Secretary Richard Riley would send expanded guidelines to all of the nation's school districts the following month.

In August 1997 Clinton issued another important memorandum on religion in the federal workplace. Working with many of the same religious leaders and advisors (including Secretary Riley), Clinton clarified that federal employees on the job can engage in religious expression to a significant degree, bosses cannot discriminate on the basis of religion, and workplaces are required to make reasonable accommodation of employee practices. Less visible and symbolically loaded than prayer in the schoolhouse, these federal workplace guidelines drew less attention, but they were still seen as significant in trying to create a culture that protects religious expression of all people.

A few months earlier the Supreme Court had declared the Religious Freedom Restoration Act unconstitutional in part on the grounds that the act exceeded Congress's power. This was disappointing to Clinton, who had supported the act and enthusiastically signed it into law. The court required the president to release revised guidelines that would give schools more flexibility in deciding how to act, which he did in May of 1998. In his radio address to announce these revised guidelines, he noted the success his original guidelines had already achieved, repeating the line that "nothing in the Constitution requires schools to be religion-free zones." He added this line against his political opponents: "Some people say there should be a constitutional amendment to allow voluntary prayer in our public schools. But there already is one; it's the first amendment."[38]

Clinton's ability to frame religion in public life had, if anything, improved, but his own personal actions had by then undermined his leadership. He had badly damaged his own capacity to employ the moral force of the presidential bully pulpit. In January 1998 Clinton faced public exposure of his relations with Monica Lewinsky. The charges of marital infidelity that had haunted him ever since his days as governor of Arkansas now paralyzed his presidency—and severely diminished his moral authority. He confronted one word every time he mentioned religion in public life: hypocrite.

When he finally got caught in his own web of deceptive and misleading statements, Clinton turned to religious language. Three weeks after a nationally televised half-apology to the American people, Clinton used the occasion of the White House prayer breakfast, on September 11, 1998, to apologize more fully. That talk was focused around this notable line: "I don't think there is a fancy way to say that I have sinned."[39]

Was Clinton truly penitent? Or was he invoking the Christian discourse of sin and redemption to gain the forgiveness of the American political community? These questions require each one of us to make our own judgment. In my view, both explanations are true; Clinton was remorseful, *and* he wanted quickly to reframe his dilemma as a familiar religious narrative. He had come to understand that his actions were not some private question, as he had suggested in his attempted apology on August 17: "This matter is between me, the two people I love most—my wife and our daughter—and our God. . . . It is private . . . nobody's business but ours."[40] He used his later speech to apologize publicly to a litany of people: his family, friends, staff members, Monica Lewinsky, and all Americans. And, interestingly, he invoked a lengthy passage from a Jewish liturgy for Yom Kippur, the annual festival of repentance. He followed that with imagery from the Psalms and the book of Proverbs. Even (or especially) in his darkest moments, Clinton turned to religious imagery from various and overlapping traditions to help him persevere. This time, this linguistic reframing was for his own benefit and, he suggested, for the "greater good" of the American people.

One lasting effect of Clinton's actions was that his ability to shape the culture into one more welcoming of religious voices in the public arena had been almost completely undermined by his failures of personal morality. As David Gergen, former senior advisor to Clinton and three other presidents, puts it, "The collateral damage was immense. He had compromised his family, friends, cabinet members, and staff. He had cheapened the political process he had worked all his life to improve. His hopes for making his second term one of high accomplishment were lost."[41]

This president who so well understood the power of symbols had disabled his own capacity to employ them to realize a new vision of America. After January 1998 Clinton could not speak effectively on issues about which he cared deeply. He had made it more difficult for Democrats to talk about faith in politics.[42] Still, even Clinton's serious leadership failures and self-destructive behavior should not make observers lose sight of his success in creating a more level and inclusive playing field for citizens of various backgrounds. That part of the Clinton legacy will never receive the headlines of the Lewinsky affair, but it nevertheless contributed to a wider and deeper public life.

Conclusions

These three examples strongly support the point that leaders have the capacity to influence the "moral environment" of their institution.[43] All of them faced difficult dilemmas, and each has admitted mistakes in his leadership.[44] All three men seemed to have understood the power of public stories and symbols even as each one underestimated the symbolic effects their actions would have. What can we learn from the successes and disappointments that Nichol, Ellison, and Clinton experienced? What general lessons might we draw?

First, each of these three figures drew successfully on the values embedded in the American civic tradition. They each cited the tradition of Jefferson, Madison, the First Amendment, and the Constitution. They appealed, in other words, to what scholar Barbara McGraw has called "America's sacred ground."[45] In the language of morals, they articulated the importance of religious freedom for every American. Clinton did this most explicitly in his address at James Madison High School in 1995. Nichol did it through his appeals to make everyone welcome on campus and in the Wren Chapel. Ellison expressed his desire to lead as a public servant who was also Muslim; his hand on Jefferson's Quran was a literal connection to the great American founder's intellectual curiosity and commitment to religious freedom.

Second, each leader noted contemporary America's significant religious diversity and the need to think increasingly broadly about mutual respect. The United States has always had religious and moral variety among its population, but growing diversity and public interaction force us to think anew about the American values that undergird religious freedom. Nichol cited the Jewish,

Muslim, and "secular" students who wanted to enjoy the Wren Chapel; Ellison spoke of the heterogeneity of his Minnesota constituents; Clinton provided a narrative about churches, synagogues, and a mosque in Arkansas.

Third, these leaders sought to acknowledge the historic role of the Christian tradition and Christianity's role in shaping civil religion in American public life. For Nichol, of course, this became a core issue, and a plaque and a glass case for the cross provided a breakthrough for his dilemma. Clinton immersed himself in his own Baptist tradition, citing biblical passages and referencing his personal faith on multiple occasions. Ellison's tack was more indirect, perhaps; his decision to employ Jefferson's Quran placed him in the American civil religion, but Jefferson was a peculiar sort of Christian.

Fourth, each leader sought to build common ground. This often occurred by recruiting a broad coalition of dissimilar constituents to support their initiatives. Each drew in an array political and religious perspectives to support their action. All three leaders managed to find or forge common ground, even when it was not clear that any existed.

Fifth, these three leaders emphasized that, when it comes to religious symbols, leadership can get personal. Nichol's family was harassed, and he lost his job, at least partly as a result of claims that he did not understand "the Tribe" he was supposed to lead. Ellison was threatened—and linked by sweeping statements about Islam to terrorism—before he ever got to office. Clinton was lambasted as a secular wolf in a Christian sheep's clothing.

Finally, each of these leaders emphasized the need—after their own trials—to anticipate and prepare for a response from the opponents of diversity. As much as leaders cite their respect for American tradition and Christian influences, some citizens still view their acts of leadership as hostile to religion in general or to Christianity in particular. Leaders who seek change will be called un-American or unpatriotic. Anticipating this type of criticism (not to mention threats and harassment) will not make it all go away, but by preemptively taking these kinds of actions, leaders can help undercut their critics.

None of these are magic bullets. Leaders and constituents who seek to build a more inclusive American public space will surely face opposition. Civic disagreement and heated public debate are certainly a healthy part of democracy. It is not simple or without cost to attempt to reshape the culture, especially on questions on which "tradition" plays a key role. Attempting to change civic and political culture in ways that question majority privilege often provokes unfair retribution from those who take their benefits for granted. The more prepared leaders can be for such challenges, the more likely they are to withstand the pressure and succeed in promoting a culture of convivencia.

8

Engaging Citizens

Instead of the leader as . . . a magic man, you could develop individuals who were bound together by a concept that benefited the larger number of individuals and provided an opportunity for them to grow into being responsible for carrying out a program.

—Ella Baker

CRISES BRING PEOPLE TOGETHER IN WAYS THAT ARE NOT USUALLY POSSIBLE. IN THE skies over Pennsylvania on September 11, 2001, passengers of United Airlines Flight 93 joined together to attack their hijackers. Some of them prayed before they did so. The passengers and crew were quite diverse in terms of religious background, race, nationality, gender, and sexual orientation. Although they died in the process, these passengers found the courage to come together to stop the terrorists' plans.

A lesser-known hijacking attempt occurred in 2007 on an Air Mauritania flight to the Canary Islands. This time the passengers and crew managed to both foil the hijacking plot and save their own lives. Their response was coordinated by the pilot, who sent coded messages over the public-address system about how and when to attack the armed gunman who was trying to take over their plane. The passenger hero of the flight made the following remark to a reporter a few days later: "If I had not been sure that I was going to die, I would not have hurled myself at the hijacker. I chose between certain death and probable death." This hero, Mohamed Uld Ahmed, continued, "I am Muslim and I have faith. I know that one day I will die, but it was not meant to be on that airplane."[1]

These two cases involved citizens leading in a moment of crisis—by drawing on resources of their own faith and acting in concert despite their differences. We should not compare our ordinary leadership with this kind of extraordinary heroism. Still, the mundane actions of convivencia, of living together in all of our variety, can also require serious risk taking and personal investment. James MacGregor Burns asserts that transforming leadership demands a high level of engagement between leaders and followers. For citizens of varied religious backgrounds, committing ourselves to public action is a matter of faith—as it was for the heroes of United 93 and Air Mauritania Flight 465. In some cases, this engagement requires leaving the comfort zone of people who look like us or believe as we do. Befriending "religious others" can make us subject to criticism in our own communities. Reaching out to fellow citizens and constituents—"leadership by showing up"—takes a lot of time and effort. And engaging in a heterogeneous society requires humility, which allows us to hold fast to our convictions while cooperating and seeking to learn from others. This chapter examines, then, the engagement of citizens and leaders that requires—if not heroism—bold, proactive collaboration.

The Hard Work of Building Coalitions

In August of 2007, long-simmering tensions within two prominent religious organizations came to a boil. Both the Anti-Defamation League (ADL) and the Council on American-Islamic Relations (CAIR) work on promoting the positive place and contribution of members of their respective religious communities in American public life. The ADL, founded in 1913, and CAIR, founded in 1994, have shone significant light on acts of hate and bigotry against Jews and Muslims, respectively, in the United States. Yet in the face of international tensions—especially in Israel and Palestine—these organizations have rarely spoken up in strong terms against the degradation of people from the other religious community.

The war of words broke out when the ADL issued a background report on the Islamic organization that stated that "[u]nfortunately, CAIR's credibility as a community relations agency promoting 'justice and mutual understanding' is tainted." It went on to catalog CAIR's alleged connections to pro-Hamas groups and anti-Semitic rhetoric. It also criticized CAIR's fund-raising efforts on behalf of the legal defense fund of the Holy Land Foundation, which had been accused of funneling donations to support Hamas.[2] Less than two weeks after releasing this report, the ADL followed up with a press release bearing this headline: "ADL Troubled by National Islamic Civil Rights Organization's

Failure to Condemn Terrorism by Name."[3] In terse language, national ADL director Abraham Foxman stated, "[I]t is deeply troubling that CAIR simply refuses to issue a clear and unequivocal condemnation of terrorists and terrorism." The ADL labeled CAIR hypocritical and claimed that, despite its lip service against anti-Semitism, it had failed to renounce "its past affiliation" with pro-Palestinian groups known for anti-Semitic ideology.[4]

Nine days later CAIR retaliated. In language that mirrored that of the ADL invectives, CAIR stated, "It is unfortunate that the ADL would employ rhetorical tactics that are used routinely by anti-Semites. These tactics raise questions about the sincerity of the ADL's stated mission to 'secure justice and fair treatment for all citizens alike.'"[5] The letter went on to identify CAIR's public efforts to denounce terrorism and named Jewish leaders who supported CAIR's work. The CAIR letter used the same divisive rhetorical style that it had denounced in the ADL's statements. In addition, CAIR's letter posed four pointed questions, three of them concerning Israel's actions in Palestine and Lebanon.

The communications from the ADL and CAIR alike used the term "unfortunate" to decry each other's actions. These very public attempts to attack the other organization's integrity made the whole exchange an unfortunate affair indeed.

It is clearly no simple matter for advocacy or human rights groups that represent minority religious communities to manage conflictual relationships, let alone form effective coalitions. American Jews and Muslims both face discrimination, whether overt or subtle. Jewish and Muslim histories in the United States are quite different, but they share the common challenge of living as minorities in a country in which roughly four-fifths of the citizens are Christians. When a major presidential candidate suggests that America was founded as a Christian nation and that a Christian leader might be more effective than a Muslim one; when presidents invoke Christian scripture in ways that non-Christians are unlikely to understand; when some churches lead the way against efforts to accommodate citizens of minority faiths, non-Christians can find it difficult to see themselves as full members of the community.

Jews have been acknowledged as a part of American culture through the vision of a "Judeo-Christian tradition" and ideas like Herberg's American "triple melting pot."[6] From a position between the mainstream and the margin, Jews have a unique relationship with other minority traditions, including Islam. Each year the Federal Bureau of Investigation (FBI) issues annual hate-crime statistics for the United States. In recent years, incidents motivated by anti-Jewish sentiment have consistently been about six times as common as anti-Islamic ones.[7] Some Jewish leaders have used these statistics to argue that anti-Semitism continues to outpace anti-Islamic thought and behavior in the

United States.[8] This is surely a complicated and heated issue. The numbers are difficult to interpret given the respective (and disputed) population figures for Jews and Muslims, the likelihood of members of the respective community to report hate crimes, the severity of different reported crimes, and related matters. One study estimates that hate crime *rates* against Jews and Muslims stand at roughly the same level—fifteen per 100,000 against Jews and twelve per 100,000 against Muslims.[9] Whatever the exact figures, Jewish and Muslim leaders should not try to gain attention by competing for the most victimized position.

American Hindus have also struggled with the question of how best to navigate their relationships with majority and minority religious communities in the United States. The tensions between Hindus and Muslims on the south Asian subcontinent have colored Hindu-Muslim relations in the United States as well. As sociologist Prema Kurien has framed it, Hindu American civic outreach in the United States reflects two strains: a "genteel multiculturalism" and a "militant Hindu nationalism." In the former approach, Hinduism is portrayed as a model community for a heterogeneous society since Hinduism itself is characterized by rich diversity and a tolerance for dissimilar beliefs. In the "genteel" strain, Hindu Americans are portrayed as "model citizens" who have embraced the American dream. In the wake of 9/11, however, Kurien notes that the militant nationalist strand reared its head and actively criticized American Muslims. Some Hindu leaders censured those who would promote Islam as a religion of peace in the United States while supporting Islamist organizations abroad.[10]

Some Muslims in America have also engaged in name-calling and stark criticism of Jews and others. Minister Louis Farrakahn has made well-publicized anti-Semitic statements throughout his three decades of leadership of the Nation of Islam. Of course, African American Muslims and the immigrant Muslim community have long debated whether the Nation of Islam is properly considered "mainstream" Islam. A very small faction of Muslim Americans—estimated at 1 percent by a 2007 survey—believes that Jews or Israel bears responsibility for the 9/11 attacks.[11]

When marginalized communities criticize each other, as these examples suggest, they too easily end up in a race to the bottom. Although it is difficult to reverse this downward trajectory, it causes needless damage to the respective religious communities. Religious and civic communities must be able to engage in frank conversation and even criticism, but those interactions achieve little if they are not conducted with basic respect for others. Leadership from within such organizations (and from our political leaders, too) can help transform these destructive conflicts into constructive exchanges.

What can be done? As a first step, leaders from all religious, civic, and political institutions must state firmly and consistently that hate crimes against people of any religion, race, ethnicity, nationality, or sexual orientation are heinous acts. Citizen groups from across the religious spectrum should work together to respond to hate crimes against any group. In the same way that political and military alliances have done, religious coalitions should ban together not only to declare solidarity but also to prepare to respond to an attack against any organization in the coalition.[12] This is a very specific way of building crossroads and connectors in the form of interreligious alliances.

While this kind of work is not easy, it can be done. Consider a group of religious communities in Britain that have banded together to promote respect for all religious communities. The Interfaith Network for the United Kingdom was established in 1987 to bring together religious organizations and related educational bodies. Immediately after the London public transport bombings on July 7, 2005, the Interfaith Network rushed to release a document titled "Looking after One Another: The Safety and Security of Our Faith Communities."[13] This initiative aims to build a broad coalition among religious groups based on three practices:

1. respond jointly—an attack on one is an attack on all
2. build on existing good intercommunity relations
3. maintain calm in times of tension

Under this rubric, the Interfaith Network suggests a variety of practical steps, including showing solidarity by standing together at the site of any attack or threat. This unity should also extend to helping victimized groups clean up or rebuild their communities or buildings. Moreover, leaders should make joint statements to the media condemning hostility against anyone based on their religious identity. The organization helpfully frames this crisis response within the context of building ongoing relations among neighboring communities, especially personal interactions between religious leaders. These networks of mutual understanding provide the "social capital" that respondents can draw on in times of crisis. In Britain as in the United States and elsewhere, we do not know what acts of hate or terror we will face, but we should prepare to respond to them. Having the basic structure—including the personal associations—in place before crisis hits makes it much easier to act together when something does happen.

In the United States, some Muslim and Jewish leaders have begun building bridges to help ease the political tensions that lead to mutual suspicion. The very day after CAIR's August 2007 letter criticizing the ADL, a leading Jewish figure addressed fifteen hundred Muslims at the annual conference of the Islamic Society of North America (ISNA). Rabbi Eric Yoffie, president of the Union for Reform Judaism (URJ), representing nine hundred congregations and 1.5 million members, offered words of conciliation and attempted to find common ground. He announced discussions between the URJ and the ISNA to create a joint dialogue between American Jews and American Muslims. He condemned the public statements of political leaders—from Christian, Jewish, and other backgrounds—who stereotype Islam as violent or extremist. In addition, he noted that Jewish sacred texts—as well as Christian and Muslim ones—contain passages that could be interpreted as condoning violence. Yoffie called for a constructive reading of these traditions that will help followers live together in peace.

Yoffie also waded into some of the most difficult questions of Jewish-Islamic relations: "Permit me to conclude with a few words about the situation in the Middle East—because this too must also be included in our dialogue." He called for common support of a two-state solution—for "a democratic Palestinian state [that] lives side by side, in peace and security, with the democratic State of Israel." He summarized his approach to this stumbling-block issue with this question: "Will we, Jews and Muslims, import the conflicts of the Middle East into America, or will we join together and send a message of peace to that troubled land?"[14]

Yoffie's appearance at the annual meeting of the largest association of Muslims in the United States took some courage. He decried those critics who are "eager to seize on any troubling statement by any Muslim thinker and pin it on Islam as a whole."[15] Yoffie himself was criticized by some for reaching out to a group that many Jews have scorned. Daniel Pipes, an outspoken critic of Islam, called Yoffie's outreach "well-intentioned but very misguided" and noted the "deep current of anti-Semitism among Muslims in the United States."[16] At the same time, two Republican members of the U.S. House sent a letter to the U.S. attorney general, in which they condemned the Islamic Society of North America and the Justice Department's decision to have a display at the conference. They decried the government officials' participation as "a precedent that radical jihadists should be the conduit between the U.S. government and the American Muslim population."[17] To many observers, labeling the ISNA—an organization headquartered in Plainfield, Indiana, with five decades of mainstream American presence and tradition—as a group of "radical jihadists" would be laughable if it were not such a serious charge. Yoffie had defended his own participation in the ISNA meeting by saying that the Bush administration was "so well represented" there.[18]

Although ADL president Abraham Foxman had vocally denounced CAIR, he had generally positive comments about Yoffie's appearance at the ISNA conference. He commented that although the ISNA "is not perfect—and no umbrella organization is at all times perfect—it has spoken against terrorism."[19] This nuanced statement is a positive sign in the midst of the tensions between Jews and Muslims in America.

The hard work of building coalitions requires patient and judicious leaders who are willing to tread lightly. In this case, it requires persons from Jewish and Muslim communities who are willing to forge connectors between their communities—to build a new path where both known and unknown minefields exist. Which dialogue and which partners should you choose, and what will you seek to accomplish? Which topics will be set aside or simply avoided because of their present difficulty? Sometimes the most vocal critics will be one's own constituents who harbor such animosity against outsiders that they fear their leaders are selling out. Leaders must also be strategic, then, in their timing and in their framing of outreach efforts.

The example of the Interfaith Network in Britain provides a helpful reminder that all faith communities—including the variety of Christian traditions—can come together to develop coalitions. Building a foundation for response in times of crisis is vital, but the most important effect of such efforts is the development of ongoing, day-to-day friendships among members of different communities.

A More Perfect Union

Those efforts to build "crossroads coalitions" often occur at the local level. After 9/11, localities across the United States were reporting suspicion of and even violence against Muslim, Arab, and south Asian communities. Richmond, Virginia, was no exception. In response, the University of Richmond, the Council for America's First Freedom, and Karamah: Muslim Women Lawyers for Human Rights established a metropolitan antibias initiative. They named it A More Perfect Union (AMPU), a phrase from the preamble to the U.S. Constitution.[20] AMPU brought in eight additional coalition partners representing Sikh, Muslim, Jewish, and interfaith communities. By holding monthly meetings of advisory boards and subcommittees, AMPU built up the connections among so-called minority communities in the Richmond area.[21]

In its first five years, AMPU undertook two major media outreach campaigns. Each sought to capture and communicate the everyday nature of a religiously diverse America. In Howard Gardner's terms, these campaigns told an inclusive story of religious freedom that would reach the "five-year-old mind" of fellow citizens. These were intentional efforts to appeal to familiar stories—the American dream, the U.S. immigrant experience, and the U.S. Constitution.

The first initiative involved the production of two public service announcements, which have been aired on cable television stations and on the Internet and earned national media recognition.[22] In the first of these public service announcements, "Lonely," a Muslim-Arab man tells the story of his family's struggles to feel welcome in America. His son, Ahmed, he says, loves the playground, but no one will play with him. The visual image shows a white mother pulling her son, who is motioning "bang, bang" with his fingers, away from the Arab American boy. The narrator's daughter, Fatima, rides the bus, but people distance themselves from her when she sits down. The visual of this bus scene echoes the civil rights struggles of African Americans, such as Montgomery in 1955–1956. The man's wife loves to shop, but she cannot get sales clerks to assist her. In the final shot, the man, bumped by harried fellow Americans on a crowded elevator, concludes with these words: "I've gotta tell you: This isn't the America I dreamed of." In thirty seconds, then, this spot attempts to show the reality that a Muslim and Arab American family faces every day—one that is in clear contrast to the familiar story of the American dream.

A companion public service announcement also highlights mundane encounters, albeit in a tenser atmosphere. This spot takes place on an airplane. A friendly, well-dressed Sikh man wearing a turban is seated on the plane. A white businessman in coat and tie is about to sit next to him. He says a polite hello to the Sikh man, but then we hear what the businessman is really thinking: "He's mad, he's mad as a hornet!" He then says to the Sikh, "Say, are you from Pakistan?" The Sikh smiles and says, "Actually, I'm from Pittsburgh." We witness the businessman's thoughts again, and he is panicked: "Pittsburgh? . . . How many people from Pittsburgh look like that? . . . Look what he's got on his head! . . . He's a sleeper! . . . We're going down!" And we hear the sound of a plane in free fall. The video ends with a voice-over comment from a narrator about the businessman's fear: "This is the problem. Education is the answer. Rethink bias at aMorePerfectUnion.info."

This public service announcement was by far the more controversial because it tapped into the anxiety many flyers have felt since 9/11. It made the Sikh appear as nice as a favorite uncle or grandfather. The problem, as the spot framed it, was only in the head of the white businessman. The tone of the announcement almost mocks him for his anxious ignorance. Although this is provocative, observers can debate whether it manages to generate a constructive conversation.

A More Perfect Union's second public media campaign also aimed to make people think, albeit without the edge of the airplane scene. On 170 public buses in Richmond, the coalition placed large advertisements written in Arabic. At the bottom of each sign, an English translation was included in smaller print. The signs stated mundane, innocuous phrases, including "plastic or paper," "rock, paper, scissors," and "I'm a little teapot." The posters then asked in English: "What did you think it said? Rethink bias at www.rethinkbias.org." The lesson? If we get to know one another and our languages, we discover that people from different backgrounds share many everyday experiences. Even the placement on buses was designed to reflect a daily activity in which diverse people's paths cross as they ride the bus together.

This campaign received significant and appreciative media coverage.[23] The public's response was strong but mixed. The feedback section on the organization's web page reveals Americans' divergent perspectives—from welcoming to despising—of Muslim neighbors. Indeed, the AMPU staff had to remove some comments that it judged were hate provoking. Still, staffers have not filtered out sharp comments such as "The only good snake is a dead snake. IF you get my meaning . . . Yes I am BIAS [sic] and don't care." Another critic grasped the focus on everyday life but was concerned that "[t]hey are just trying to get us used to Arabic signs. Later when they put up the real Jihad messages we will ignore them." (This commentator did not specify who "they" were.) On the other side, various commentators applauded the signs: "Most of the comments listed here [on the feedback page] are telling us exactly why this campaign is so sorely needed."[24]

A More Perfect Union chose an intentionally provocative public outreach strategy that focused on stories. With assistance from two public relations firms, the coalition has sought to make mutual understanding a matter of daily life. The echoes of African American civil rights struggles are important— particularly in the context of Richmond, the former Confederate capital and a site of massive resistance against school integration.

Religious leaders and political leaders stepped forward to endorse the project. For example, then lieutenant governor Tim Kaine spoke at an *Eid-al Adha* community dinner (associated with the *Hajj*, or pilgrimage to Mecca) and framed the AMPU initiative within Jefferson's vision of religious freedom. Yet it was the citizen-leaders who moved this project from an idea to a visible presence in the metropolitan region. Principals from secular and religious communities joined together to take the coalition's work to their members and to the wider community. These citizens built a public education effort around media promotions, as well as packets of educational materials for faith communities, public schools, civic groups, and legislators. Related educational information was posted on the coalition's website. Through its Internet presence and the edgy nature of its media campaigns, the public education effort sought to appeal to young people in particular.

A More Perfect Union has struggled to find an identity as a coalition of identity-based organizations. In a community of overcommitted citizen-leaders, the coalition found it difficult to accomplish groundbreaking work with a small staff and busy volunteers. The institutional home moved from a university to an interfaith organization, the Virginia Interfaith Center for Public Policy. The work of A More Perfect Union continues on a shoestring budget. Whether the initiative will achieve enduring social change—and thus fit that crucial criterion of transforming leadership—remains to be seen. Yet the effort offers a vivid example of how local people from many major religious traditions, as well as none at all, have sought to communicate a lofty message about everyday encounters.

For citizens building an interreligious network, finding common cause on civic issues—such as fighting bias—may be more straightforward than broaching theological or dogmatic questions. Citizens need not be theologians to achieve convivencia with their neighbors.

Leadership by Showing Up

How should political leaders interact with the vibrant and varied religious communities and networks that help make up American civil society? We have seen how members and leaders of different religious groups forge coalitions at interreligious crossroads. For their part, political leaders help shape a level playing field that encourages such connections. Beyond the important symbolic work of shaping the culture, successful leaders engage directly with their constituents, too. This is "leadership by showing up." Public leaders help transform our politics when they attend a wide array of events—such as the observance of holy days, dedications of new buildings, and discussions of policy issues—not just to campaign but also to connect. This work of "showing up" at events across the constituent spectrum can also expand a leader's vision.

Business experts and scholars refer to "management by wandering around" or "management by walking about." A widely read book by Tom Peters and Robert Waterman Jr., *In Search of Excellence: Lessons from America's Best-run Companies*, highlights the practice.[25] In firms like IBM and Hewlett-Packard (HP), executives engage tirelessly in informal interactions with employees at all levels of their mammoth organizations. The costs of this practice are high,

Peters and Waterman admit, in terms of the time and commitment it requires of leaders. Yet it is a fundamental part of what makes these companies excellent. The authors highlight three reasons for leading in this way: Most important, effective managers need to remain in close touch with what their followers actually think and do. Second, leaders who interact frequently can communicate their own vision and priorities for the organization in person. Third, as an HP executive puts it, "[I]t is just plain fun," and thus such interaction tends to energize the leaders, as well as their followers.[26]

Of course, political and business leaders face different contexts and opportunities for interaction with their followers.[27] Nonetheless, the lessons of management by walking about, or "MBWA," are suggestive for political leaders. Of course, it matters whether they are town council representatives or president of the United States. The president cannot simply wander around the local mall or into a local PTA meeting. Or, if he or she does, it is against the Secret Service detail's better wisdom. Yet, connecting with constituents is important for political leaders at all levels partly because of the symbolic importance of being in touch with constituents' reality. On one trip to Virginia, President George W. Bush stopped his motorcade at a roadside fruit stand and chatted with the locals as he bought a pumpkin. He received regional press as a leader who was connected to the local people. It did not matter that, as the press soon revealed, his staffers had carefully planned the stop.[28] Contrast that image with that of his father, President George H. W. Bush, who was mocked as an out-of-touch leader when he seemed not to know how a supermarket bar-code scanner works.[29] Whether or not the journalist's account of the elder Bush's amazement was accurate, the public's perception of him contributed to his defeat in 1992. The symbolism of being connected to one's constituents is inevitably important.[30]

This is the significance of leadership by showing up. The interactions cannot and probably should not be as informal as what management experts suggest CEOs should practice. And they should be more substantive than detours to fruit stands. The overall schedule and array of visits to religious communities and civic associations should be carefully planned—and not just for reasons of politics, though a leader's self-interest is an unavoidable and an appropriate consideration. Good leaders understand the importance of engaging all sides of society—by showing up with a wide range of communities in their purview.

I have already noted that the Islamic Society of North America has its headquarters in Indiana. The Muslim Alliance of Indiana claims to include 280,000 "Muslim Hoosiers" and provides a seven-page list of Islamic organizations around the state.[31] In 2005 and 2006 Governor Mitch Daniels of Indiana hosted leaders of the state's Islamic community for Iftar dinners to break the fast during the holy month of Ramadan. Daniels had reached out to Muslim leaders as part of his 2004 election campaign and, based on those relationships, hosted annual events first at the statehouse and then at the governor's residence. A Republican and a Presbyterian, Daniels told the Muslim crowd in 2006: "All God's people are equal in his eyes. I am glad to welcome you to this home. You should think of this as your home." Indiana Muslim leaders report that Daniels has maintained ongoing connections with their communities between these high-profile events.[32]

Governor Tim Kaine of Virginia has likewise visited various faith communities in his commonwealth. Northern Virginia in particular is home to a very large number of Muslim, Hindu, Sikh, and Buddhist communities, alongside Christian and Jewish ones. When the Dar Al Noor Mosque was dedicated in Manassas, Virginia, in 2007, Kaine was present to greet the crowd in Arabic and to speak proudly of Virginia, America, and their heritage of religious freedom. The imam, Sheikh Rashid Lamptey, said of Kaine, "We like the way he is. He is an outreach person—reaching out and bridging the gap, building bridges and getting closer to us. That is what we want. We want to be included."[33] Earlier in 2007, Kaine had addressed the Muslim American Society's annual dinner in Washington, D.C. He has met with Hindu, Jewish, Catholic, and Protestant groups as well.

Not all Americans see this wide-ranging "leadership by showing up" as a positive development. Kaine, for example, has received stinging rebukes from critics in Virginia and beyond. Some Virginia Republican leaders accused Kaine, in the words of Delegate C. Todd Gilbert, of "cozying up to organizations and individuals that have radical agendas." They claimed to have begun an investigation of Kaine's and fellow Democrats' ties to the Muslim American Society and the Dar Al Hijrah Islamic Center in northern Virginia. Kaine's communications director replied by saying, "Politics and campaigning have stooped to a new low when the governor of Virginia's effort to reach out to people of all faiths and races is characterized by an association with terrorists."[34]

Kaine had earlier received criticism when a Muslim appointee of his was accused of having, years earlier, made controversial comments about Israel. Esam Omeish, president of the Muslim American Society, had been serving on the Virginia Commission on Immigration in 2007 when videos surfaced of Omeish condemning Israeli incursions in Lebanon against Palestinians and referring to the *"jihad* way" against injustice. (*Jihad* in Arabic means "struggle," which can be but is not necessarily tied to violence.) Kaine felt pressured to ask Omeish to resign his position on the commission, which he did, although Democrats and Republicans alike defended Omeish as an accomplished surgeon, a community leader, and a civic award winner in northern Virginia.[35]

For many Americans, engaging with religious minorities, especially Muslims, remains a political taboo. Fortunately, leaders of both major parties—such as Daniels and Kaine, who are devout Christians (a Protestant and a Roman Catholic, respectively)—have taken the initiative to extend the vision of religious freedom and civic participation to various minority communities.

Such interactions between leaders and citizens can be a tricky business in another way. There is a fine line between engaging followers on their terms for mutual learning and doing so in a way that appears to push a political agenda. Contrast the two visits of President George W. Bush to the Islamic Center of Washington, D.C. I have already identified his visit to this center six days after the 9/11 terrorist attacks as a highly significant act of responsible, enlightened leadership. On that occasion Bush began his brief public statement by thanking the community leaders for their hospitality. By the words he chose and through his presence, he demonstrated that he was standing with American Muslims. He spoke out directly against any acts of hate aimed at these Americans, who, as Bush put it, "love America as much as I do." "In our anger and emotion, our fellow Americans must treat each other with respect." His language reflected the level of informality that works for management by walking around: "I want to thank you all for giving me a chance to come by." This was Bush drawing on his own folksy style without losing the sense of gravitas appropriate to the moment.

In June 2007 the president returned to the Islamic Center of Washington for a fiftieth anniversary rededication ceremony. Invoking an image of convivencia, Bush said, "This Muslim center sits quietly down the road from a synagogue, a Lutheran church, a Catholic parish, a Greek Orthodox chapel, a Buddhist temple—each with faithful followers who practice their deeply held beliefs and live side by side in peace." He extolled the virtues of religious freedom guaranteed by the First Amendment. "It is a basic compact under which people of faith agree not to impose their spiritual vision on others, and in return to practice their own beliefs as they see fit. This is the promise of our Constitution, and the calling of our conscience, and a source of our strength." Much like in September of 2001, Bush condemned radical extremists as enemies of true Islam.

Yet from here the president went on to specifics about the war on terror and used the occasion to prod moderate Muslims to condemn violence in the name of Islam. He went beyond this general point and reverted to stump-speech language that the "efforts under way in Afghanistan and Iraq are central in this struggle" against terrorism. He framed the war on terror in these terms: "I have invested the heart of my presidency in helping Muslims fight terrorism, and claim their liberty, and find their own unique paths to prosperity and peace."[36]

Thus the appearance to rededicate the Islamic Center became a speech about the war on terror and a call to Muslims to help him. According to a 2007 survey, Muslims in the United States disapproved, by a three-to-one margin, of the invasion of Iraq, and fewer than half of American Muslims saw the war on terror as "a sincere effort to reduce terrorism."[37] Bush had come to honor the fifty years of the Islamic Center in Washington and to announce that he would appoint a U.S. special envoy to the Organization of the Islamic Conference, but those aims were transformed into a defense of the war on terror and actions in Iraq.

There is no clean line between civic community building and political maneuvering, yet these two speeches reveal a clear difference in tone and message. In Bush's earlier visit, his words sought to elevate Americans' treatment of one another; he clearly stated that Muslims are part of the American community. In the later speech, Bush used a special occasion in the Muslim community to push for political support on an issue that is highly charged in the American public at large and within that religious community in particular.

Admittedly, leadership by showing up is no simple practice. A leader who declines invitations will be criticized for overlooking that community. A leader who accepts might well be linked with that community and held accountable for anything any of its members have ever done. Other groups will criticize leaders for not visiting their communities, too. In the moment, their words and gestures and tone will be weighed for hidden meanings. Yet all of these challenges go with the territory of leadership. Genuine, human interaction with myriad individuals and communities is essential. In their analysis of management by walking around, Peters and Waterman highlight executives who log two hundred thousand airline miles a year to accomplish the levels of interaction they need to lead successfully.[38] Analogously, political leaders face grueling demands to appear before and interact with people from many backgrounds. The scheduling and coordinating of such visits must be done thoughtfully to ensure that the visits are representative of America's many civic, moral, and religious communities. Leadership by showing up and engaging diverse constituents is hard work. But there is no substitute for this kind of personal investment.

With Humility from All

For leaders and citizens who are willing to engage one another across lines of difference, one virtue arguably stands above all others: humility. Humility does not seem to come easily to politicians. Mac Davis's country song comes to mind: "O Lord, it's hard to be humble when you're perfect in every way."[39] These lyrics actually invert language in the Psalms that acknowledges humans' obvious lack of perfection and humility. Our religious and political leaders would do well to recognize these deficits.

Political philosopher Richard Rorty famously dismissed religion as a "conversation stopper" in public debate.[40] He had plenty of evidence to back him up. Playing the "Because God told me so" card ends the game because it is a claim to have certain access to ultimate truth. Some secularists, however, have their own absolute worldview. They can be dogmatic in excluding religion from public life. The arrogance is evident in the title of Christopher Hitchens's recent book: *God Is Not Great: How Religion Poisons Everything*.[41] Is Hitchens any more open minded than the religious dogmatists he skewers in his book? All absolutists lack humility.

John Danforth, a Republican and an Episcopal priest, took on those Christians who claimed to know God's truth for themselves, their nation, and the world and who were prepared to use political means to enact it. In 2004 and 2005 the former senator published two opinion essays in the *New York Times:* "In the Name of Politics" and "Onward Moderate Christian Soldiers."[42] The principal target of Danforth's criticism was the Christian Right, which is an important segment of the Republican base. In his subsequent book, *Faith and Politics,* Danforth also criticized Christian liberals, whom he sees as being too certain in their own peace-and-justice activism.[43] His main targets, though, were conservative Christians within his own party.

Danforth had served in the U.S. Senate as a moderate Republican and had earned respect on both sides of the aisle. He later served briefly under George W. Bush as the U.S. ambassador to the United Nations. Arguably, his most controversial moment in politics came when he sponsored Clarence Thomas for the U.S. Supreme Court. Thomas had been Danforth's assistant in the Missouri attorney general's office. During Thomas's Senate confirmation hearings in 1991, Danforth loyally stood by Thomas after Anita Hill alleged that Thomas had used inappropriate sexual language with her while serving as her boss at the Equal Employment Opportunity Commission. Danforth's loyalty to Thomas buttressed his significant clout with the Republican party's conservative base, and as a member of the clergy he garnered further credibility on issues of faith, morality, and politics.

When Danforth spoke out, then, against religious conservatives, people listened. He offered a critique of political leaders who were "adopting a sectarian agenda" and making their party "the political extension of a religious movement."[44] He went on to describe a better way to welcome faith into political life. That preferred path, Danforth suggested, begins with the "spirit of humility."

Danforth describes humility both as a way of understanding our human limitations and as an attitude for relating to our fellow leaders and citizens. Danforth calls himself a moderate Christian. He says that moderates are not certain about how to apply their faith directly into policies and laws, and he views this as a healthy thing. Playing on the word "certainty," he writes: "To assert that I am on God's side and you are not, that I know God's will and you do not, and that I will use the power of government to advance my understanding of God's kingdom is certain to produce hostility." Danforth is subtly referring to the famous words of Abraham Lincoln, who, as we have seen, shifted his views during the Civil War to accept, as he matured, the ambiguous and imperfect motives of the humans who are willing to fight one another in the name of God.

In calling his own position moderate, Danforth invokes at least three senses of the term *moderation*. The first is the theological and philosophical belief in humans' imperfection. We are not God.[45] Second, moderates are called to be bridge builders and to act with respect and in humility toward the various factions that seek to have their way. Third, moderation, in Danforth's view, implies a politically middle-of-the-road perspective. Danforth describes this moderate political position, at least for Republicans, as including faith in a limited government and a strong private sector with global free trade.[46]

It is clear that the first two kinds of moderation—"we are not God" and "we should build bridges"—can readily lead to politically moderate positions. Yet it is not necessary to be politically middle-of-the-road to demonstrate humility. Rather, if we are to transform our politics, it is critically important that people with conservative and liberal positions also embrace the humility that Danforth extols. In other words, the fact that Danforth is a moderate should not imply that humility requires everyone to stand in the political middle.

The first two kinds of moderation that Danforth discusses correspond to two forms of humility. *Epistemic humility* relates to what we know about faith and the human limitations thereof. *Interpersonal humility* concerns how we act toward others based on that faith. Epistemic and interpersonal humility are distinct things. For example, I could be uncertain about what I know about God but still come across as an arrogant jerk. Conversely, I might think I am certain beyond any doubt on questions of God, salvation, truth, and my vocation but still express humility in every human interaction. Since both forms of humility are enormously important for good leadership, they each deserve some discussion.

John Locke is an early (and perhaps the most eloquent) voice on the importance of epistemic humility for political leadership. For Locke, who wrote *A Letter concerning Toleration* while in exile, political leaders had no special religious power, no special religious revelation: "Princes, indeed, are born superior unto other men in power, but in nature equal. Neither the right, nor the art of ruling, does necessarily carry along with it the certain knowledge of other things; and least of all true religion."[47] Locke's worry was that monarchs used their political power to privilege their own tradition. Even worse, they persecuted those from other sects. Locke's point should be read as a general warning that religious views should never become the law of the land through political power. Many of us may think that we have special access to religious knowledge, but few of us have the political power to impose our worldview. Leadership scholar Terry L. Price suggests that, given their privileges and status, leaders are particularly likely to lack epistemic humility—and this is doubly dangerous given their political clout to impose their views on the rest of us.[48]

What would epistemic humility look like in practice? No U.S. president has expressed this stance more fully or elegantly than Lincoln in his second inaugural address. After noting that each side in the Civil War had failed to foresee how terrible the human costs to both sides would be, Lincoln turns to a theological description of the Union and the Confederacy (quoted in the introduction), in which he decried the self-righteous presumption of equating one's own cause with God's will. Lincoln notes that no one can understand God's providence, including the role of the "offense of slavery." Lincoln moves directly from his point about epistemic humility to chasten his Union supporters not to gloat and not to lord victory over the Confederates, who were headed for defeat. He makes his meaning plain with these closing words:

> With malice toward none, with charity for all, with firmness in the right as God gives us to see the right, let us strive on to finish the work we are in, to bind up the nation's wounds, to care for him who shall have borne the battle and for his widow and his orphan, to do all which may achieve and cherish a just and lasting peace among ourselves and with all nations.[49]

These are words spoken firmly but in a spirit of epistemic humility that knows we are not God.

Lincoln's repudiation of any gloating on the part of the victorious Union points toward the second kind of humility—interpersonal humility. People are often mistaken. Even or especially when we strongly believe we are right, we are not justified in arrogant or disrespectful treatment of our constituents or fellow citizens. Interpersonal humility is a virtue that helps demonstrate leaders' respect for devout and diverse constituents.

Danforth, of course, equates interpersonal humility with moderation. So, too, does Aristotle. Aristotle describes the virtue of magnanimity, which stands between vanity and excessive humility. For Aristotle, only honorable men, well trained in the virtues, are able to achieve magnanimity; common people cannot attain it.[50] Aristotle, after all, was not a democrat, and his conception of magnanimity carried both the humility associated with proper self-regard and the honor that only elites could earn.

In our democracy we focus on humility, a virtue attainable by leaders and citizens alike. For the vain, humility requires the loss of arrogance. This applies to all those, whether leaders or citizens, who believe that they are somehow superior—more American, perhaps—than others of a different religious background. People on the margins of society are, however, more likely to suffer the vice of excessive humility than that of vanity.[51] Alternatively, they are placed on the defensive because more powerful figures presume to speak for them. Humility should not be mistaken for self-deprecation or meekness.

Conclusions: Equals Meeting at the Crossroads

Building coalitions, showing up with diverse constituencies, and acting with humility are some of the most difficult parts of effective leadership. What do they have in common? In short, they require civic and political interaction based on mutual respect. The positions we hold—president, chairperson, citizen—stand atop our foundational assumption of moral equality: All people merit equal treatment within the political order.[52] This also means that citizens share equal responsibility to participate.

What does this look like in practice? First, our leaders must help shape our culture so that the legal guarantees of equality are realized in everyday life. No law requires that any of us build coalitions or connectors across the categories that divide us. Yet building coalitions is the part of leadership that overcomes stereotypes that not only keep groups divided but also disfavor some people on account of their religion. Of course, Americans are free simply to embrace a live-and-let-live attitude—mere coexistence—in contrast to convivencia.[53] Leaders model that spirit of convivencia when they show up and engage their constituents at community events. In addition, they can model humility in all that they do. It bears emphasizing that exercising mutual respect rarely requires waging extensive theological debates. The distinction between "civic-political debate" and "theological debate" is not clear-cut for many people who cannot readily separate their political convictions from their theological or philosophical ones. Still, we can show mutual respect for people very different from ourselves—and work with them for positive social changes—without settling questions of theological truth.

Likewise, leaders are certainly entitled to hold and express their own religious faith, as long as they are aware of the danger that it may readily be conflated with the public faith of their locality, state, or nation. When leaders represent a political body, they can certainly demonstrate respect for the practices, celebrations, and even beliefs of many religious groups without suggesting that they share them. This is why a political leader's overall calendar, including outreach to a vast array of religious, civic, and moral associations, should place in context any single visit to any community. I have highlighted leaders who have framed their visits to constituent events in terms of familiar American narratives such as moral equality and the political freedom of religion guaranteed by the Constitution.

The time and effort it takes to show up and listen to multiple constituencies is one way that leaders model interpersonal humility. Or course, it is certainly possible to show up at a community event and manage to offend the host organization. Politicians seem to find creative ways to make missteps even on seemingly benign, festive occasions. This is just another reason that it is better to listen than to say too much.

The concept of "showing up" admittedly runs the risk of seeming too minimal in its demands on leaders. By "showing up" I mean leaders' literally being present for person-to-person interaction with their followers from all sides, who together represent the wide range of perspectives and backgrounds. But it also requires additional steps from the leaders: admitting the possibility that they can learn from others or even be corrected by them; challenging their own assertions and those of constituents; risking embarrassment and offense; and withstanding the criticism of critics who would prefer that leaders be less inclusive in their outreach. These are elements that transform "drive-by" photo opportunities into the genuine engagement of leadership.

What I have called epistemic humility stands at the heart of the practice of mutual respect. If we are certain that we are right—as in D. James Kennedy's mission to "Reclaim America for Christ" or in Hitchens's claim that "Religion poisons everything"—we will have trouble respecting citizens from different perspectives. Humility about the limits of our knowledge is especially hard for those people that we set apart as special, by election or appointment, to be our political leaders. They are indeed special—it is their privileged access to political power that leads us to exclaim that, in terms of religious knowledge, they are just as limited as everyone else. James Madison put it well: We must *reject* the view that "the Civil Magistrate is a competent Judge of Religious Truth," for this is "an arrogant pretension falsified by the contradictory opinions of Rulers in all ages, and throughout the world."[54]

This epistemic humility does not ask us to discard our religious convictions. Rather, it is a modest assertion that we can conduct much of our civic and political life without attempting to resolve questions of ultimate truth. We owe basic respect to our neighbors and fellow citizens not because we agree with their religious convictions but because it is part of the laws, moral fabric, and civic customs of the country. Indeed, many religious and philosophical traditions affirm this sense of mutual respect. If citizens understand their respectful actions in light of their own faith-based worldview, so much the better.

"Showing up" to learn from one another, expressing humility, and forging coalitions are important steps that move mutual respect from an abstract idea into a way of living.

9

Educating Leaders and Citizens

Do you not know, O people, that I have made you into tribes and nations so that you may know each other?
—Surah al-Hujurat 49:13

Knowledge Deficits

WHAT IS THE DIFFERENCE BETWEEN A SUNNI AND A SHIITE? PERHAPS THIS sounds like the start of a joke. When many of our leaders cannot answer the question, however, the joke is on us. Jeff Stein, a respected Washington journalist, has posed this question to counterterrorism officials and political leaders of both parties. Many respondents at the FBI and on Capitol Hill recognized that understanding religious identity is crucial; these leaders were steering the U.S. mission in Iraq and dealing with Iran (mostly Shia) and al Qaeda (mostly Sunni), but many of them could not, in fact, correctly define the differences.[1] What Peter Beinart of the *New Republic* wrote about foreign policy might also apply to leadership: It "is not only about opinions; it is also about facts."[2] Leadership in our religiously and culturally complex society requires a basic level of religious and cultural knowledge.

Yet some leaders seem unembarrassed by their lack of knowledge about religious identity—even when it relates directly to U.S. interests. Senator Trent Lott once appeared dumbfounded that Sunnis and Shia were fighting one another in Iraq: "It's hard for Americans, all of us, including me, to understand what's wrong with these people. Why do they hate each other? Why do Sunnis kill Shiites? How do they tell the difference? They all look the same to me."[3] Lott was reveling in his own ignorance not only of Iraq but also of the United States. By placing "Americans, all of us," in contrast to Sunnis and Shiites, he overlooked the fact that more than one million Americans are Sunni and hundreds of thousands of Americans are Shiite.[4]

We should not be surprised that our public officials lack the basic religious literacy they need to lead in a diverse nation and world. The American populace from which leaders arise fares no better. I am not talking about knowing the nuances of obscure doctrine but simply the basic beliefs and everyday practices of our neighbors. Stephen Prothero, in *Religious Literacy: What Every American Needs to Know—and Doesn't*, documents the profound lack of knowledge about even the Christian tradition that some 85 percent of Americans claim as their preference.[5] He agrees with George Gallup's description of America as "a nation of biblical illiterates." Half of U.S. citizens cannot name even one of the four Christian gospels, and a majority cannot name Genesis as the first book of the Bible. With such ignorance in a country whose population is predominantly Christian, it is hardly a wonder, then, that only 10 percent of teenagers in the United States can name all five major world religions; 15 percent cannot identify even one.[6] Seen a different way, this 15 percent does not recognize that Christianity is one of the major traditions—the one, in fact, with the most adherents, at roughly two billion worldwide.

This deficit of religious knowledge creates a number of problems for our civic and political leadership. When politicians consult their faith in deliberating public policy, do they know what their own tradition has taught on the topic at hand? Can they identify the fault lines of debate among fellow believers?

Leaders invoke religious imagery in their speeches and statements. Given the problem of religious illiteracy that Prothero documents, though, they should not presume that even believers in their own tradition understand their allusions. During his run for the 2008 Republican nomination for the presidency, Mike Huckabee frequently mentioned biblical stories. He was admittedly targeting a conservative Christian base within his party—consistent with television ads that labeled him a "Christian leader." As one reporter noted, however, it was not clear that many Christians could recognize the references he was making.[7]

Additionally, people who grew up in a religious or moral environment outside of the Christian tradition are arguably even less likely to understand the references to Christian scripture. In his first inaugural address, George W. Bush referred to the parable of the Good Samaritan, from the New Testament's Gospel of Luke. CBS journalist Dick Meyer, who is Jewish, said on the air, "There were a few phrases in the speech I just didn't get. One was, 'When we see that wounded traveler on the road to Jericho, we will not pass by on the other side.'"[8]

This case of the president, a journalist, and the Good Samaritan raises a set of fascinating questions. Whose problem is it that there was a communication gap? Should the president (and the president's speechwriters) keep in mind that not all citizens are of the same religious tradition? Yes. Should a national journalist recognize an allusion to an important story from the majority religion? Probably. Should the president find ways to draw on rich religious imagery in ways that are equally accessible to all citizens from whatever tradition? Certainly.

For example, in this case Bush might have said, "My religious tradition teaches me that when we see a wounded traveler on the side of the road, we must not pass by on the other side." This is a matter of nuance, but it makes a difference, especially for religious "outsiders." It identifies the source of the leader's allusion and acknowledges that not all citizens have that source in common. And it invites everyone into public action.

The challenge of religious knowledge in a diverse society—knowledge about our own traditions and those of others—is a serious one for public leadership. In order to address the deficit, religious understanding must become a greater element of our civic education. If we are to have citizens who are able to talk to one another, treat one another with respect, and collaborate on matters common to their neighborhoods, schools, and jobs, then they must understand the various aspects of one another's identity.

This civic education must attend to knowledge of multiple traditions. It is helpful to know some facts about various holidays, attire, and food practices, for example. Each of these topics is contested within any given religious tradition—a reality that makes learning the so-called basics no simple matter of memorization. In addition, we must cultivate a culture that encourages continued learning about our neighbors, their beliefs, and their practices. Such a culture will be marked by a respectful curiosity. We need not be walking encyclopedias of religious belief and practice; rather, we need to develop the tools and the expectations that make it possible for people to ask each other their respectful questions.

In light of this challenge of illiteracy, this chapter explores the education of leaders and citizens about religion in its many forms. What role should our schools and colleges play in preparing students for citizenship in a religiously diverse America and world? How should we think about our public culture beyond formal schooling? What role do religious and moral associations—Tocqueville's "schools of virtue"—play in this rich civil society? When we interact at our public crossroads, how can we keep the focus on our common problems while understanding that people are coming from different places? What do we need to know about our fellow citizens, and how can we learn it? The answer, I think, looks less like formal interfaith dialogue and more like an everyday interaction among neighbors.

Schooling and Civics: A European Perspective

American public schools help prepare students to contribute productively as citizens. The rhetoric of just what "productive contribution" means may have shifted in recent decades, but preparation for meaningful work and civic participation remain fundamental goals of public education. In the coming years, citizens will not meet their full potential if they do not understand religion's role in society.

How far can schools go before they cross a line from teaching about religion to teaching religion—or at least being accused of teaching religion? Are students currently learning about various religious and cultural traditions or only about Christianity? These are questions that U.S. public school systems have encountered and should proactively address. Similar questions have challenged other nations as well—and many have offered answers quite different from our own.

Stephen Prothero, recounting a conversation with an Austrian colleague about Europeans and Americans, notes a paradox: Europeans tend to be knowledgeable about religion, but they do not believe it, while Americans tend to be believers but do not really know about the tradition in which they believe.[9] In Spain, for example, the Roman Catholic Church has no official establishment, but it does, under a policy of "cooperation" with the government, receive significant financial and other benefits from the state. As one part of this arrangement, students in public schools receive religious instruction during school hours. For most students, this means learning about Catholicism from nuns, priests, or others whom the public school employs to teach Catholicism. Jewish, Protestant, and Muslim students may opt to receive instruction in their own tradition.

In 2006 the Spanish Catholic press Ediciones SM published a primary school textbook for Muslim students titled Descubrir el Islam: Religión islámica. Primaria (Discover Islam: Islamic Religion, First Grade).[10] These partner institutions intend to publish an additional textbook every year until they have completed a text for every grade level. The text, a collaboration between Spain's Islamic communities and the Foundation for Pluralism and Convivencia, was reportedly the first textbook for Muslim schoolchildren in Europe that was written in a national language—Castilian Spanish—rather than Arabic.[11]

This collaborative initiative is intended to address the growing concern about how best to welcome and integrate Muslim immigrants into Spanish society. In the wake of the 2004 Madrid train bombings, this issue is pressing. The textbook's publication was hailed as consistent with Prime Minister Zapatero's sweeping call for an Alliance of Civilizations. Diplomats from many European countries attended a formal ceremony that celebrated the textbook, thus helping Spain in its effort to become a leader in proactively integrating Muslims into civic life.[12]

Yet overall progress on religious instruction for Spanish Muslims in the public schools has been slow and uneven. Figures from Spain's Ministry of Education and Science has indicated that, as of early 2007, only 33 teachers of Islamic religion were employed by the Spanish government throughout the nation. In comparison, the public school systems employ a total of fifteen thousand teachers of Catholicism. These 33 teachers of Islam certainly cannot reach the 24,000 students officially on record with their local registries as Muslims. The Islamic Commission of Spain estimates that at least 74,000 Muslim students overall are enrolled; other sources have estimated at least 100,000. The 33 teachers are distributed very unevenly across Spain; in fact, 21 of them are located in the two Spanish territories in north Africa, Ceuta and Melilla. This leaves only 12 teachers on the Spanish mainland—10 in Andalusia and 2 in Aragon. The other autonomous regions have essentially refused to enact the promise of instruction for Muslim students that was made in the 1992 accord between the Islamic Commission and the Spanish government.[13]

The Spanish case, as in other European countries with some level of state support for religion, directly addresses religion as a matter of civic and political life. This approach is both good and bad. It can provide a more immediate framework (with financial support) for addressing issues of integration than the U.S. context allows. In practice, however, students from minority religions in Spain and elsewhere in Europe have thus far not received equal opportunity to learn their tradition. This is a serious issue that comes with state sponsorship of religion.

American Experiments

For observers in the United States, state-funded religious instruction by tradition seems quite strange. Meanwhile, American schools continue to struggle to reach and welcome students from various religious traditions. How should the public schools teach students about their own tradition (if at all)? How should they properly encourage students to learn about the plethora of religious traditions in the United States and worldwide?

The 1995 Clinton memorandum on religion in public schools helped clarify these issues: Schools must not attempt to inculcate particular religious beliefs or practices, but they may teach about religion as it relates to an understanding of history, society, culture, and the arts. Public schools may teach about specific civic values—like trust, service, and citizenship—as long as they do not teach religious doctrine.

Recent experiments have moved in the direction of focusing on a particular cultural group in a school's educational programs. The Khalil Gibran International Academy opened in 2007 in Brooklyn. A New York City public school founded in partnership with the Arab American Family Support Center, the academy features intensive language training in Arabic and related cultural programs. The school faced controversy before its doors even opened. Critics accused the principal, Debbie Almontaser, of supporting pro-Islamist messages. Almontaser also got into hot water when she tried to explain that T-shirts bearing the message "Intifada NYC"—being sold in New York—should not be seen as an affront to Jews. She later relented and called this T-shirt message unacceptable because of the term's allusion to the violent struggle in Israel-Palestine. By then, however, her critics had pushed her out—and they had managed to paint the Khalil Gibran Academy not as one of many theme-based public schools in the city but as more akin to a radical *madrassa*.[14] These critics later decried the public school officials' appointment of a new principal who was Jewish, calling her a smokescreen for the Islamic radicalization they feared would occur at the school.

Also opening its doors in the 2007–2008 school year was the Ben Gamla Charter School in Hollywood, Florida, whose mission is to provide "a unique bilingual, bi-literate, and bi-cultural curriculum" with intensive teaching in Hebrew. The school serves kosher food and is led by a rabbi. The school notes that it will teach Jewish history as part of its curriculum, and one-third of its children have Israeli parents. Critics have suggested that this publicly funded charter school may violate the separation of church and state, given that it is, in effect, providing a Jewish-focused curriculum and cultural experience for an almost exclusively Jewish student body.[15]

These two schools have received an undue proportion of public attention with regard to diversity and American identity. Critics worry about social fragmentation along cultural and religious lines. The Khalil Gibran Academy—named after a Lebanese American mystic of Christian background—welcomes students of any upbringing, but critics are correct that many (but not all) of the Arab American students in the school are also Muslim. An even greater proportion of the students at Ben Gamla are Jewish. Together, the opening of these two schools raises the key question of how American public education will continue to address the growing religious and cultural variety in our midst—and with what results. Are these specialized schools means for a wide or a narrow civic education?

Whatever the context and composition of students, the rule still holds that schools may teach about religion, but they may not teach students to be religious. And whatever the context, schools have the obligation to prepare their students to live productively and respectfully within a diverse American society and world. There are potential costs and benefits for students, whether from minority or majority groups, to attending schools arranged by themes that appeal to certain identity groups.

In overall terms, the challenge of building crossroads is much more difficult when students are divided up by identity, affinity, or affiliation. Similarly, homeschooling—unless it incorporates activities that connect diverse students—can deprive its pupils of a crossroads education. Indeed, this same point highlights the troubling fact that U.S. public schools have in the past three decades become increasingly segregated on the basis of race.[16] Educational separation largely along lines of religion, culture, race, or ethnicity—whether de facto or de jure and whether voluntary or residential based—reflects more closely the vision of communalism than a society marked by convivencia. The latter requires regular crossing of paths of people very different from each other, and no site is more important for this interaction than school.

A Wider U.S. View

Despite our fascination with unique schools such as Khalil Gibran and Ben Gamla, most students are educated in less newsworthy public schools. Due to the activism of Christian creationists, the debates over religion in these schools have focused on science classes more than on social studies. Indeed, the biology classroom has become a leading arena in the culture wars. School board elections across the country have moved from deep inside the local paper to the front page of the *New York Times*. In some cases candidates have, after winning, revealed themselves to have been "stealth candidates" for creationism.

Alongside the creation-evolution controversy, debates over social studies have focused on the role of religious beliefs and communities in history and in contemporary society. In a number of states, educators and parents have criticized the content of the curriculum and, more specifically, the test questions that students must answer on their statewide examinations. Which peoples and groups do they cover? Are the founders, for instance, described as Christian believers or as deists? Do the cultural or religious practices of Native Americans receive attention in the state or national histories? If so, are they portrayed in a positive light? What about Jews, Hindus, Chinese Americans, Catholics, and so on? Are they part of the story, how are they described, and are they on the test?

Many teachers have expressed a willingness and even a desire to teach about religion in their social studies, literature, and related courses. However, most of them did not formally study religion, and they may consider themselves believers but not be particularly literate about the nuances of their own or other traditions. A number of organizations have developed curricula, seminars, and resources for teachers to help them teach about religion in the public school classroom. Not surprisingly, the materials differ according to the political and religious affiliations of those groups.

Many of the most respected organizations, however, stand above the culture wars. Their agenda is to promote—in ways generally acceptable to multiple parties—the public understanding of religion and conscience in its disparate forms. Two such organizations are the Council for America's First Freedom and the First Amendment Center. The Council for America's First Freedom (CAFF), located in Richmond, Virginia, describes itself as "a politically and religiously neutral 501(c)(3) organization that provides educational programs that increase understanding and respect for religious freedom."[17] To determine the goals and practical challenges of teaching about religion in the public schools, CAFF conducted a six-month-long Internet survey of educators and students. It designed a series of educational resources focused around the principles of the First Amendment, as well as the national and global realities of religious pluralism. Robert Seiple, a former U.S. ambassador-at-large for International Religious Freedom, served as president and CEO of CAFF from 2006 until 2008; he used his stature to push CAFF's vision for public education about religion.

The First Amendment Center (FAC), with offices at Vanderbilt University in Nashville, Tennessee, and in Washington, D.C., also frames its work in terms of religious freedom and disestablishment. Founded in 1991 by veteran journalist John Seigenthaler Sr., FAC has developed into a prominent voice on issues of religious freedom and public education, particularly through the work of Charles Haynes. The U.S. Department of Education has distributed information prepared by FAC on what is permissible to teach about religion in the schools to all public schools in the country.[18]

Despite organizations such as these, the debate over how educators teach about religion in the public schools has spawned what we might call the textbook wars. Not-for-profit education organizations from various religious traditions now work as consultants with textbook authors and editors to incorporate the histories and perspectives of multiple groups of Americans. Such efforts to widen the American narrative from a Christian or so-called Judeo-Christian framework have sparked criticism from conservatives. Predictably, one of the traditions that has received harsh treatment is Islam. The Council on Islamic Education (CIE), located in Fountain Valley, California, offers lesson plans and topical resources for teachers at all grade levels to help students understand Islam. It has borne the brunt of criticism from Christian conservatives. Gilbert T. Sewall and his American Textbook Council condemn publishers who yield to pressure from the CIE and other "Muslims and allied multiculturalists" to "whitewash" Islamic history in their textbooks.[19] The experts Sewall cites are scholars, such as Samuel Huntington and Daniel Pipes, who see a clash of civilizations. Thus those who would offer a multiperspective account of U.S. history and contemporary society are discounted as "politically correct" ideologues.

It is unfortunate that the teaching about religious diversity in public school education has become a political hot potato. Despite the heated rhetoric, though, public school teachers and officials, independent not-for-profit groups, and religious educators forge ahead with designing textbooks, standardized tests, and related materials that help teach about the role of religion in American life. These educators are immersed in the very ordinary and important work of making their schools an educational crossroads.

Private Religious Schools

It is also important to consider the role of private schools—religiously affiliated institutions in particular. Catholics founded parochial schools in the nineteenth century to help maintain Catholic identity in a Protestant-dominated U.S. society. Some Protestants expressed their disdain for the separatism that such Catholic schools purportedly fueled. The editorial I cited earlier—"Pluralism: National Menace"—took aim at the increasing significance of Catholicism in public life, focusing on the fact that students in parochial schools would not readily develop a sense of patriotic identity needed in the Cold War.[20] Some of this anti-Catholic rhetoric still exists, certainly, but for the most part Catholics enjoy a more comfortable position in the American mainstream. Further, the declining numbers of priests and nuns have led to fewer parochial schools.

Jewish schools have also been accused of being undemocratic; debates within the Jewish community about the importance of religious schools and public schools continue. Most recently, the concern about schools for students from "immigrant" traditions, especially Islam, have focused on similar issues: Will these students learn how to integrate themselves into American society, or are they learning to be separate from (or even hostile to) American democracy?

The recent expansion of Protestant schools—many labeled nondenominational and/or fundamentalist—has received attention in the culture wars, but from the opposite side. Even as Catholic or Jewish or Muslim schools draw criticism from political conservatives, liberals rebuke conservative Protestant schools for their rejection of contemporary society. Proponents of these schools defend them as sanctuaries against what they call the corruption and moral relativism of contemporary life. Some of this criticism is aimed at educators who teach about diversity in their classrooms. According to these conservatives, the better days of Protestant values in public schools—like the classroom Bible studies that Bill Clinton ironically recalled from his Arkansas days—have been transformed into education about multiculturalism, which critics decry as relativism. Thus, progressives criticize conservative Christian schools on the grounds that they are out of touch with contemporary public life.

Sociologist James Davison Hunter acknowledges the challenge of religious schools to American democratic life. Author of *The Culture Wars* and *The Death of Character*, Hunter worries about how American democracy can hold together when we have become fragmented and have in large part lost the capacity, in his view, to teach common moral values to our children. But he and coauthor David Franz are unwilling to join the critics of Islamic and other religious schools who claim that "instruct[ing] children in one particular religious tradition necessarily pose[s] a threat to democracy." Rather, he insists that we look at the content of the classroom and the culture that schools create in order to determine how well they prepare students for citizenship in a diverse America.[21] The real risk of these schools, whether Protestant nondenominational, Catholic, Jewish, or Islamic, is isolation from the public school experience, which, seen in its best light, exposes students to a wide range of people and perspectives. Yet, as I have noted, public school practices do not align with the noble hopes we have for them. De facto segregation by race and socioeconomic status is more of a challenge to American democracy than is segregation by religious tradition. Given these imperfections in public and private schooling, the formal education of our children is not a sufficient means for expanding our religious knowledge, but it is certainly a necessary part of the picture.

Higher Education and Public Education

By the time students arrive on a college or university campus, they have learned at least one account of U.S. history and contemporary society. They have received some sort of religious or moral instruction from their parents, guardians, or other family members. So, on the one hand, the best opportunity for students to form their social understanding and deepest commitments has already passed.

On the other hand, college is an occasion for exploration, critical thinking, and development of one's own understandings of the world. In the U.S. system of higher education, a broad general education in the liberal arts is the foundation of the curriculum at most schools. At the University of Richmond, where I teach, the responsibility to educate students for citizenship is part of the university's mission statement: "A Richmond education prepares students to live lives of purpose, thoughtful inquiry, and responsible leadership in a global and pluralistic society."[22] This type of language is not uncommon in higher education, but do the universities and colleges live up to their mission?

In their important book *Educating Citizens: Preparing America's Undergraduates for Lives of Moral and Civic Responsibility*, Anne Colby, Thomas Erlich, Elizabeth Beaumont, and Jason Stephens argue that higher education must prepare students to contribute to a pluralistic society that faces serious division and social challenges. They offer powerful strategies and report on effective programs on campuses around the country. A surprising element of this influential book, however, is the relative lack of mention of the need for religious literacy or for understanding religious diversity in the pluralistic society the authors describe. Within the discussion of a curriculum to foster citizenship, the authors refer to a few courses with religious themes—citing one because it does *not* grapple adequately with questions of contemporary citizenship and at least two for engaging issues related to crossing religious boundaries. In terms of the noncurricular activities on campus, religious and spiritual organizations receive only a page and a half of discussion. This is scant attention for a topic that is clearly crucial for the questions the authors believe are vital.[23]

Stephen Prothero might say that it is a good thing these authors do not link religious literacy and moral-civic development. He worries that religion may be reduced to talk of civic values without any wider view of specific religious traditions.[24] On this concern I concur fully with Prothero. Yet it seems important to focus on learning *both* the content of particular religious traditions and the virtues of good citizenship. The capacity for civic engagement requires literacy about multiple religions; conversely, learning about America's religions demands the capacity to interact constructively with diverse fellow citizens.

Higher education also plays a significant role in educating leaders and citizens. Many religion scholars have fashioned themselves into public educators—or public intellectuals—who help shape a society-wide discussion about religion. They have taken the insights of the academic study of religion and helped communicate them to wider public audiences.

Yet these and other scholars are underutilized when it comes to informing and educating our leaders. If a scholar is to have an influence on leaders, it is usually by anecdote or happenstance—an advisor sees a relevant book and passes it on to his boss, or a professor is in the right place at the right time to share her perspective with a leader. In one example of such auspicious influence, Yale law professor Stephen Carter's book *The Culture of Disbelief* was picked up by Bill Clinton and subsequently helped spark public discussion of religion and secularism. Despite these isolated occasions, there remains a host of issues on which expertise in religious studies could be of real value beyond the academic community.

A negative example is illustrative. In 2007 Laurie Goodstein of the *New York Times* reported that the U.S. Bureau of Prisons had enacted a policy to remove most religious books from the shelves of federal prison libraries. Concerned about prisoners reading works deemed radical, officials from the Bureau of Prisons decided to create a list of up to 150 books and 150 multimedia materials in each of twenty religious groupings. Only those "approved" books and resources could remain on prison library shelves; all others were taken away. Thus, if a library owned only a few of the approved books, its shelves were to become almost empty. In defense of this program, bureau officials stated that they had worked with professors in seminaries and "at the American Academy of Religion," Goodstein reported. As it turned out, a few days later the executive director of the American Academy of Religion (AAR), Jack Fitzmeier, sent an e-mail to all of the organization's academic section leaders to clarify that no one on the staff of the AAR had been consulted on the composition of these lists. It appears likely that only one or a few scholars from among the more than ten thousand AAR members had been consulted.[25]

As the chairperson of the Religion and the Social Sciences section of the AAR, I was quite surprised to learn of this program. Like many of my colleagues, I found it hard to believe that such a plan could withstand either constitutional or public scrutiny. The Bureau of Prisons almost immediately received intense public pressure from citizens, scholars, and politicians who had been contacted by their constituents. This pressure came from Left, Right, and Center. Less than three weeks later, the bureau revoked its policy and agreed to return the banned books to their shelves. It announced that it would find a more targeted way to identify books that might incite violence.[26]

The Bureau of Prisons has said it will not make public its list of experts. It appears clear, however, that many scholars in religious studies could have advised the bureau that its policy was wrongheaded. Had the bureau sought wider expertise from the relevant officials or scholars in religious studies, it would have in all probability avoided this embarrassing mistake in leadership. The burden of connecting experts from higher education with public officials falls on both groups.

Sharing Our Stories

Formal educational institutions are certainly fundamental in preparing leaders and citizens for public participation. Yet there is also a more informal but equally significant aspect of civic education: the ongoing public conversations that take place at workplaces, PTAs, voluntary organizations, religious communities, and neighborhood meetings.

When Tocqueville cited religious communities as vital sources of public virtue for American democracy, he did not emphasize the need for citizens in the various faith communities to learn from one another. Building a strong civic fabric today, though, requires that we promote interaction among members of the various religious and moral associations. If we are to understand our neighbor's habits and holidays, customs and beliefs, we must ask about them. It is one thing to memorize the Four Noble Truths and the Eightfold Path of Buddhism; it is quite another to learn from a Buddhist neighbor why he tolls a bell each morning for meditation.[27] At the institutional level, the work of the Interfaith Council for the United Kingdom stands as a good example. It helps leaders of various religious communities develop long-standing friendships and networks so that in times of crisis they may respond together. Similarly, interreligious networks in cities across the United States, such as A More Perfect Union, have developed coalitions to address social and public-policy issues. Diverse people connect to address global issues, as well as to improve local race relations and public education.

This is a vision of a flourishing civil society. What stands between this vision and current reality? Mutual ignorance and lack of interaction among our communities remain so great that often our next-door neighbors are foreign to us. It will take a different way of viewing our neighbors—and ourselves—to change that reality. The great moral philosopher Adam Smith tells a story about humans who remain distant, or abstract, from one another: "Let us suppose that the great empire of China, with all its myriads of inhabitants, was suddenly swallowed up by an earthquake, and let us consider how a man of humanity in Europe, who had no sort of connection with that part of the world, would be affected upon receiving intelligence of this dreadful calamity."[28] The European would be saddened, Smith notes, yet he would rather quickly return to his own life and activities. But were the cultured European "to lose his little finger to-morrow, he would not sleep to-night; but, provided he never saw them, he will snore with the most profound security over the ruin of a hundred millions of his brethren."[29]

Smith knew that without a sense of sympathetic (or empathetic) connection to other people, we simply will not have a proper moral understanding. Without empathy, we will see human suffering on a massive scale—Smith's tale was tragically realized in the 2008 earthquakes in China—as less significant than our little finger. If we were closely connected to even one of those victims, however, our thoughts and actions might change significantly.[30]

Writing in a post-9/11 context, Martha Nussbaum considers the dangers of depending too much on empathy and compassion. We are likely to feel the most empathy with people who are like us—in terms of appearance, culture, belief, or nationality. A dependence on our sentiments can thus lead us to favor those who are most like us and to disfavor those who seem to be different. Yet Nussbaum also challenges us to have a critical appreciation for the other lesson in Smith's parable: If the Chinese victims of the earthquake were somehow less distant from us—culturally, geographically, or otherwise—our circle of sympathy would be widened.[31] Nussbaum, drawing on Smith, believes we can employ our moral imagination to know strangers better—whether they live next door or across the world.

Knowing each other, then, is a key element in this vision of a transformed politics, of an active public life characterized by convivencia. Nussbaum is right to remind us that our sympathy and commitments can still lead us to favoritism, though, so we still must hold on to the core legal rules and moral norms that protect each one of us as equals. The guarantees of the First Amendment in particular stand as a firm framework for our conversations, interactions, and shared work. At the same time, Smith and Nussbaum are correct that without a capacity to imagine ourselves in our neighbor's shoes, these legal and moral guarantees will not motivate us to uphold them. Furthermore, to put it succinctly, we are more likely to know what our neighbor's shoes feel like if we ask to try them on for size. Of course, each of us must be willing to reciprocate.

The idea of an ongoing public conversation should suggest activities that range from individual discussions with neighbors to public events sponsored by local religious and civic associations, as well as town hall meetings and candidate forums. Admittedly, this vision places a lot of confidence in citizens' capacity for respectful interaction and discourse. It is a vision ultimately grounded in the hope that, when citizens make an effort to learn from one another, they both increase their *knowledge* of the other's beliefs and commitments and expand their *capacity to empathize* with those fellow human beings.

We will not always (or even usually) agree with each other's beliefs or practices. Indeed, this vision of sharing our stories is not based on the assumptions of universalism—which suggests that if we talk to one another, we will eventually discover that we are really saying the same thing, just with different language. Rather, on both theological and political fronts, it is clear that often we are *not* saying the same thing. On the other hand, we have reason to hope that we can discover common ground, not merely about our common humanity but also about our beliefs and policy solutions. Only through public conversation can we know for sure.

The Role of the Media

One institution deserves special consideration in this chapter on educating citizens and leaders about our diverse and devout country. It is easy enough to bash the media for bias or for simplifying the news into sound bites. Turn on a cable news program in the evening, and you will typically find a split screen with two or more experts shouting over one another. The same list of talking heads appears on air to represent various "interests"—Christians, Jews, Muslims, African Americans, women's groups, and so on. And within these broader categories are specialized roles. When it is time to hear from a liberal Christian voice on social issues, only a couple of regulars predictably appear onscreen. Covering an African American protest? Two or three experts are likely to comment. What about God in public life? For both the "God defenders" and the "separationists" (as if these were the only two sides to this complex issue), the networks seem to use a very small Rolodex.

A professor of mine in divinity school once talked about receiving a call from a religion reporter asking him about Christian understandings of war and peace. The reporter asked what a "just war" is. My professor responded by making reference to the Protestant Reformation. The journalist's next question was, "Can you remind me what the Reformation was?" The professor, exasperated, told the reporter not to quote him and never to call him back. Perhaps the professor should not have been surprised that the same lack of religious knowledge among the general populace also extends to members of the media. Scholars also hesitate to speak with journalists because, as experts trained to draw out the finer points of their field, they are reluctant to reduce their topic (or worse, to help a reporter distort it) to a sound bite or bullet points.

A word in defense of many members of the journalism profession is also due. The task of communicating the complexity of current religious issues to a broad public audience requires background understanding of faith communities, beliefs, and practices and a comprehension of how these and other issues interconnect. The topic at hand may be a political, economic, social, or environmental question. It could be principally domestic or international. I have met or spoken with many journalists who cover religion, and they are almost always professional and knowledgeable. We ask a lot of journalists who cover such a wide beat and do so under difficult constraints.

These journalists, of course, have tremendous power to shape the public conversation. That is why the demands on them are so high. Yet, to paraphrase Chester Bowles, journalism is too important to leave to journalists alone. The responsibility for good reporting on religion in public life falls to a wider set of stakeholders.

First, scholars of religion must do a better job of sharing their insights with journalists. Christian Smith of the University of Notre Dame is correct to say that scholars do not owe it to reporters to give them a crash course in religion; journalists should be trained in their topic before calling the scholars.[32] But reporters will inevitably need to rely to some extent on scholars who are specialists in their area. Scholars should view their interactions with journalists as part of their responsibility for public education.

Besides the patient teaching that religion scholars should undertake (even when it is annoying so to do), it also falls on institutions of higher education to help provide precisely the background training that Smith recommends. The Nieman Fellows program at Harvard University typically includes a number of journalists who enroll at Harvard Divinity School to learn more about their subject. The Center on Religion and the Professions, housed at the School of Journalism at the University of Missouri, promotes religious literacy for journalists and other professionals who address religion in their work. Trinity College's Center for the Study of Religion in Public Life also pays particular attention to journalism. Programs at the American Academy of Religion help scholars learn to speak more effectively with reporters. These efforts are helping to improve the quality of media coverage of religion.

In addition, in conversation with journalists, political leaders and their institutions should think carefully about how they frame matters of religion and public life. For example, in 2006 the European Union (EU) announced that it was reviewing the terms it would use in referring to acts of terrorism committed by some people self-identifying as Muslims. The internal development of a "lexicon" to talk about this issue was a sensitive matter, and the EU was sure to face charges of political correctness. An EU official told Reuters that EU leaders or staffers would no longer use the term *Islamic terrorism* because of its suggestion that Islam and terrorism are integrally linked. In Europe or the United States it is rare to hear an analogous term (e.g., *Christian terrorism*) even to describe people like Mike Bray, a minister in a small Lutheran faction who bombed abortion clinics, or Timothy McVeigh and Terry Nichols, whose beliefs are linked to fringe Christian groups and who bombed the Murrah Federal Building in Oklahoma City.[33] (In fact, initial media reports of that 1995 attack suggested that it had probably been the work of "Islamic terrorists.") Many leaders and their media staffers have uncritically accepted terms and conceptual frameworks that fail to encourage a more complex understanding. Unfortunately, the matter also becomes politicized when candidates accuse their opponents of being soft for refusing to label as terrorists those who would harm the United States. Others counterattack with charges of pandering, but these terms matter beyond campaign bickering. General John Abizaid, former head of the U.S. Central Command, has said that the U.S. military's work on the ground in Iraq and elsewhere in the Middle East became more difficult when the label "Islamic terror" was employed.[34]

Some will ask, How should we talk about people who are motivated by faith to use indiscriminate violence? Are they not religious terrorists?[35] Do some people who are using violence not label *themselves*—proudly, defiantly—as Muslims, Jews, Christians, or Hindus? Yes, they do. The challenge is to identify such persons as religious terrorists without suggesting that others with that religious affiliation are also terrorists. There is no simple term of choice. Rather, it requires careful journalism that describes the contexts, motivations, and identities of the actors without making unsubstantiated generalizations about wider categories of people.

Political leaders bear much of the responsibility for how the linkages between religion and conflict are generalized in our public discourse. Some journalists also employ easy labels that can have untold and unintended consequences. Of course, if citizens and religious groups were to build more interreligious crossroads and connectors, then the media would have more local, tangible stories of cooperation to report. This would go a long way in overcoming the religion-as-conflict model that too easily pervades not only our media but our politics as well. Thus, reporters, scholars, political leaders, citizens, and institutions should be carefully thinking together about how to produce more nuanced coverage of a devout and diverse America.

Conclusions: A Lot to Learn Together

We need greater public understanding of religion in its many forms. We have political and military leaders who cannot distinguish among the major Islamic communities with whom they deal regularly. Some politicians defend the display of the Ten Commandments, but few citizens could list a majority of those commandments. (More reason to post them in public, some might say.) Since 9/11, Muslims, Sikhs, Hindus, Jews, and Christians who simply appeared "foreign" have endured acts of hate or distrust against their communities, their possessions, and their bodies and spirits.[36] Our president seemingly did not realize that the term *crusade* would conjure negative sentiments within and against the Muslim community. A leading political candidate misidentified the book of Job as a text of the New Testament. We all have a lot to learn together.

Such teaching and learning will take place in formal educational settings and beyond. In terms of our schools, the question is not whether we should teach about religion and its varied forms; it is how we should do so. I have given a glimpse of the flash points and ongoing battles about which content and whose influence will prevail in setting the curriculum of our public schools. Beyond the inflammatory rhetoric and public disputes, many educators and parents are working effectively with organizations—religious and otherwise—to provide instruction that reflects the diverse religious voices who have shaped and continue to shape the country and the world. The limits of specialized, charter, and magnet school curricula and enrollment are yet to be determined with any clarity, but the same guidelines should apply. Schools may—and should—teach about religion but not teach or train in the religion itself. This may be a fine line in many instances, and it will call for public voices both to provide input to and to express trust in our educators.

Professors and administrators in institutions of higher learning must see that they have a responsibility to expand their role as teachers of the public at large. I have outlined some efforts that are already under way. A key leadership challenge in this area will be for wise officials to develop programs that are sufficiently diverse, in terms of the worldview and background of the participating scholars, to remain above charges of political entanglement or partisanship. It is surely difficult to remain protected from charges of taking sides. The more that educators can teach about religion from multiple perspectives, the more easily they will be able to respond to the inevitable criticism.

Our religious and civic leaders must also devise new ways to increase experiential knowledge through activities that connect different communities and enable them to learn about each other. Given Prothero's account of our own illiteracy, faith communities would be well advised to improve teaching of their own tradition to their own members. Other civic communities—such as PTAs, civic clubs, and neighborhood associations—can readily create informal opportunities for people of a wide variety of backgrounds to share their stories with one another. Even workplaces, perhaps the most diverse public spaces in society, can include brown-bag lunches and other informal "around-the-water-cooler" opportunities for employees to learn about each other.[37]

Journalists are powerful figures because they frame issues and throw a spotlight on certain events that become part of our ongoing public conversation. We should all view journalism as a profession, with the requisite responsibilities, that has repercussions for the way in which we live our lives. Other parties can play a collaborative role with journalists to ensure quality reporting on religion in our public life.

As the preceding chapter notes, political leaders can do a great deal to shape a culture of respectful curiosity and mutual interaction. Their own leadership by "showing up" and engaging constituents creates a model for others to emulate. They can use moderation in addressing issues of religion in the public schools, whatever "side" they fall on. They can be forward thinking in the language they employ to talk about the leading issues of our day, such as immigration and homeland security. These heated issues pit racial, ethnic, and religious communities against one another—sometimes with the threat of violence. Politicians must think carefully about the consequences of their words, which others can use in ways the leaders themselves would never have endorsed. High-profile leaders cannot control how others take their words out of their context, but they can be cautious in invoking language that could clearly become provocative. Leaders can help start the conversation, but engaged citizens need the capacity, willingness, and knowledge to carry it forward.

10

What We Can Do Now

With a good conscience our only sure reward, with history the final judge of our deeds, let us go forth to lead the land we love, asking His blessing and His help, but knowing that here on earth God's work must truly be our own.
—John F. Kennedy

Starting from Here

LEADING A DIVERSE SOCIETY IS A TREMENDOUS CHALLENGE PRECISELY BECAUSE ITS citizens and leaders come from disparate religious and cultural worldviews. While understanding ourselves and others better is helpful, it is no guarantee that we will all get along. Often the fiercest fights occur among family. Leaders must also shape a culture of mutual respect by using their influence to project an inclusive vision of America. They can invoke the First Amendment— arguably America's most distinctive contribution to democratic governance—as the guide for how citizens of many different convictions and commitments can live well together.

Good leaders recognize the power of stories and symbols and employ them effectively to realize their vision. Lyndon Johnson signed the most significant immigration act of our time at the foot of the Statue of Liberty; Bill Clinton chose to appear at James Madison High School to reorient the place of religion in public schools; and George W. Bush visited the Islamic Center of Washington, D.C., in the days after 9/11 in order to show the country that Muslims are equals in the American story.

I have suggested that we should tell the modern-day story of American religious freedom in terms of crossroads and connectors. We are following many paths, but we live on common ground. Our paths intersect in some places, but we can also build new connectors—as people in many traditions, congregations, and coalitions are doing. At the crossroads that already exist, we can continually redesign and improve our interactions.

We recognize that our own paths will be changed by the encounters we have along the way with people who are very different from us in appearance, language, and custom. At restaurants, shopping centers, and workplaces we can learn powerful lessons about living in a diverse society. For leaders, engaging with the variety of communities in the country requires both significant personal investment and the taking of certain political risks. It demands leaders who are willing to stand with immigrant communities, religious minorities, and others who do not look like the political mainstream, and it calls for leaders to risk being labeled as outsiders themselves. I have identified people such as governors Mitch Daniels and Tim Kaine, who ventured beyond their comfort zones, blazing trails to transform their respective political cultures.

Building crossroads and connectors calls on each of us to exercise humility. Many of America's most significant leaders have spoken of the need to express a humble spirit—even if they have not always lived up to it. James Madison knew that political leaders were not competent arbiters of religious truth, and Abraham Lincoln refused to claim moral superiority even at a time of political and moral triumph. Bill Clinton called for an increased role of religion in public life, but he urged humility and asked leaders, in that humility, not to claim God for their side. Politically moderate senators John Danforth and John Warner made their careers by quietly standing up for freedom of thought and expression and taking a stand against colleagues who wished to divide people by religion or any other category.

Majorities, Minorities, and Convivencia

Nearly two centuries after his observations of American democracy, Tocqueville's comments about religion and moral associations endure. Those associations have proliferated into a broad set of overlapping networks. What would the French aristocrat have thought about the public-service announcements produced by A More Perfect Union? Or about Hindu scout troops and Buddhist civic festivals? Interfaith social action alliances and annual conventions for atheists? We must expand Tocqueville's understanding of Christianity and democracy to address a wider collection of religious and moral belief systems in American civil society. How do we do this?

The answer lies in Tocqueville's own writings. Tocqueville called on leaders to protect the voice and interests of minority factions against what he called the tyranny of the majority. He also cherished the tradition of religious freedom. Valuing freedom and protecting minorities are more fundamental dimensions of Tocqueville's work than the boundaries he placed on democratic religion. In a Tocquevillian society, the vitality of local voluntary associations (and local governing bodies) will prevent us from falling prey to our own excesses or the tyranny of others.

As leadership scholar J. Thomas Wren has shown, Tocqueville believed that an active civil society served as a proxy for traditional leadership under an elite. Wren concludes that, for Tocqueville, "private, voluntary associations held the potential of resurrecting the classical ideal of the leader."[1] Leaders, in turn, have the responsibility of helping support the flourishing of such religious, civic, and moral associations. In brief, leadership in a vibrant democracy requires both the culture shaping of leaders and the participation of citizens.

Tocqueville did not see into the future, and his inability to envision a positive democratic role for traditions beyond Christianity is hardly surprising. He never had the opportunity to "get used to" many people, in Appiah's terms, who were not Christians. In the early to mid-nineteenth century Muslims and Hindus and Buddhists remained, in France and America, those "exotic" specimens who were defined in terms of and in contrast to Christians. How could he have imagined a fuller view of the world's religious and moral traditions when they were little more than curiosities in his experience?

Today the question becomes, how do we stretch our imaginations beyond Tocqueville's and our experiences beyond our comfort zones? How can we learn to live together in the best spirit of convivencia? We need both the lofty goals of transforming leadership and the down-to-earth, everyday notion of getting used to one another. We also need initiatives that educate leaders and citizens about religious diversity. These are starting points for leaders' and citizens' interactions across dividing lines.

Recall Robert Putnam's analysis of civic engagement in contexts marked by significant cultural (and religious) differences. People tend to turn inward, to the detriment of both *bonding* (within relatively similar groups) and *bridging* (across different groups) social capital.[2] Civic engagement is arguably more complex today than it was Tocqueville's day, and it is at least as needed now as it was then. In this democratic work, there is room for citizens of all backgrounds—those from majority and minority religious backgrounds and the unaffiliated, too. Clearly, given American demographics, churches and Christian associations are predominant sources of bonding capital. And given the breadth and variety of Christian denominations, it will also take a great deal of bridging in order to span Catholicism, Mormonism, and Orthodoxy, as well as the African American, mainline, and evangelical strands of Protestantism.

Likewise, various traditions beyond Christianity have opportunities for both bonding and bridging. The bonding within minority communities is a vital source of membership and participation, especially for groups that, for one reason or another, are disconnected from public life. This bonding is, at the first level, essential to support people who may have no other community to which to belong. Bridging is important, too. I noted earlier that largely immigrant religious groups in the United States (e.g., Hindu or Buddhist communities) may appear to be homogeneous to outsiders, but a great deal of bridging may also be required among people who are quite diverse in their cultural, linguistic, political, national, and socioeconomic backgrounds. I have likewise noted both the value and the challenge of bridging *across* different minority religious communities, and I have discussed the efforts of interreligious groups as examples of bridging among the majority and various minority communities. This work to bridge divides is a fundamental aspect of the inclusive vision of leadership I have presented.

The social capital that this bridging and bonding create has benefits even for people outside of the networks. In economic terms, social capital has "positive externalities."[3] The more that Americans can promote social bonding and bridging in general, the more these processes tend to benefit everyone involved. In a society of cultural and religious enclaves (the approach we have called "communalism"), bonding within one religious community might not affect people from others. However, our vision of crossroads, connectors, and convivencia offers multiple points that link various groups. Stated more directly, whether we are in a majority, minority, or unaffiliated category—or some overlap of those—we all have an interest in increasing religious networks and bonds of trust.

With Citizens on All Sides

Here are ten initiatives that citizens can undertake to help realize a vision of leadership to build crossroads and connectors:

1. *We should give our political leaders a chance to succeed.* It is so easy for us to "pile on" to a mounting collective cynicism about our leaders. Currently, CNN

WHAT WE CAN DO NOW 163

runs a regular feature called "Keeping them honest," which essentially identifies scandalous or self-serving actions by politicians. As the fourth estate, the media have a clear responsibility to serve as watchdogs for the people. Yet this duty must not be reduced to sensationalism. Journalists' critical eye should be reasoned and also point out good and effective leadership when it happens. As citizens evaluating our leaders, we should adopt the strategy of "trust, then verify." Trust is a bedrock value for functioning democracies. This does not diminish the importance of verifying what our leaders tell us, however, which is part of the accountability process of an active citizenry. The mutual engagement requires a sense of investment by citizens, as well as leaders. By inviting leaders to community events, citizens should give leaders an opportunity to take seriously the call to "show up" and engage their constituents. This means, however, that citizens also need to commit to participating in those programs.

2. *We should reject leaders who cater to base motives.* Experts tell us that, as much as citizens express a distaste for campaign attack ads, they are still effective for causing undecided voters to stay home rather than vote for the candidate under attack. We must consciously strive to change the culture of the public sphere. How? We should tell our leaders to stop the conflict-driven politics through all of the traditional and high-tech mechanisms at our disposal. We can reward—through our votes, our contributions, our praise on blogs—those politicians who take the high road in their rhetoric and their actions and who accomplish tasks through bipartisan collaboration. Politicians who use direct or coded words of discrimination against minority people or groups should be called out for their unacceptable provocation. The 2008 elections provided some evidence that politicians, including McCain, Obama, and Huckabee, exceeded expectations because they generally (at least early on) resisted diving into negative campaigning. Of course, each of the three went to great lengths to tell the voters that they were taking the high road—but we cannot fault them too much for that.

3. *We should appeal to fellow citizens' higher motives.* As we place expectations on our leaders to renounce fearmongering and stereotyping, we must also hold ourselves and our neighbors to higher standards. The talk-radio strategy of citizen engagement mocks those who believe or practice differently. We must not engage in ad hominem attacks or question any citizen's patriotism. It is admirable to appeal to the ancient virtue of civility and emphasize that public meetings should be conducted with respect for all. At the same time, the need to appeal to the better side of fellow citizens has at least as much to do with convivencia and the bustle of everyday life.

4. *We should treat each person as an individual with distinct commitments.* As the Declaration of Independence states, we owe it to each American,

whether Muslim, Mormon, Aristotelian, or atheist, to treat everyone as persons "endowed by their Creator with certain unalienable rights." The vision I have laid out in this book attends carefully to questions of religious, spiritual, and moral commitments. I have sought, at the same time, to suggest that these beliefs and practices are not static. Neither are one's affiliations, as a recent Pew survey on religion indicates.[4] Yet, in this time of so-called identity politics, it is easy to group people by their ethnicity or religion or class.[5] The next step on this slippery slope might be to say that all African Americans believe a certain thing or that all Muslims behave a certain way. This is the kind of logic that reinforces stereotypes and fails to honor each person's worthiness of equal regard in our society. We must not fail in this way. This is particularly important in our moment when our leaders make broad—and incorrect—statements about Muslims, Hindus, Latinos and Latinas, poor people, and so on. Such statements are surely incorrect because almost any sweeping statement about any group does not hold.

5. *We should engage in religious, moral, and civic associations.* I take for granted the intrinsic value of participating in religious congregations and other kinds of communities. People do not join churches, temples, or social clubs so that they can contribute to the national civic fabric. Yet American democracy is richer for the active religious and civic groups that are present among us. As I have discussed earlier, both the bridging and bonding forms of engagement benefit many in our diverse democracy. The example of A More Perfect Union illustrates that associations often band together to form a coalition. Or a school PTA, a nonprofit agency, and a neighborhood association work together to build a playground. In many of these cases, there is little way to distinguish the boundaries of one association from another. Neither can we separate the bridging from the bonding functions at these crossroads.

6. *We should build new forms of social connections.* Should we sell our TV and pull the plug from our Internet connection? No, but we must continue to find ways to integrate the benefits of these technologies with face-to-face and communal interaction and thereby create new forms of social networks. How can Facebook.com or Myspace.com promote religiously diverse groups and communities? Some have stated that our civic participation has not declined; it has merely shifted. In the religious sphere, participation can mean traditional weekly attendance, but it might also mean Bible studies, book groups, workplace network groups, involvement in "parachurch" or interfaith coalitions, and even religiously themed social networks online. From a wider perspective, our crossroads are increasingly located in children's activities. There is strong support for the idea that children are increasingly overscheduled, and many parents find themselves acting as scheduling coordinators and chauffeurs. Supporting

children in short-term activities—perhaps meeting other adults similarly shut-
tling their kids—is not the same thing as longer-term membership in an organization. Yet meaningful relationships do form, say, among parents of children
on sports teams. Family-to-family relationships develop at community pools.
One challenge of this type of connecting is that many children's activities occur
around residential patterns that group people who are similar in socioeconomic,
racial-ethnic, and religious situations. There may be little opportunity for the
path crossing that is fundamental for developing a diverse democracy.

7. *We must stretch our comfort zones.* We can challenge ourselves to go beyond
simply bonding with neighbors and fellow citizens who tend to look and believe
as we do. As David Brooks has written, we have structured our lives so that we
are surrounded by "people like us." Sure, it is exciting to get to know a person or
family from another part of America or the world, but at times it can be embarrassing, too. Can I ask this person why she dresses this way? Do I explain why
I choose not to drink this drink or eat this food? Is he going to misunderstand
my invitation? There is no substitute for the individual acts of citizens who
make the effort to build ties. Such comfort-zone stretching also takes place in
our organizations—our churches and synagogues, mosques and temples, our
PTAs, our civic clubs and sports teams. We build coalitions, formal or informal,
to work on neighborhood or wider issues of common concern, like promoting
healthy activities for our kids. Once we build up trust, we tackle political or social
change. All of these things call us to leave our comfort zones.

8. *We must identify areas of disagreement and conflict.* It is also uncomfort-
able to admit that even well-meaning people do not always agree. Some people
who work on issues of faith and diversity hold a deep-seated belief that, when
it really comes down to it, "people are just people" and that differences dissolve
when diverse people build trust and communication. I do not believe that this
is the case. I have seen (and experienced) genuine, respectful disagreements
on issues of politics, religion, and culture. Disagreements, however, are much
easier to address than conflicts among people who are not willing to face them
head on. Honest engagement among diverse parties requires devising ways to
settle conflicts without coming to blows. This is a place where our discussions
of both interpersonal and epistemic humility come to the fore. As some of the
examples in this book show, however, confronting conflicts does not necessarily mean arriving at perfect or comprehensive solutions. On the contrary, Max
Weber's image of political work as "a strong and slow boring of hard boards"
comes to mind.[6] Transformative leadership offers a promise of significant
progress, but it seems most often to occur through the plodding work of a wide
range of citizens willing to grapple with seemingly insignificant issues in order
to effect change.

9. *We must increase our religious literacy.* In my work on religion and public life, I have heard from many well-intentioned Americans who simply do not know much about religion. They are sometimes embarrassed about this. None of us, even those of us who have had an opportunity to study religion, can know about it all. I have also come to the firm conviction that fellow citizens, especially from often-misunderstood minority traditions, are generally happy to be asked to share what they believe or why they practice their faith as they do. The key, of course, is the tone of the questioning, the spirit of the inquiry. Facing hostile interrogations in the post-9/11 era, Islamic centers and mosques across the country have tried to turn lemons into lemonade, hosting open houses and preparing programs and materials that explain what role their community plays in U.S. society. Muslim Americans have tried to shift their place in the public conversation from a defensive posture to a constructive, proactive sharing of their identity. How much better it is when all Americans, especially those from the mainstream, show a respectful curiosity, so that we might learn more. This practice draws on the better angels of our nature and that of our neighbors. It assumes that if we create a level playing field, all of the parties can learn from one another. Our religious and civic associations can host educational programs. In our workplaces and neighborhood associations, we can schedule open forums for discussions of our own commitments. Topics could include religious practices or beliefs, and they could also encompass a broader array of cultural topics to include hobbies, special talents or interests, and so on.

10. *We should practice critical and curious thinking.* All of these ways of engagement involve a willingness to treat our leaders and fellow citizens with respect and to expect the same attitude in return. Some ways call for even more openness to a variety of people and exposure to new ideas. None of these requires us to check our critical thinking skills, values, or convictions at the door. Indeed, genuine mutual respect means being willing and able to communicate disagreement. At times individual citizens and citizen-led groups will need to issue hard challenges—or even protest—to their leaders. Citizens in an association may disagree among themselves on how to balance their group's interests with the rights of outsiders. In every case, critical thinking requires openness to alternative points of view. It should also include the capacity (and moral obligation) to communicate to fellow citizens our reasons for believing or acting in the ways that we do in public life. Being critical calls us to exercise our judgment, based on our commitments, and to share our views with our fellow citizens. We must also have the flexibility to reach consensus on matters of policy and common life, even if it is not the way we would do it if we were king. After all, we are democratic citizens who might as well get used to one another.

Some of these ideas are more specific than others. Some are more difficult. I hope that they help us move from merely tolerating one another to getting along in a spirit of convivencia. Shaping the culture through stories and symbols, engaging one another with humility to build meaningful coalitions, and educating one another about our myriad and overlapping traditions—these are elements of building crossroads and connectors. Leadership for a devout and diverse America is about what our leaders do in Washington and our statehouses and city halls. But it is also about ordinary people doing extraordinary things with diverse, fellow citizens on their street, in their PTA, or across town. It is time to reach out to all sides.

Epilogue:
Memo to the President

Memorandum

To: President Barack Obama
From: Douglas A. Hicks
Subject: Leading a Devout and Diverse America

Congratulations on your election. I know that you are already hard at work, shifting gears from campaigning to governing. It is an honor and a privilege to offer you this memo as you prepare to lead the people of the United States. I respectfully submit these ideas for your consideration.

You will be leading the most religiously, racially, and ethnically varied citizenry in America's history. We may be the most diverse democracy anywhere, ever. Leading this broad spectrum of Americans will certainly be a daunting challenge, but I hope that you don't envision it as *only* a challenge. Our religious diversity is also a remarkable resource, one of the things that makes America great.

Devotion is a powerful force for good and for ill. Religious literacy, for lack of a better term, will be critical to your administration's success. Understanding the dynamics of spiritual and cultural identity—in the Middle East, Central Asia, India, and sub-Saharan Africa, for instance—is correctly called the missing dimension in statecraft. And at home, the issues of homeland security, immigration, and economic health all require attention to religious and cultural differences among the American people.

I know you are a person of deep faith and strong conscience. You have communicated empathy for your fellow Americans and respect their particular and wide-ranging identities. During the campaign you have held up our tradition of religious freedom as one of the greatest of America's political traditions. At the same time, you experienced the divisiveness that comes when religion meets politics.

Thus, one challenge of leadership is to shape the public square in ways that encourage citizens to express their deepest commitments and still get along. In Spain, they have a word for living together in peace—*convivencia*. Perhaps you could help translate this idea into our own politics. You set the tone for a culture of public spiritedness.

So a big question for you at the start of your presidency is, What messages will your leadership send to a devout and diverse citizenry?

Like it or not, citizens from across denominations and traditions, devout practitioners and the unaffiliated alike, will see you as a kind of spiritual leader. If G. K. Chesterton was correct that "America is a nation with the soul of a church," then you will be ordained as the high priest of our civil religion. You did not ask for this role, but it comes with the office.

To your stack of preparatory reading materials, please add Robert Bellah's classic essay, "Civil Religion in America," and note the ways our greatest presidents have drawn richly and deeply on Christian scriptures in particular to shape a common American identity. They avoided easy proof texting and pious pandering. Please attend also to Bellah's air of skepticism as to whether civil religion can retain the critical (or prophetic) edge needed to resist merely fueling American exceptionalism or triumphalism. Lincoln is the great model here. As he matured in leadership, he refused to claim that God was on the Union's side. Rather, Lincoln's second inaugural invoked God's judgment on all parties for their complicity in the sin of slavery and the need for humble resolve.

Writing in 1967, Bellah was limited by the Protestant-Catholic-Jew framework of American diversity. Your declarations about faith and morality should speak to a country that now reflects the world.

In no single speech will you be able to identify the laundry list of America's faith traditions. Indeed, you should not become so concerned about connecting with every moral and religious view that you are afraid to talk about faith. But over time, Americans "from A to Z—atheist to Zoroastrian," as one former White House staffer has put it—should recognize themselves in your speeches and remarks.

As president, then, you have the power to frame the ways in which diverse and devout citizens interact with one another. You have the opportunity to use your bully pulpit to support America's first freedom and offer an inclusive vision of our common life. We need public education of our leaders and our citizens to understand and teach the value of religious diversity. Your words and actions will encourage citizens to respect and engage with others from all backgrounds.

Here are six general principles to guide you:

1. *Your words matter.* Your labels for America will not be mere descriptions. As "image maker in chief," your words will help shape reality. Are we a Christian nation? If you say we are, then many Christians will be empowered. At least some from outside the Christian community will believe they are less than equal citizens. Images of Christian America perpetuate the view that non-Christians are visitors in someone else's home. Refer to churches, but do not forget synagogues, mosques, temples, ashrams, gurdwaras, and other houses of worship that contribute to America's civil society. Is the war on terror actually a clash of civilizations? If you say it is, then people may associate Islam as a whole with violence, without carefully distinguishing between radicals who choose violence and the vast majority of others who peacefully stand apart from them. Survey data indicate that the cognitive linkage between Islam and violence is already prevalent in the United States. Your appearances at mosques and Islamic celebrations are an invaluable part of the equation, but those significant acts of symbolism will be rendered irrelevant if, especially when crises occur, you or your staff use sweeping language. When President Bush called the war on terrorism a crusade, many Americans girded their loins for battle, but Muslim Americans took offense—and took cover. A single ill-thought reference can hamper all of the efforts to uphold mutual respect. Your team must be relentlessly consistent in that message. What metaphor should you use? I respectfully suggest that you describe America as a crossroads of many great religious and moral traditions. We share common ground, but our paths are distinct. And we must not simply pass by one another—or worse, crash into each other. Instead, crossroads emphasizes the connections that we can build.

2. *Your presence matters.* You will have crushing demands on your time. There seemingly will not be enough hours even to monitor current crises and to carry on your predecessors' traditions. That is, between the most urgent matters and established ceremonial occasions, how could you find the time to support the religious institutions and moral associations thriving across the country? Still, there is no substitute for "management by walking around." In terms of the presidency, this means building into your schedule the religious and cultural events that reflect America. Fortunately, some of these already fit within established precedent, and others qualify as connecting with supporters, but showing up at an array of community events requires moving beyond those

expected activities. Remember, too, to "think religion" beyond December. Many faiths bulk up minor festivals to stand alongside Christmas, but be there for the most significant festivals throughout the year. The Muslim, Jewish, Hindu, and Christian communities alike expect to see politicians at their community events during election season. But for local religious and civic communities to receive the current president—although not to hear you use the occasion for a politicized agenda—is a powerful symbol of an inclusive America.

3. *The White House workplace culture matters.* You can model your own vision of American society through the culture you create among employees in your administration. Former staffers note vast differences in the workplace environments created under recent presidents. There has been a lot of talk—not just in the United States but in European countries as well—about how leaders should build a leadership team to reflect the country's diversity. Gender- and racial-ethnic diversity usually top the list, and religion is rarely noted. This is fully appropriate, especially in the U.S. context, as religion cannot and should not be a test for office. But note the ways diverse staffers function together once they are assembled. Is the workplace welcoming to employees from varied backgrounds? Would staffers wearing religiously mandated attire or observing dietary restrictions face any hurdles fitting in? Are there appropriate venues for staffers to talk together about their "personal" religion and morality and their "public" roles? Are you curious about religion and respectful of others? Again, you set the tone.

4. *Policies matter.* The highly symbolic matters of language, personal presence, and work environment are more than window dressing. Indeed, they do as much as anything else to shape a respectful culture and to appeal to the better angels of our nature in dealing with religious difference. It should also go without saying that the policies your administration implements with respect to religion and religious and moral diversity also influence the ground rules of that culture. Do your policies reflect equal treatment of the religiously affiliated and the unaffiliated alike? Do Christians and Jews, Muslims and Hindus, humanists and atheists all get a fair shake? It is not just the appearance of equality before the law (de jure) but also the effects in practice (de facto) that merit your concern. The community and faith-based initiatives, now spread throughout the executive branch, should be carefully evaluated and not only according to the rhetoric of equal eligibility; your administration should also determine whether the recipients of funding are roughly proportional to the religious, racial, and ethnic composition of the social-service sector. This work of oversight will raise challenging issues about how to assess fairness, but they are precisely the kinds of questions that should be a part of public debate.

5. *Your own faith matters.* How should you draw on your own faith and religious identity in your role as president? Deeply and carefully. The American people have already asked you about your beliefs and practices, and you told your own story throughout the campaign. In office, you should not hesitate to find time for prayer, reflection, or worship in your own tradition if you find that to be of personal or public value for your leadership. You should make every effort to explain the ways in which your own convictions, which are not held by all Americans, inform your political values and decision making. Just as important, you should make efforts to ensure a clear distinction between your personal faith and the office of the president. Put in terms of the First Amendment, your religion must not receive any established or preferential status. More than any actual privileging, you should seek to avoid even the appearance of preferential status for your tradition. Remember, too, that your own faith matters, but it is not all that matters. Religion's role in your leadership has to do with the faith and practices of all Americans.

6. *Humility matters.* Leadership scholar Terry L. Price has written about the ways leaders fail because of the very position they hold. They come to think that, at the top, the everyday rules of morality no longer apply to them. Strive to maintain humility in your own leadership. It will infuse the culture of the whole administration. I mean two kinds of humility: interpersonal and epistemic. In terms of religion, there is no need for you to wear your faith on your sleeve, and if you do, it will make you appear smug. It will also set you up to be called a hypocrite. As for the epistemic, or knowledge-based, part of humility, beware John Locke's particular cautions about religious ideas and political power, remembering that political office gives you no special religious insight. You will certainly receive moral and political pressure from many Americans—who may lack humility—asking you to use your power to legislate their morality. Perhaps those who share your faith will be the most vocal and most convincing in your mind. Give proper place to doubt. They might be wrong. You might be wrong. Or both. This disposition will help you also to appreciate those who argue the other side, and perhaps your own humility will bring out their better angels as well.

Now on to some tactical points that can help you translate these principles into practice:

A. *Identify and charge advisors to keep the public vision on your agenda.* Religious freedom, civic engagement, and mutual respect are abstract concepts. They will not cry out for your time on a daily basis, and their needs are not as immediate as responding to domestic or international crises. In Stephen Covey's terms, promoting engagement and respect is a very *important* but not an *urgent* matter; your successful leadership depends on not losing sight of long-term priorities amid the immediate. You should also recall that responding well to crises often depends on your own attention to religious factors—so religious understanding can sometimes become urgent. You can be sure that this important-but-not-always-urgent issue gets proper attention by charging people around you to make religion and America's diversity a part of your agenda. What are the impacts of *policy x* on American Muslims? Evangelical Christians? Mormons? Your Office of Public Liaison will help filter comments to you from devout and diverse constituents. Even closer to your daily work, you could also appoint your chief of staff or key domestic and international advisors to pose such questions relentlessly. By charging specific staffers to help you communicate a vision of a religiously diverse America, you allow the related issues to get attention in the midst of and to inform more immediate demands.

B. *Establish crash courses in religious literacy for key staffers.* Former administration officials speak of their dire need to understand religious ideas, identities, and practices so that they could do their work well. No one now needs to be convinced of the value of knowing the differences between Shiites and Sunnis in Iraq or of grasping the complexities of Kurdish identity. The Muslim community in the United States is as varied as the American Christian community or as the Muslim community abroad. Sikhs and Jains are regularly confused with Hindus. For that matter, not all secularists are atheists. These facts matter greatly for domestic and international policy. Even in very abbreviated format, short courses can save your administration (and the public) from embarrassment, failed policy, or both. Who can offer such courses? Federal agencies that already train employees and rising leaders can play a part by revising their curricula. For a fuller picture, scholars in politics and religious studies at U.S. universities could develop such courses. Ideally, you would instruct some government agents to work with scholars in order to design fitting programs.

C. *Your religious outreach should be as broad as possible.* Your administration's religious outreach should extend across the gamut of traditions in this country. It is easy to fall into building connections only with religious communities in your own political base; these are, after all, people and groups who have helped you to reach the White House. The effectiveness of your leadership, however, will be enhanced by communication with people who tend to disagree with you. In fact, your interactions with the faith communities do not always need to have some immediate policy agenda or goal. Good leadership requires hearing skeptical perspectives and giving full consideration to alternative points of view. Bill Clinton directed his staff to coordinate religious

MEMO TO THE PRESIDENT   175

outreach breakfasts that included religious conservatives who tended not to agree with him. These were give-and-take sessions conducted with the aim of two-way listening and learning. The team of religious outreach staffers you assemble in the Office of Public Liaison should have contacts in America's various religious communities.

D. *Work with American communities as bridge leaders on international questions.* One of the most fundamental agenda items for your domestic and foreign policy agendas is this: You can help all Americans to clearly distinguish the campaign against al Qaeda from animosity against Islam as a whole. Our leaders and citizens must isolate radical extremists motivated to use violence from the approximately 1.4 billion adherents of Islam around the world. Look to the millions of Muslims in this country as bridge figures and potential allies between the United States and the Islamic world. These Americans have faced marginalization and even hate crimes in this country. Remember that, like American Christians and Jews, the American Muslim community is not uniform and has no single spokesperson. Past U.S. presidents have effectively appealed to bridge leaders among the Jewish community on policy questions concerning Israel. Similar strategies can also help relations with India and China, which have their own diverse populations. Start with your own political supporters in the various U.S. subcommunities, but be sure to identify bridge leaders across partisan divides. This is one important way that America's diversity can be a resource for your own leadership.

E. *Renew and expand public diplomacy efforts abroad.* The Bush administration appointed Karen Hughes, a trusted confidante and former high-profile official, as undersecretary of state on matters of public diplomacy, a welcome acknowledgment that helped America's image abroad. Yet her diplomatic efforts were framed almost entirely by the war on terror, as Hughes publicly took Muslims and others to task for not condemning terrorism more explicitly. When public diplomacy is so closely aligned with the war on terror, foreign observers readily interpret the program as just another part of a U.S. propaganda effort. To the greatest extent possible, public diplomacy should set the framework for international relations. In this approach, U.S. leaders will appeal to friends in foreign governments who would cooperate in distinguishing terrorists from the rest of the population. This whole effort will require time and a commitment to building strong relations with various foreign leaders. Public diplomacy moves more slowly than military campaigns, but there is little doubt that the more proactive approach can save lives and build trust.

F. *In crises, invoke a broad and deep American civil religion.* As president, you and your team are charged to confront the unthinkable, to prepare for severe crises. This certainly includes acts of terrorism, but it extends far beyond them.

Prepare words and symbolic acts that would appeal to citizens' higher motives. You can send a strong signal of an inclusive American identity, especially at times when religious or racial-ethnic minorities are at risk. In Richmond in the late 1960s, teams of African American and white men, along with teams of African American and white women, organized themselves in case of national or local race-based violence. They were prepared to walk side by side through the streets of the former Confederate capital. This was a proactive sign of solidarity in times of high tension. What symbols and language will you draw on when crises hit? Charge members of your staff to turn now to the bridge leaders and other contacts in America's religious communities and prepare together. In the moments of response to catastrophe, invoke the profound images of American civil religion in the broadest possible language. If you cite passages from Christian or other scripture, frame them as texts treasured by some Americans that might provide comfort to all Americans. In moments of temptation to vengeance, be careful not to fuel American intolerance or belligerence. At these times, even more than the usual ones, you must exercise leadership by empathizing with citizens, showing wise restraint of anger, and drawing people together in solidarity.

Thank you for taking the time to consider these issues. Religion, as Richard Rorty said, can be—and certainly has often been—a "conversation stopper." But, among America's devout and diverse citizenry, you have an opportunity to help frame an ongoing public conversation in which religion is a rich resource. This is heady stuff, easily pushed aside, and that is why identifying and charging some of the people close to you to keep religious diversity front and center is essential for your leadership. Let there be no doubt that your leadership is much needed; if you fail to frame an inclusive approach, there will be more of the same, a politics of religious division and fear. I encourage you to stand with integrity and openness about your own faith but to reach out as broadly as possible to "God on all sides"—to the crossroads of communities and traditions that is America today.

Acknowledgments

I AM GRATEFUL TO MANY PEOPLE AND INSTITUTIONS FOR THEIR PART IN THE making of this book. The opportunity to discuss religion and public leadership with colleagues near and far has been the highlight of my work on it. Acknowledging these people reminds me that I am part of many overlapping communities that sustain my own learning.

This book provides evidence—some obvious and some subtle—of my incalculable intellectual debt to my teachers at Davidson College, Duke University, and Harvard University. It hardly does justice merely to list them: Charles E. Ratliff Jr., Clark G. Ross, Lois A. Kemp, R. David Kaylor, Frederick Herzog, Thomas A. Langford, Mary McClintock Fulkerson, Thomas E. McCollough, Harvey Cox, John Rawls, Cornel West, Diana L. Eck, Amartya K. Sen, and Ronald F. Thiemann. Each has taught me to grapple with the moral and political questions that arise in communities of people with diverse backgrounds and deeply held commitments.

Generous readers devoted their time and energy to review this entire manuscript. For their extremely thoughtful comments I thank Edward L. Ayers, Catherine L. Bagwell, Fred L. Bagwell, G. Scott Davis, George R. Goethals, Grove Harris, Robert A. Johnson Jr., Peter Iver Kaufman, Elizabeth A. Kelly, Molly Marsh, Lucretia McCulley, Rebecca Todd Peters, Terry L. Price, Mark Valeri, Thad Williamson, and Jonathan Zur. I also express my thanks to the anonymous reviewers from Oxford University Press for their helpful responses.

Other colleagues provided important information on specific areas of expertise. Scott Alexander and Azizah Y. al-Hibri have helped me understand more fully the challenges Muslim Americans have faced since September 11, 2001.

Amy Sullivan, Shaun Casey, Michael Nelson, Mike McCurry, and Maureen Shea shared insights on religion and the presidency. Amy L. Howard made useful suggestions about the "cross controversy" at William and Mary. Zenobia L. Hikes confirmed the overall contours of my account of the Virginia Tech leadership in response to the campus tragedy there. Joanne B. Ciulla, Kevin P. Colleary, Alan Ehrenhalt, Mark Valeri, and especially Rebecca Todd Peters, Terry L. Price, and Thad Williamson offered valuable help in framing the project from proposal to final draft. For my discussions of Spain and *convivencia*, I thank Antonio Robles-Egea, Francisco Carmona, Cecilia Hita Alonso, Javier Jordán, Santiago Delgado, José María Contreras, and Juan Ramón Ferreiro Galguera.

For responding to seemingly ceaseless and obscure research inquiries—some of which I believed had no answer—Lucretia McCulley deserves special recognition. For their creative and careful efforts on research and editing, I also want to thank Elizabeth A. Kelly, Emily Neuberger, Connie Ng, Cassie Price, Jess Scrimale, and Tammy Tripp. I am grateful for my wonderful faculty colleagues at the Jepson School of Leadership Studies, who model an intellectually diverse community thinking together about public leadership. I thank John W. Rosenblum, Kenneth P. Ruscio, J. Thomas Wren, and Sandra J. Peart for leading the Jepson School and for encouraging me on this book. The students in the course Leadership and Religious Values from various semesters over the past decade helped me develop these ideas. I also want to acknowledge my colleagues in the Bonner Center for Civic Engagement for their commitment to community-based learning that bridges many divides.

Thanks are also due to the team at Oxford University Press. My editor, Theo Calderara, offered outstanding ideas that greatly improved the book. I also want to acknowledge the efforts of Meechal Hoffman, Keith Faivre, Carol Hoke, Betsy DeJesu, Michelle Rafferty, and Brian Hughes.

I received generous institutional support for the research and writing of this book. From my home institution, the University of Richmond, I was provided a sabbatical grant and additional research funds from the Jepson School of Leadership Studies. Union Theological Seminary and Presbyterian School of Christian Education (Union-PSCE) in Richmond, Virginia, welcomed me as a visiting associate professor during my sabbatical and offered a wonderful office in the tower of the William Smith Morton Library. In 2006 the Pluralism Project at Harvard University provided me a research grant. An earlier (2001) summer stipend from the National Endowment for the Humanities helped me frame this project vis-à-vis my previous book on religion and leadership in the workplace. Finally, Spain's Ministry of Education and Science awarded me a Foreign Researcher Sabbatical Grant in 2007 (SAB-2005-0090), which allowed me to complete research in the Department of Political Science at the University of Granada in the spring of 2007.

As valuable as this collegial and institutional support has been, my deepest gratitude belongs to family. My parents, Harry E. and Susan V. Hicks, and my parents-in-law, Fred L. and Ann S. Bagwell, do not always agree with me on matters of religion in politics, but we share an appreciation for the challenges it creates for our public life.

My daughter, Ada Neill Hicks, entered the world in the midst of my writing this book and changed my world forever. Her brother, Noah Shaffer Hicks, had already been visiting me at the computer to send e-mails, view buses, and type his name. Their mother and my dear spouse, Catherine Lake Bagwell, hold our team together even as she makes her own scholarly contributions on ADHD and children's friendships. In constant conversation with Catherine, I pursued the ideas of this book even as we chased Ada and Noah across the plazas of Granada and the parks of Richmond. Catherine would concur with me that, in their curious attention to the diverse people and contexts they have encountered, Ada and Noah have given us new eyes to see God on all sides. I dedicate this book to these three beloved family members.

Notes

CHAPTER I

1. Massimo Rubboli, "'The Battle is God's': Patriotic Sermons during the American Civil War," paper presented at the "War Sermons" conference, Université de Provence Aix-Marseille 1, Nov. 17–19, 2005.

2. Abraham Lincoln, "Meditation on the Divine Will," in *The Collected Works of Abraham Lincoln,* ed. Roy P. Basler, 8 vols. (New Brunswick, N.J.: Rutgers University Press, 1953), vol. 5, 403–404.

3. Roy P. Basler, ed., *The Collected Works of Abraham Lincoln,* 8 vols. (New Brunswick, N.J.: Rutgers University Press, 1953), vol. 5: 332–33.

4. For a rich account of this new religious diversity in the United States see Diana Eck, *A New Religious America: How a "Christian Country" Has Now Become the World's Most Religiously Diverse Nation* (paperback ed., San Francisco: Harper San Francisco, 2002).

5. Maureen Shea, interview by author (June 28, 2007).

6. *Editor and Publisher* staff, "Ann Coulter on CNBC Show: Jews Need 'Perfecting,'" http://www.editorandpublisher.com/eandp/news/article_display.jsp?vnu_content_id=1003657196, accessed Nov. 7, 2007; Ann Coulter, "Calvin and Hobbes—and Muhammad," *Anncoulter.com* (Feb. 8, 2006), http://www.anncoulter.com/cgi-local/article.cgi?article=99, accessed Nov. 10, 2007; Sam Harris, *Letter to a Christian Nation* (New York: Knopf, 2006), viii–ix.

7. Erik Eckholm, "Muslim Voters Detect a Snub from Obama," *New York Times* (June 24, 2008), A1, A20.

8. Dan Gilgoff, "John McCain: Constitution Established a 'Christian Nation,'" *Beliefnet.com,* http://www.beliefnet.com/story/220/story_22001.html, accessed Oct. 3, 2007.

9. BBC News, "Infinite Justice, Out—Enduring Freedom, In," Sept. 25, 2001, http://news.bbc.co.uk/2/hi/americas/1563722.stm, accessed Mar. 10, 2008.

10. George W. Bush, "President's Remarks at National Day of Prayer and Remembrance," Sept. 14, 2001, http://www.whitehouse.gov/news/releases/2001/09/20010914–2.html, accessed Mar. 10, 2008.

11. George W. Bush, "Address to a Joint Session of Congress and the American People," Sept. 20, 2001, http://www.whitehouse.gov/news/releases/2001/09/20010920–8.html, accessed Mar. 10, 2008.

12. Basler, *Collected Works of Abraham Lincoln,* vol. 5, 262–71.

13. "Correspondence of the *Boston Journal:* The President's Entry into Richmond," *Littell's Living Age,* no. 1090 (Apr. 22, 1865), 137–38, http://cdl.library.cornell.edu/cgi bin/moa/pageviewer?frames=1&cite=&coll=moa&view=50&root=%2Fmoa%2Flivn%2 Flivn0085%2F&tif=00109.TIF&pagenum=137, accessed Nov. 8, 2007.

14. Thomas Jefferson, "Letter to Benjamin Waterhouse," July 19, 1822, in Norman Cousins, ed., *In God We Trust: The Religious Beliefs and Ideas of the American Founding Fathers* (New York: Harper and Brothers, 1958), 162.

CHAPTER 2

1. Robert Ajemian, "Where Is the Real George Bush; the Vice President Must Now Step Out from Reagan's Shadow," *Time* 129 (Jan. 26, 1987), 20–21.

2. Fredrick Kunkle, "Fairfax Native Says Allen's Words Sting," *Washington Post* (Aug. 25, 2006), B9.

3. Peter Hardin, "Immigration Foe Goode Says Mexican Flag 'Riles' Him," *Richmond Times-Dispatch* (May 25, 2007), B1.

4. Nancy Frazier O'Brien, "U.S. Congress More Religiously Diverse; Catholics Still Well Represented," *Catholic News Service,* Jan. 16, 2007, http://www.catholicnews.com/data/stories/cns/0700279.htm, accessed Nov. 7, 2007; Mary K. Brunskill, "Rep. Pete Stark Becomes First Congressman to Publicly Declare He's an Atheist," *All Headline News,* Mar. 14, 2007.

5. The full text of Goode's letter is available at http://abcnews.go.com/Politics/story?id=2743475, accessed Nov. 7, 2007; see also Rex Bowman, "Goode Refuses to Apologize for Letter," *Richmond Times-Dispatch* (Dec. 22, 2006), A1.

6. Diana L. Eck, *A New Religious America: How a "Christian Country" Has Now Become the World's Most Religiously Diverse Nation,* rev. ed. (San Francisco: HarperSanFrancisco, 2002), 239–51.

7. Pew Research Center, *Muslim Americans: Middle Class and Mostly Mainstream* (May 22, 2007), 18–19, http://pewresearch.org/pubs/483/muslim-americans, accessed Mar. 21, 2008.

8. "Ellison: Lawmaker Has 'A Lot to Learn about Islam,'" *CNN.com,* Dec. 21, 2006, http://www.cnn.com/2006/POLITICS/12/21/quran.congress/index.html, accessed Aug. 20, 2007.

9. Ibid.

10. Transcript of Nikki Giovanni's convocation address (Apr. 17, 2007), http://www.vt.edu/remember/archive/giovanni_transcript.html, accessed Mar. 9, 2008.

11. Caine O'Rear, "Bush Addresses Grieving Community," *Richmond.com*, Apr. 17, 2007, http://www.richmond.com/news-features/731, accessed Mar. 21, 2008.

12. A.J. Hostetler, "Virginians Come Together to Mourn; Tech Victims Remembered with Moments of Silence, Tears, Bells, and Balloons," *Richmond Times-Dispatch* (Apr. 21, 2007), A3.

13. Audio of Governor Tim Kaine's speech accessed and transcribed from "Virginia Tech Shootings," from the Official Site of the Governor of Virginia, http://www.gover nor.virginia.gov/TempContent/Tech-Archive.cfm, accessed Aug. 10, 2007.

14. For a discussion see Eck, *New Religious America*, xiv–xvi. See also Douglas A. Hicks, *Religion and the Workplace: Pluralism, Spirituality, Leadership* (New York: Cambridge University Press, 2003), 12–13.

15. Janet I. Tu and Lornet Turnbull, "Christmas Trees Going Back Up at Sea-Tac," *Seattle Times*, Dec. 12, 2006, http://archives.seattletimes.nwsource.com/cgi-bin/texis.cgi/web/vortex/display?slug=seatactrees12m&date=20061212&query=trees+menorah+rabbi, accessed Nov. 10, 2007.

16. David Van Biema, "Minnesota's Teetotal Taxis," *Time* (Jan. 19, 2007), http://www.time.com/time/magazine/article/0,9171,1580390,00.html, accessed Feb. 1, 2007.

17. Associated Press, "Minneapolis Airport Approves Stiffer Penalties for Cabbies Who Refuse Customers with Alcohol," *International Herald Tribune*, Apr. 16, 2007, http://www.iht.com/articles/ap/2007/04/16/america/NA-GEN-US-Muslim-Cabbies-Alcohol.php, accessed Nov. 8, 2007.

18. "Governor's Ethnic American Advisory Council," Office of Personnel Management, State of Oklahoma, Minutes of Meeting, Feb. 16, 2007, http://www.ok.gov/opm/HR_and_Employee_Services/Ethnic_American_Advisory_Council.html, accessed Nov. 8, 2007.

19. Mick Hinton, "Legislator to Find Home for Quran," *Tulsa World* (Oct. 25, 2007), A1.

20. "Judge: Woman Can't Cover Face on Driver's License," *CNN.com*, June 10, 2003, http://www.cnn.com/2003/LAW/06/06/florida.license.veil, accessed Nov. 7, 2007.

21. Philip Jenkins, *God's Continent: Christianity, Islam, and Europe's Religious Crisis* (New York: Oxford University Press, 2007), especially 283–87.

22. Jack Straw, "I Want to Unveil My Views on an Important Issue," *Lancashire Telegraph*, Oct. 5, 2006, 12; Graeme Wilson, "Brown Breaks Ranks to Back Straw over Lifting Muslim Veils," *Telegraph News*, Dec. 10, 2006, http://www.telegraph.co.uk/news/uknews/1531106/Brown-breaks-ranks-to-back-Straw-over-lifting-Muslim-veils.html, accessed June 16, 2008.

23. Pew Forum on Religion and Public Life, *U.S. Religious Landscape Survey. Report 1: Diverse and Dynamic* (Washington, D.C.: Pew Research Center, February 2008).

24. Ibid., 22.

25. Michael J. Sandel, *Liberalism and the Limits of Justice* (New York: Cambridge University Press, 1982), 147–54.

26. Immanuel Kant, "An Answer to the Question: What Is Enlightenment?" in *Kant: Political Writings*, ed. Hans Reiss, Cambridge Texts in the History of Political Thought (New York: Cambridge University Press, 1991).

27. Immanuel Kant, "Religion within the Boundaries of Mere Reason," in *Kant: Religion within the Boundaries of Mere Reason and Other Writings,* trans. Allen Wood and George di Giovanni, Cambridge Texts in the History of Philosophy (New York: Cambridge University Press, 1999). An important text in leadership ethics that argues for a Kantian view of morality is Terry L. Price, *Leadership Ethics: An Introduction* (New York: Cambridge University Press, 2009).

28. Pew Forum on Religion and Public Life, *U.S. Religious Landscape,* 37.

29. John Locke, *A Letter concerning Toleration* (Amherst, N.Y.: Prometheus, 1990).

30. On the question of when the magistrate believes that some issue is a matter of state jurisdiction but citizens disagree, Locke writes, "Who shall be the judge between them? I answer, God alone; for there is no judge upon earth between the supreme magistrate and the people. . . . But what shall be done in the mean while? . . . You will say then the magistrate being the stronger will have his will, and carry his point. Without doubt. But the question is not here concerning the doubtfulness of the event, but the rule of right." Ibid., 61.

31. Charles Marsh, *God's Long Summer: Stories of Faith and Civil Rights* (Princeton, N.J.: Princeton University Press, 1997).

32. I am grateful to Edward L. Ayers for suggesting these categories.

33. George Gallup and D. Michael Lindsay, *Surveying the Religious Landscape: Trends in U.S. Beliefs* (Harrisburg, Penn.: Morehouse, 1999). For a discussion of the trends in this participation rate since 1940 see Robert Putnam, *Bowling Alone: The Collapse and Revival of American Community* (New York: Simon and Schuster, 2000), 69–72.

34. See the discussion in chapter 3.

35. Jo Ann Gibson Robinson, *The Montgomery Bus Boycott and the Women Who Started It: The Memoir of Jo Ann Gibson Robinson,* ed. David J. Garrow (Knoxville: University of Tennessee Press, 1987).

36. Putnam, *Bowling Alone,* 111–13.

37. The Metanexus Institute is sponsoring a major research initiative on this topic: See http://www.metanexus.net/spiritual_capital/.

38. Putnam, *Bowling Alone,* 66.

39. Ibid., 22, 362.

40. Alisdair MacIntyre, *After Virtue: A Study in Moral Theory* (Notre Dame, Ind.: University of Notre Dame Press, 1981), 207.

41. Robert N. Bellah, "Civil Religion in America," *Daedalus* 96 (Winter 1967): 1–21.

42. George W. Bush is an exception to this generalization. I have discussed this in some detail in Douglas A. Hicks, "Ethical Diversity and the Leader's Religious Commitments," in *The Quest for Moral Leaders: Essays on Leadership Ethics,* ed. Joanne B. Ciulla, Terry L. Price, and Susan E. Murphy, 45–61 (Northampton, Mass.: Edward Elgar, 2005).

43. Bellah, "Civil Religion in America," 12.

CHAPTER 3

1. "Pluralism—National Menace," *Christian Century* (June 13, 1951).

2. Jenkins poses a similar comparison between the integration of Catholics into American society and Muslims within Western European society, though he says that it

is still unclear whether the latter process will overcome the current challenges and social tensions; Philip Jenkins, *God's Continent: Christianity, Islam, and Europe's Religious Crisis* (New York: Oxford University Press, 2007), 22–25.

3. Neil MacFarquhar, "Fears of Inquiry Dampen Giving by U.S. Muslims," *New York Times* (Oct. 30, 2006), A1. This case against the Holy Land Foundation was declared a mistrial, though federal authorities vowed to bring the case again to trial. Leslie Eaton, "U.S. Prosecution of Muslim Group Ends in Mistrial," *New York Times* (Oct. 23, 2007), A1.

4. MacFarquhar, "Fears of Inquiry."

5. One prominent organization, the Council on American-Islamic Relations (CAIR), compiles a list of such condemnations of terrorism at "Islamic Statements against Terrorism in the Wake of the September 11 Mass Murders," http://www.cair.com/AmericanMuslims/AntiTerrorism/IslamicStatementsAgainstTerrorism.aspx, accessed Nov. 7, 2007.

6. Renee Montagne, "Filmmakers Shatter Arab Stereotypes in Hollywood," National Public Radio (Sept. 13, 2006), http://www.npr.org/templates/story/story.php?storyId=6064305, accessed Sept. 28, 2007.

7. For one American's perspective on this European-American comparison see George Weigel, *The Cube and the Cathedral: Europe, America, and Politics without God* (New York: Basic Books, 2005). See also Jenkins, *God's Continent*, 22–25.

8. See chapter 2.

9. Alexis de Tocqueville, *Democracy in America* (Garden City, N.Y.: Anchor Doubleday, 1969), 292.

10. The First Amendment reads as follows: "Congress shall make no law respecting an establishment of religion, or prohibiting the free exercise thereof; or abridging the freedom of speech, or of the press; or the right of the people peaceably to assemble, and to petition the Government for a redress of grievances."

11. George Will, "God of Our Fathers," *New York Times Book Review* (Oct. 22, 2006), 10; Barry Alan Shain, *The Myth of American Individualism: The Protestant Origins of American Political Thought* (Princeton, N.J.: Princeton University Press, 1994); Barbara A. McGraw, *Rediscovering America's Sacred Ground: Public Religion and Pursuit of the Good in a Pluralistic America* (Albany: SUNY Press, 2003).

12. Ronald F. Thiemann, *Religion in Public Life: A Dilemma for Democracy* (Washington, D.C.: Georgetown University Press, 1996), 19–33.

13. Cornel West, "The Democratic Soul," *Religion and Values in Public Life, Center for the Study of Values in Public Life at Harvard Divinity School* 6(1) (Fall 1997): 4.

14. Tocqueville, *Democracy in America*, 294.

15. Ibid., 292.

16. George W. Bush, "President Highlights Faith-based Initiative at Leadership Conference," Omni Shoreham Hotel, Washington, D.C. (Mar. 1, 2005), http://www.whitehouse.gov/news/releases/2005/03/20050301-4.html, accessed Nov. 7, 2007.

17. Tocqueville, *Democracy in America*, 295.

18. Ibid.

19. Ibid., 531.

20. Ibid., 534–35.

21. An interesting discussion of the role of political leaders in promoting civic piety among their people is found in James M. Sloat, "The Subtle Significance of Sincere Belief: Tocqueville's Account of Religious Belief and Democratic Stability," *Journal of Church and State* 42(4) (Autumn 2000): 759–79.

22. Tocqueville, *Democracy in America*, 542–46.

23. Ibid., 544.

24. Ibid., 546.

25. Ibid., 544.

26. Ibid., 290.

27. Ibid., 290–91.

28. Ibid., 292.

29. Ibid., 445.

30. Ibid., 292.

31. Ibid., 316.

32. Ibid.

33. Ibid., 317.

34. James Kloppenberg, "Life Everlasting," *Religion and Values in Public Life, Center for the Study of Values in Public Life at Harvard Divinity School* 5(4) (Summer 1997), 1–3.

35. Tocqueville, *Democracy in America*, 250–51.

36. Ibid., 255–56.

37. For a fuller discussion of immigration and religious diversity see Diana L. Eck, Rebecca K. Gould, and Douglas A. Hicks. "Encountering Religious Diversity: Historical Perspectives," Diana L. Eck and the Pluralism Project at Harvard University, *On Common Ground: World Religions in America*, CD-ROM (New York: Columbia University Press, 1997).

38. See Diana Eck, *A New Religious America: How a "Christian Country" Has Now Become the World's Most Religiously Diverse Nation*, rev. ed. (San Francisco: HarperSanFrancisco, 2002), 48–54.

39. William R. Hutchison, in his fine historical examination, *Religious Pluralism in America: The Contentious History of a Founding Ideal* (New Haven, Conn.: Yale University Press, 2003), also notes this roughly contemporaneous use of the symphony metaphor by Zangwill and Kallen. In overall terms Hutchison's book offers a comprehensive history of American thought on pluralism.

40. Israel Zangwill, *The Melting Pot: Drama in Four Acts* (New York: The Macmillan Company, 1921), 33.

41. Philip Gleason. "The Melting Pot: Symbol of Fusion or Confusion?" *American Quarterly* 16(1) (Spring 1964): 20–46, esp. 22–23.

42. Zangwill, *Melting Pot*, 34.

43. Quoted in Arthur M. Schlesinger Jr., *The Disuniting of America: Reflections on a Multicultural Society*, rev. and enlarged ed. (New York: Norton, 1998), 41.

44. Horace Kallen, "Democracy versus the Melting-Pot," *Nation* 100(2590) (1915), 219.

45. Ibid.

46. Ibid.

47. Ibid., 220. Both Cornel West and Diana Eck have suggested the image of jazz as preferable to that of a symphony as a vision of pluralism, precisely to incorporate the improvisational and interactive nature of the common enterprise. Cornel West, *Race Matters* (Boston: Beacon, 1993); Eck, *New Religious America*, 58–59.

48. Kallen, "Democracy versus the Melting-Pot," 220.

49. Israel Zangwill, "Afterword," (1914) to *Melting Pot*, 204–207. The reference to "black and yellow" in the play is on page 184.

50. Sidney Ratner, "Horace M. Kallen and Cultural Pluralism," *Modern Judaism* 4 (May 1984): 185–200, 190.

51. Address of Senator John F. Kennedy to the Greater Houston Ministerial Association, Sept. 12, 1960, http://www.jfklibrary.org/Historical+Resources/Archives/Reference+Desk/Speeches/JFK/JFK+Pre-Pres/Address+of+Senator+John+F.+Kennedy+to+the+Greater+Houston+Ministerial+Association.htm, accessed Nov. 7, 2007.

52. For a discussion of Kennedy, religion, and the presidency see Shaun Casey, *The Making of a Catholic President: Kennedy versus Nixon 1960* (New York: Oxford University Press, 2009).

53. Will Herberg, *Protestant, Catholic, Jew: An Essay in American Religious Sociology*, new ed., completely rev. (Garden City, N.Y.: Anchor Books, 1960), 39.

54. Ibid., 114.

55. Ibid., 40.

56. Eck, *New Religious America*, 63–64.

57. For a discussion of the public role of these religions see Stephen Prothero, ed., *A Nation of Religions: The Politics of Pluralism in Multireligious America* (Chapel Hill: University of North Carolina Press, 2006); for a look at Islam in America see Geneive Abdo, *Mecca and Main Street: Muslim Life in America after 9/11* (New York: Oxford University Press, 2006). Robert Wuthnow discusses the impact of this diversity particularly for U.S. Christians in *America and the Challenge of Religious Diversity* (Princeton, N.J.: Princeton University Press, 2005).

58. Dwight Hopkins, *Religions/Globalizations: Theories and Cases* (Durham, NC: Duke University Press: 2001), 8.

59. Eck, *New Religious America;* Eck and the Pluralism Project at Harvard University, *On Common Ground*.

60. Lyndon B. Johnson, "Remarks at the Signing of the Immigration Bill, Liberty Island, New York," Oct. 3, 1965, http://www.lbjlib.utexas.edu/johnson/archives.hom/speeches.hom/651003.asp, accessed November 7, 2007.

61. Ibid.

62. Eck, *New Religious America*, 366–70.

63. Hans Kung and Karl-Josel Kuschel, eds., *A Global Ethic: The Declaration of the Parliament of the World's Religions* (New York: Continuum, 1993).

CHAPTER 4

1. For a fuller discussion see Douglas A. Hicks, *Religion and the Workplace: Pluralism, Spirituality, Leadership* (New York: Cambridge University Press, 2003), 14–16.

2. One exception, during the Democratic primary campaign in 2007, was John Edwards. He received mocking criticism from Republicans who asserted that he did not understand the threat al Qaeda posed to America. See Mike Allen, "Edwards Rejects 'The War on Terror,'" *Time* (May 2, 2007), http://www.time.com/time/nation/article/0,8599,1616724,00.html, accessed Nov. 7, 2007.

3. George W. Bush, "President's Address to the Nation" (Sept. 11, 2006), http://www.whitehouse.gove/news/releases/2006/09/print/20060911–3.html, accessed Mar. 13, 2008.

4. Ibid.

5. Samuel P. Huntington, "The Clash of Civilizations?" *Foreign Affairs* 72(3) (1993): 22.

6. Tony Blankley, "Is There a Clash of Civilizations? Islam, Democracy, and U.S.—Middle East and Central Asia Policy," hearing before the Subcommittee on the Middle East and Central Asia of the Committee on International Relations, serial no. 109–210 (Sept. 14, 2006), 45.

7. John McCain, "McCain Speaks at Columbia University" (May 16, 2006), http://mccain.senate.gov/public/index.cfm?FuseAction=PressOffice.PressReleases&ContentRecord_id=544c3108-bec5–4951-abe6-f4501ca4dfd4&Region_id=&Issue_id=e2d83197–0adb-4a53–994a-9eb58268b452, accessed Mar. 14, 2008.

8. George W. Bush, "'Islam Is Peace,' Says President: Remarks by the President at Islamic Center of Washington, D.C." http://www.whitehouse.gov/news/releases/2001/09/20010917–11.html, accessed Sept. 24, 2007.

9. John Hawkins, "Interview with Tom Tancredo," *Right Wing News* (2007), http://www.rightwingnews.com/interviews/tancredo.php, accessed Nov. 10, 2007. The comments about bombing Mecca were reported by Associated Press following Tancredo's comments on an Orlando, FL, radio show on July 15, 2007; see "Tancredo: If They Nuke Us, Bomb Mecca," *FoxNews.com*, July 18, 2005, http://www.foxnews.com/story/0,2933,162795,00.html, accessed Nov. 7, 2007.

10. George W. Bush, White House Press Conference (Sept. 16, 2001), http://www.whitehouse.gov/news/releases/2001/09/20010916–2.html, accessed Oct. 13, 2006; George W. Bush "President Rallies the Troops in Alaska" (Feb. 16, 2002), http://www.whitehouse.gov/news/releases/2002/02/20020216–1.html, accessed Oct. 13, 2006.

11. Bruce Lincoln, "Bush's God Talk: Analyzing the President's Theology," *Christian Century* (Oct. 5, 2004): 22–29; Ron Suskind, "Without a Doubt," *New York Times Magazine* (Oct. 17, 2004), 44–51, 64, 102, 106; Carl M. Cannon, "Bush and God," *National Journal* (Jan. 3, 2004): 12–18.

12. James Davison Hunter, *Culture Wars: The Struggle to Define America* (New York: Basic Books, 1991).

13. Brooks, "One America, Slightly Divisible," *Atlantic Monthly* (Dec. 2001): 53–65.

14. David Von Drehle, "Political Split Is Pervasive; Clash of Cultures Is Driven by Targeted Appeals and Reinforced by Geography," *Washington Post* (Apr. 25, 2004), A01.

15. Pew Research Center, *Muslim Americans: Middle Class and Mostly Mainstream*, May 22, 2007, http://pewresearch.org/pubs/483/muslim-americans, accessed Mar. 21, 2008, 7.

16. A Pew Research Center poll suggests that the 2004 numbers were 71 percent for Kerry and 14 percent for Bush (and 15 percent "other/don't know"); ibid., 41.

17. Pulsar Research and Consulting, "*Time* Poll: Survey on Faith and the Presidential Election," May 10–13, 2007, http://www.pulsarresearch.com/PDF/TIME_Report.pdf, accessed Mar. 15, 2008; Pew Research Center for the People and the Press, "Religion in Campaign '08: Clinton and Giuliani Seen as Not Highly Religious; Romney's Religion Raises Concerns," Washington, D.C.: Sept. 6, 2007, http://pewforum.org/surveys/campaign08/, accessed Mar. 15, 2008; Amy Sullivan, *The Party Faithful: How and Why Democrats Are Closing the God Gap* (New York: Scribner, 2008); Jimmy Carter, quoted in Robert Scheer, "The Playboy Interview: Jimmy Carter," *Playboy* 23(11) (Nov. 1976), 63–86. In his important book on evangelicals in public life, D. Michael Lindsay offers a good discussion of evangelicals and the White House in *Faith in the Halls of Power: How Evangelicals Joined the American Elite* (New York: Oxford University Press, 2007), 15–37.

18. CNN, "Situation Room: Special Edition: Sojourners Presidential Forum," George Washington University (June 4, 2007), http://transcripts.cnn.com/TRAN SCRIPTS/0706/04/sitroom.03.html, accessed Sept. 2, 2007. Edwards offered a less wordy answer in an interview with David Kuo of Beliefnet:

DAVID KUO   Do you think that America is a Christian nation?

EDWARDS   That's a good question. I never thought of it quite that way. There's a lot of America that's Christian. I would not describe us, though, on the whole, as a Christian nation. I guess the word "Christian" is what bothers me, even though I'm a Christian. I think that America is a nation of faith. I do believe that. Certainly by way of heritage—there's a powerful Christian thread through all of American history.

David Kuo, "John Edwards: 'My Faith Came Roaring Back,'" *Beliefnet.com*, undated, http://www.beliefnet.com/story/213/story_21312_1.html, accessed Sept. 1, 2007.

19. See the discussion in chapter 2.

20. "Terrorist Attack Aftermath: General's Remarks on Islam Draw Fire," *Facts. com, Facts on File World News Digest* (Oct. 23, 2003).

21. Samuel P. Huntington, *Who Are We?: The Challenges to America's National Identity* (New York: Simon and Schuster, 2004), 83.

22. Ibid., 85.

23. Ibid., 98–103.

24. Ibid., 100.

25. Ibid., 101.

26. Ibid., 103.

27. Ibid., 364–65.

28. See chapter 2.

29. In his book *Religion in Public Life: A Dilemma for Democracy* (Washington, D.C.: Georgetown University Press, 1996), Ronald F. Thiemann asserts that mutual respect, a fuller commitment than mere tolerance of difference, is more fitting for contemporary America than the value of toleration as articulated in America's founding documents. See pages 136–37.

30. "The 25 Most Influential Evangelicals in America," *Time* (Feb. 7, 2005), http://www.time.com/time/covers/1101050207, accessed May 21, 2007.

31. David Barton, radio interview by D. James Kennedy, quoted in Deborah Caldwell, "David Barton and the 'Myth' of Church-State Separation," *Beliefnet* (2006) http://www.beliefnet.com/story/154/story_15469.html, accessed June 21, 2007.

32. Wayne Slater, "GOP Buttons on Their Shirts and Faith on Their Sleeves: Republican Convention Draws Religious Conservatives," *Dallas Morning News* (June 4, 2006).

33. Kurt W. Peterson, "American Idol: David Barton's Dream of a Christian Nation," *Christian Century* (Oct. 31, 2006): 20.

34. Caldwell, "David Barton and the 'Myth.'"

35. Christian Smith, *Christian America? What Evangelicals Really Want* (Berkeley: University of California Press, 2000), 26–37; quote on p. 36.

36. Alan Wolfe, *One Nation After All: What Middle-class Americans Really Think About* (New York: Penguin, 1999).

37. For a survey and analysis of American Muslims' views of identity questions see Pew Research Center, *Muslim Americans,* 29–34, 36. See also Bernd Debusman, "In U.S., Fear and Distrust of Muslims Runs Deep," *Reuters.com* (Feb. 25, 2007), http://www.reuters.com/article/topNews/idUSARM55127020070225, accessed Nov. 7, 2007.

38. David Barton, "An Historical Perspective on a Muslim Being Sworn into Congress on the Koran" (January 2007), http://www.mfc.org/SOS/AnHistoricalPerspectiveonaMuslimBeingSwornintoCongressontheKoran.pdf, accessed Oct. 15, 2007.

39. Pew Research Center, *Muslim Americans,* 37.

40. The Pew researchers note a number of factors—language barriers, technological issues, and immigrants' fear of being contacted or identified—that make this figure a conservative estimate.

41. Ibid., 9–14.

42. Ibid., 23–27.

43. Ibid., 49.

44. Ibid., 53–54.

45. Arthur Allen Cohen, *The Myth of the Judeo-Christian Tradition* (New York: Harper and Row, 1969).

46. For a recent concise discussion see Stephen Prothero, *Religious Literacy: What Every American Needs to Know—and Doesn't* (San Francisco: HarperSanFrancisco, 2007), 153–55.

47. Richard Berke, "With a Crackle, Religion Enters G.O.P. Meeting," *New York Times* (Nov. 18, 1992), 23.

48. Ronald Smothers, "Jewish Groups Criticize Remarks by a Governor as 'un-American,'" *New York Times* (Nov. 20, 1992), A14.

49. Grove Harris, "Wiccan Invocation: A Canary in the Mineshaft of the United States," background paper prepared by the Pluralism Project at Harvard University (Jan. 23, 2007), http://www.pluralism.org/research/profiles/display.php?profile=73769, accessed Oct. 15, 2007.

50. Proponents of this model portray the colonists and the American founders as Christians dedicated to establishing, in John Winthrop's biblical phrase, "A city set upon a hill." It is, however, a selective reading of U.S. history; deists and secularists are incorrectly viewed as devout Christians, and other parties are left out of the narrative altogether (George Will, "God of Our Fathers," *New York Times Book Review* [Oct. 22, 2006], 10). For one significant account of religion in the period see Frank Lambert, *The Founding Fathers and the Place of Religion in America* (Princeton, N.J.: Princeton University Press, 2003).

51. Thomas Jefferson, *The Autobiography of Thomas Jefferson, 1743–1790,* ed. Paul Leicester Ford (Philadelphia: University of Pennsylvania Press, 2005 [1914]), 71.

CHAPTER 5

1. George W. Bush, "President's Remarks to the Nation" (Sept. 11, 2002), http://www. whitehouse.gov/news/releases/2002/09/20020911-3.html, accessed Mar. 13, 2008.

2. For a detailed discussion of Bush's personal faith vis-à-vis his leadership, see Douglas A. Hicks, "Ethical Diversity and the Leader's Religious Commitments," in *The Quest for Moral Leaders: Essays on Leadership Ethics,* ed. Joanne B. Ciulla, Terry L. Price, and Susan E. Murphy, 45–61 (Northampton, Mass.: Edward Elgar, 2005).

3. David Kuo, *Tempting Faith: An Inside Story of Political Seduction* (New York: Free Press, 2006); John Danforth, *Faith and Politics: How the "Moral Values" Debate Divides America and How to Move Forward Together* (New York: Viking, 2006).

4. Sam Harris, *Letter to a Christian Nation* (New York: Knopf, 2006), vii.

5. Ibid., 29.

6. Sam Harris, *The End of Faith: Religion, Terror, and the Future of Reason* (New York: Norton, 2004), 48.

7. Richard Dawkins, *The God Delusion* (Boston: Houghton Mifflin, 2006); Christopher Hitchens, *God Is Not Great: How Religion Poisons Everything* (New York: Twelve, 2007).

8. See, for instance, Barry W. Lynn, *Piety and Politics: The Right-wing Assault on Religious Freedom* (New York: Harmony, 2006), 248.

9. Robert Fuller, *Religion and the Life Cycle* (Philadelphia: Fortress, 1988); Wade Clark Roof, *A Generation of Seekers: The Spiritual Journeys of the Baby Boom Generation* (San Francisco: HarperSanFrancisco, 1993).

10. Douglas A. Hicks, "Spiritual and Religious Diversity in the Workplace: Implications for Leadership," *Leadership Quarterly* 13(4) (Oct. 2002): 379–96; Douglas A. Hicks, *Religion and the Workplace: Pluralism, Spirituality, Leadership* (New York: Cambridge University Press, Nov. 24, 2003), esp. chap. 3.

11. Pew Research Center for the People and the Press, "Religion In Campaign '08: Clinton and Giuliani Seen as Not Highly Religious; Romney's Religion Raises Concerns," Pew Forum on Religion and Public Life, Washington, D.C., Sept. 6, 2007, http://pewforum.org/surveys/campaign08/, accessed Mar. 15, 2008, 12.

12. Amy Sullivan, *The Party Faithful: How and Why Democrats Are Closing the God Gap.* New York: Scribner, 2008.

13. Alex Beam, "Dean's Conversion Experience," *Boston Globe* (Dec. 11, 2003), B17.

14. Catholic News Service, "Kerry Addresses Faith, Values, but Rejects Bishops on Life Issues," Oct. 25, 2004, http://www.catholicnews.com/data/stories/cns/0405879. htm, accessed Nov. 7, 2007.

15. Amy Sullivan, "Faith of the Candidates," *Time* poll (July 12, 2007) *Time.com*, http://www.time.com/time/politics/article/0,8599,1642653,00.html, accessed Oct. 17, 2007.

16. For a discussion see "The Enemy Within," *Snopes.com*, http://www.snopes. com/politics/obama/muslim.asp, accessed Oct. 26, 2007.

17. Dan Gilgoff, "John McCain: Constitution Established a 'Christian Nation,'" interview, *Beliefnet.com*, http://www.beliefnet.com/story/220/story_22001.html, accessed Oct. 3, 2007.

18. Michael Gerson, "Giuliani's Abortion Muddle," *Washington Post* (May 23, 2007), A21, http://www.washingtonpost.com/wp-dyn/content/article/2007/05/22/ AR2007052201176.html, accessed Nov. 7, 2007.

19. Paula Zahn, "Politics and Religion: Democratic Presidential Candidates on Faith," *Paula Zahn Now*, CNN (June 4, 2007).

20. Immanuel Kant, "An Answer to the Question: What Is Enlightenment?" in *Kant: Political Writings*, ed. Hans Reiss, 54–60, Cambridge Texts in the History of Political Thought (New York: Cambridge University Press, 1991).

21. Jean-Jacques Rousseau, *On the Social Contract*, trans. Judith R. Masters and ed. Roger D. Masters (New York: St. Martin's, 1978), book 4, chap. 8. Robert Bellah's account of civil religion in America is more hopeful than Rousseau's and less suspicious of confessional religion; see chapter 2.

22. John Rawls, "The Idea of Public Reason," (lecture 6) in *Political Liberalism*, John Dewey Essays in Philosophy 4 (New York: Columbia University Press, 1993).

23. Douglas A. Hicks, *Inequality and Christian Ethics*, New Studies in Christian Ethics 16 (New York: Cambridge University Press, 2000), 93–101.

24. John Rawls, "The Idea of Public Reason Revisited," *University of Chicago Law Review* 64 (1997): 765–807.

25. Hicks, *Inequality and Christian Ethics*. See also Michael J. Sandel, "A Response to Rawls' Political Liberalism," in Michael J. Sandel, *Liberalism and the Limits of Justice*, 2d ed. (New York: Cambridge University Press, 1998), 184–218. Sandel discusses both the moral and the political costs of restricting public discourse to the terms of public reason.

26. John R. Bowen, *Why the French Don't Like Headscarves: Islam, the State, and Public Space* (Princeton, N.J.: Princeton University Press, 2007), 11–15.

27. Ibid., 244.

28. UN Special Rapporteur on Freedom of Religion or Belief, as quoted in *State Department International Religious Freedom Report 2006*, released by the Bureau of Democracy, Human Rights, and Labor, http://www.state.gov/g/drl/rls/irf/2006/ 71380.htm

29. "French Sikhs Ask Chirac to Spare Turbans from Ban," Reuters News Service (Jan. 9, 2004), http://in.news.yahoo.com/040109/137/2atgc.html, accessed Sept. 21, 2007.

30. "Annual Report of the United States Commission on International Religious Freedom," *U.S. Commission on International Religious Freedom* (May 2004): 52, http://www.uscirf.gov/countries/publications/currentreport/2004annualrpt.pdf, accessed Oct. 19, 2007.

31. Martin Luther King Jr., "Letter from Birmingham Jail," Apr. 16, 1963, in *A Testament of Hope: The Essential Writings and Speeches of Martin Luther King, Jr.*, ed. James M. Washington (San Francisco: HarperSanFrancisco, 1986), 297–98.

CHAPTER 6

1. Diana L. Eck and the Pluralism Project at Harvard University, *On Common Ground: World Religions in America*, CD-ROM (New York: Columbia University Press, 1997).

2. M. R. Sahuquillo "La inmigración cambia el mapa religioso," *El País* (Mar. 31, 2007), 33.

3. Ibid.

4. Ramón Gorriarán, "El terrorismo vuelve a convertirse en la principal preocupación de los españoles," *El Ideal* (Granada, Spain) (Feb. 23, 2007), 34.

5. Islamic Community in Spain, "Islam in Granada: Welcome to the Islamic Capital of Europe," pamphlet (Mar. 2007).

6. Dr. Javier Jordán, Department of Political Science, University of Granada, Spain, interview by author (Mar. 13, 2007).

7. Dr. Cecilia Hita Alonso, Department of Sociology, University of Granada, Spain, interview by author (April 23, 2007).

8. Dr. Francisco Carmona, Department of Sociology, University of Granada, Spain, interview by author (Mar. 16, 2007).

9. The term was introduced into the medieval context by the academic Américo Castro in the 1940s. Jonathan Ray, "Beyond Tolerance and Persecution: Reassessing Our Approach to Medieval Convivencia," *Jewish Social Studies* 11(2) (Winter 2005), 1–18; Ray cites Castro's *España en su historia* (Madrid, 1948), 200–209. One book that gives a generally positive account of this period is María Rosa Menocal, *The Ornament of the West: How Muslims, Jews, and Christians Created a Culture of Tolerance in Medieval Spain* (New York: Little, Brown, 2002). Another book on Spain's al Andalus period that gives centrality of place to convivencia is David Levering Lewis, *God's Crucible: Islam and the Making of Europe, 570 to 1215* (New York: Norton, 2008). Philip Jenkins offers a more chastened reading of the reality of convivencia's limits in light of the more repressive elements of Islamic rule; see his *God's Continent: Christianity, Islam, and Europe's Religious Crisis* (New York: Oxford University Press, 2007), 103–106.

10. Quoting the leader known as Omar, in Rafael Vílchez, "Los musulmanes de Órgiva dispondrán de un cementerio propio en el municipio," *El Ideal* (Granada, Spain) (Mar. 15, 2007), 19.

11. La Fundación Pluralismo y Convivencia, http://www.pluralismoyconvivencia.es/.

12. Dr. José María Contreras, La Fundación Pluralismo y Convivencia, Madrid, interview by author (Mar. 30, 2007).

13. Some scholars distinguish between assimilation and integration as two different approaches to dealing with cultural difference. Here I follow Contreras's usage of integration.

14. Ibid.

15. Hita Alonso, interview. I note that in some contexts this communal autonomy argument is labeled *multiculturalism*—as Hita Alonso has done—but in some U.S. contexts, multiculturalism encompasses certain aspects of mutual engagement across religious and cultural identity groups. This latter notion makes multiculturalism closer to the inclusive vision of convivencia that I am advocating. One work that carefully explores the complex uses of multiculturalism is Will Kymlicka, *Multicultural Citizenship: A Liberal Theory of Minority Rights* (New York: Oxford University Press, 1995).

16. See my discussion on Indian religious diversity and communalism in Douglas A. Hicks, *Religion and the Workplace: Pluralism, Spirituality, Leadership* (New York: Cambridge University Press, 2003), 138–45.

17. William Johnson Everett, "Religion and Federal Republicanism: Cases from India's Struggle," *Journal of Church and State* 37 (1995): 67.

18. Indian Constitution of 1950, article 44. See also Ralph Buultjens, "India: Religion, Political Legitimacy, and the Secular State," *Annals of the American Academy of PSS* 483 (1986): 108.

19. Rowan Williams, "Archbishop's Lecture—Civil and Religious Law in England: A Religious Perspective," Feb. 7, 2008, archbishop of Canterbury official website, http://www.bishopthorpepalace.co.uk/1575, accessed Mar. 16, 2008.

20. John F. Burns, "Top Anglicans Rally to Besieged Bishop," *New York Times* (Feb. 12, 2008), A11.

21. Kwame Anthony Appiah, *Cosmopolitanism: Ethics in a World of Strangers* (New York: Norton, 2006); Kwame Anthony Appiah, "The Case for Contamination," *New York Times Magazine* (Jan. 1, 2006), 30–37, 52.

22. Robert Putnam, "*E Pluribus Unum:* Diversity and Community in the Twenty-first Century—The 2006 Johan Skytte Prize Lecture," *Scandinavian Political Studies* 30(2) (2007): 149.

23. Ibid., 138–39.

24. For a colorful critique of cosmopolitanism see Robert Pinsky, "Eros against Esperanto," in *For Love of Country: Debating the Limits of Patriotism, Martha C. Nussbaum with Respondents*, ed. Joshua Cohen (Boston: Beacon, 1996), 85–90.

25. Max Weber's translators H. H. Gerth and C. Wright Mills explain that "[t]he much-discussed 'ideal type,' a key term in Weber's methodological discussion, refers to the construction of certain elements of reality into a logically precise conception." Ideal types are "logically controlled and unambiguous conceptions . . . removed from historical reality" that allow the analyst better to understand actual cases. See H. H. Gerth and C. Wright Mills, "Introduction" to *From Max Weber: Essays in Sociology*, trans. and ed. H. H. Gerth and C. Wright Mills (New York: Oxford University Press, 1946), 59–60.

26. Huntington's own frame allows for "torn countries," which typically sit at the geographical boundary between civilization-based blocs. Situated between the Islamic world and the West, Turkey is the most frequently discussed example. But in

Huntington's view, being a torn country is not a comfortable or even sustainable state. Samuel P. Huntington, "Clash of Civilizations?" *Foreign Affairs* 72(3) (1993): 22–49.

27. Two reference essays are George R. Elder, "Crossroads," in *Encyclopedia of Religion*, ed. Lindsay Jones, vol. 3, 2d ed. (Detroit: Macmillan Reference USA, 2005), 2070–71, Gale Virtual Reference Library, http://go.galegroup.com/ps/start.do?p=GVRL&u=vic_uor, accessed June 26, 2008; and J. A. MacCullough, "Cross-roads," in *Encyclopaedia of Religion and Ethics*, ed. James Hastings, vol. 4 (New York: Charles Scribner's Sons, 1924), 330–35.

28. See Nancy S. Huber and Michael Harvey, eds., *Leadership at the Crossroads* (College Park, Md.: James MacGregor Burns Academy of Leadership, 2006); Joanne B. Ciulla, Donelson R. Forsyth, George R. Goethals, Crystal L. Hoyt, Michael A. Genovese, and Lori Cox Han, eds., *Leadership at the Crossroads*, 3 vols. (Westport, Conn.: Praeger, 2008).

29. For a discussion of the Yoruba god Eshu-Elegba, who either lives at or embodies the crossroads, see Robert Farris Thompson, *Flash of the Spirit: African and Afro-American Art and Philosophy* (New York: Random House, 1983), esp. 18–19.

30. Greg Andrews, "City's Mall Gamble Paid Off: After 10 Years, Circle Centre at Core of Rejuvenated Downtown," *Indianapolis Business Journal* (Sept. 5, 2005), 1.

31. Thad Williamson, *Sprawl, Justice, and Citizenship: The Civic Costs of the American Way of Life* (New York: Oxford University Press, forthcoming); Kevin M. Leyden, "Social Capital and the Built Environment: The Importance of Walkable Neighborhoods," *American Journal of Public Health* 93(9) (Sept. 2003): 1546–51.

32. Malcolm Gladwell, *The Tipping Point: How Little Things Can Make a Big Difference* (New York: Little, Brown, 2000).

33. On this point, convivencia is similar to the approach of Ronald A. Heifetz in his *Leadership without Easy Answers* (Cambridge, Mass.: Belknap, 1994).

34. Howard Gardner, in collaboration with Emma Laskin, *Leading Minds: An Anatomy of Leadership* (New York: Basic Books, 1995), 28–29.

35. Ibid., 316–17. These "lead stories" are quoted as Gardner states them.

36. Ibid., 10–11. In contrast to what Gardner calls the innovative leader, the visionary leader "actually creates a new story, one not known to most individuals before, and achieves at least a measure of success in conveying this story effectively to others."

37. First Amendment Center, "State of the First Amendment 2007," Final Annotated Survey, Sept. 12, 2007, http://www.firstamendmentcenter.org/PDF/SOFA2007results.pdf, accessed Mar. 16, 2008, 5.

38. Dr. Seuss, "The Zax," in *"The Sneetches" and Other Stories* (New York: Random House, 1961), 25–36, 32.

39. Ibid., 35.

40. James MacGregor Burns, *Leadership* (New York: Harper Torchbooks, 1978). I have analyzed Burns's approach in further detail in Douglas A. Hicks, "Public-sector Leadership, Development, and Ethics: The State of the Literature and Central Questions for Future Work," in *World Ethics Forum: Conference Proceedings*, ed. Charles Sampford and Carmel Connors (Queensland, Australia: Institute for Ethics, Governance, and Law, 2007).

41. Ibid., 17–19.

42. Ibid., 19–20.

43. Ibid., 20.

44. Burns has continued to write about the active agency or participation of citizens, as well as formal leaders, who together engage to make lasting social change. See James MacGregor Burns, *Transforming Leadership* (New York: Grove, 2004).

45. James MacGregor Burns and Georgia Sorenson, *Dead Center: Clinton-Gore Leadership and the Perils of Moderation* (New York: Scribner, 2001).

CHAPTER 7

1. See chapter 2 for a discussion of Congressman Virgil Goode's response to Ellison.

2. See, for example, Edward T. Hall, *The Silent Language* (New York: Anchor, 1959); Edgar H. Schein, *Organizational Culture and Leadership,* 2d ed. (San Francisco: Jossey-Bass, 1992).

3. According to a search for this phrase in the electronic presidential document archives at the University of California–Santa Barbara (UCSB), Nixon invoked this phrase 9 times, including once to end a speech defending his actions in the Watergate scandal. Jimmy Carter used it 4 times. Reagan used it 73 times, beginning with his acceptance speech at the 1980 Republican convention. George H. W. Bush used it 36 times, Bill Clinton 111 times, and George W. Bush, in just his first term, used it in 362 speeches. Presidency Project at UCSB, http://www.presidency.ucsb.edu/index_docs.php, accessed Mar. 18, 2008.

4. Schein, *Organizational Culture and Leadership;* Terrence E. Deal and Allan A. Kennedy, *Corporate Cultures* (Boston: Addison-Wesley, 1982).

5. For an interesting discussion see Joanne B. Ciulla, "Leadership Ethics: Mapping the Territory," in Joanne B. Ciulla, ed., *Ethics: The Heart of Leadership* (Westport, Conn.: Praeger, 1998), 3–25.

6. Susan Goodson (church historian, Bruton Parish Church), "History of the Wren Cross," letter to the editor, *Virginia Gazette* (Williamsburg, Va.) (Nov. 11, 2006), 25A.

7. The 1947 Supreme Court case *Everson v. Board of Education,* 330 U.S. 1 (1947), "incorporated" religious establishment so that state governments and not just the federal government were prohibited from establishing any religion.

8. "W&M Removes Chapel Cross to Be Inclusive: College Officials Cite Chapel's Use for Many Nonreligious Events," *Richmond Times-Dispatch* (Oct. 29, 2007).

9. Fredrick Kunkle, "School's Move toward Inclusion Creates a Rift; Upset about Cross's Removal, William and Mary Alumni Mount Online Protest," *Washington Post* (Dec. 26, 2006), B1.

10. Andrew R. McRoberts and Constance B. McRoberts, "At William and Mary, Cross Becomes a Lightning Rod," *Washington Post* (Feb. 18, 2007), B08.

11. Ibid.

12. Gene R. Nichol, "Nichol Discusses Wren Cross Decision with BOV," remarks prepared for the William and Mary Board of Visitors, College of William and Mary (Nov. 20, 2006), www.wm.edu/news/index.php?id=7026, accessed Aug. 16, 2007.

13. Gene R. Nichol, "Nichol Discusses Cross Decision in Message to Campus Community," College of William and Mary (Dec. 20, 2006), http://www.wm.edu/news/?id=7102, accessed Aug. 16, 2007.

14. Ibid.

15. Ibid.

16. McRoberts and McRoberts, "Cross Becomes a Lightning Rod."

17. "President and Board Accept Committee Recommendation on Wren Cross," *William and Mary News* (Mar. 6, 2007), http://wm.edu/news/?id=7456, accessed Aug. 16, 2007.

18. Ibid.

19. Leaders of SaveTheWrenCross.org, "Cross Returned to Wren Chapel," http://www.savethewrencross.org/stwcstatement.php, accessed Aug. 16, 2007.

20. A timeline of Nichol's tenure and the process of his departure is provided in Bill Geroux, "Nichol Leaving W&M for UNC; Ex-president's Departure Would Mark the Final Chapter in His Stormy Tenure," *Richmond Times-Dispatch* (Mar. 14, 2008), A1, A11.

21. Gene R. Nichol, "A Statement from President Nichol," e-mail to William and Mary students and alumni, Feb. 12, 2008.

22. Ibid.

23. Omar Sacirbey, "Ellison Not First to Forgo Bible for Oath," *Christian Century* (Dec. 26, 2006): 14–15; Jennifer Siegel, "Koch Calls for Pundit's Ouster from Shoah Council," *Jewish Daily Forward* (Dec. 8, 2006), www.forward.com/articles/kock-calls-for-pundits-ouster-from-shoah-council/, accessed Aug. 20, 2007.

24. Dennis Prager, "America, Not Keith Ellison, Decides What Book a Congressman Takes His Oath On," Townhall.com (Nov. 28, 2006), http://www.townhall.com/columnists/DennisPrager/2006/11/28/america,_not_keith_ellison,_decides_what_book_a_congressman_takes_his_oath_on, accessed Mar. 13, 2008.

25. Tad Vezner, "Request for Rare Quran Uncovers Minnesota Tie," *St. Paul (Minn.) Pioneer Press* (Jan. 4, 2007).

26. Michelle Norris, interview with Mark Dimunation, "Ellison to Take Oath on Thomas Jefferson's Quran," *All Things Considered,* National Public Radio (Jan. 3, 2007).

27. Kevin Hayes, "How Thomas Jefferson Read the Qur'an," *Early American Literature* 39(2) (2004): 247–61, esp. 252–55.

28. David Barton, "An Historical Perspective on a Muslim Being Sworn into Congress on the Koran," *WallBuilders* (Jan. 2007), www.wallbuilders.com/resources/misc/ellison.pdf, accessed June 21, 2007.

29. Hayes, "How Thomas Jefferson Read the Qur'an," 259.

30. Ibid.

31. Frederic J. Frommer, "Congressman to Be Sworn in Using Quran," *Associated Press* (Jan. 4, 2007), http://abcnews.go.com/Politics/wireStory?id=2768341, accessed Aug. 20, 2007.

32. William J. Clinton, "Remarks at the White House Interfaith Breakfast," American Presidency Project, University of California–Santa Barbara (Aug. 30, 1993), http://www.presidency.ucsb.edu/ws/?pid=47007, accessed Aug. 29, 2007.

33. Ibid.

34. Ibid.

35. William J. Clinton, "Religious Liberty in America," July 12, 1995, *William J. Clinton Foundation*, http://www.clintonfoundation.org/legacy/071295-speech-by-president-on-religious-liberties.htm, accessed Aug. 29, 2007.

36. William J. Clinton, "Memorandum on Religious Expression in Public Schools," July 12, 2007, Public Papers of the Presidents, *31 Weekly Comp. Pres. Doc.*

37. "Education: Clinton Sets School Prayer Guidelines," *Facts on File World News Digest* (July 20, 1995), *Facts.com*, Facts on File News Services, accessed Aug. 29, 2007.

38. William J. Clinton, "Presidential Radio Address on Prayer in School," May 30, 1998, *William J. Clinton Foundation*, http://www.clintonfoundation.org/legacy/053098-presidential-radio-address-on-prayer-in-school.htm, accessed Nov. 7, 2007.

39. William J. Clinton, "Remarks by the President at Religious Leaders Breakfast," Sept. 11, 1998, *William J. Clinton Foundation*, http://www.clintonfoundation.org/legacy/091198-speech-by-president-at-religious-leaders-breakfast.htm, accessed Mar. 15, 2008.

40. William J. Clinton, "Addressing the Nation," Aug. 17, 1998, *PBS Online Newshour*, http://www.pbs.org/newshour/lewinsky_address/address.html, accessed Mar. 15, 2008.

41. David Gergen, *Eyewitness to Power: The Essence of Leadership* (New York: Simon and Schuster, 2000), 317.

42. Amy Sullivan colorfully and aptly develops this history in her book *The Party Faithful: How and Why Democrats Are Closing the God Gap* (New York: Scribner, 2008).

43. Joanne Ciulla, "Messages from the Environment: The Influences of Policies and Practices on Employee Responsibility," in *Communicating Employee Responsibilities and Rights: A Modern Management Mandate,* ed. Chimezie A. B. Osigweh Yg (New York: Quorum, 1987), 133–40.

44. In July 2007 Keith Ellison encountered harsh criticism for his remarks critical of the Bush administration, including an analogy between George Bush and Adolf Hitler. He apologized publically, though he maintained that Bush had used the events of 9/11 to fuel Americans' fears for support of his foreign policy and military actions. Frederic J. Frommer, "Ellison Says He Was Wrong to Compare Bush 9/11 Response to Nazis," *Associated Press State and Local Wire*, July 17, 2007.

45. Barbara McGraw, *Rediscovering America's Sacred Ground: Public Religion and Pursuit of the Good in a Pluralistic America* (Albany: SUNY Press, 2003).

CHAPTER 8

1. Tomás Bárbulo, "Ataqué al bandido porque estaba sequro de que iba a morir," *El País* (Feb. 12, 2007), 24.

2. "Council on American-Islamic Relations," *Anti-Defamation League* (Aug. 8, 2007), www.adl.org/Israel/cair.asp, accessed Sept. 5, 2007.

3. "ADL Troubled by National Islamic Civil Rights Organization's Failure to Condemn Terrorism by Name," *Anti-Defamation League* (Aug. 21, 2007), http://www.adl.org/PresRele/Teror_92/5115_92.htm, accessed Sept. 5, 2007.

4. Ibid.

5. "An Open Letter from CAIR to the ADL," *Council on American-Islamic Relations* (Aug. 30, 2007), http://www.cair.com/default.asp?Page=articleView&id=2939&theType =NR, accessed Sept. 5, 2007.

6. Will Herberg, *Protestant, Catholic, Jew: An Essay in American Religious Sociology,* new ed., completely rev. (Garden City, N.Y.: Anchor, 1960).

7. The FBI's Uniform Crime Report annual hate-crime reports are located at www. fbi.gov/ucr/ucr.htm, accessed June 25, 2007. The relevant figures are listed in table 1 of each year's report.

8. For example, the ADL's national director, Abraham Foxman, has stated, "There's a feeling that there's a lot of Islamophobia out there. While there is, anti-Jewish hate crimes predominate." Quoted in Chanan Tigay, "For Jews, FBI Hate Crime Report Has Some Good News, Some Bad," Jewish Telegraphic Agency (Nov. 24, 2004).

9. Rebecca Stotzer, *Comparison of Hate Crime Rates across Protected and Unprotected Groups* (Los Angeles: Williams Institute at the UCLA School of Law, 2007). This calculation uses a rather conservative estimate for the Muslim population in the United States, 1.74 million persons, based on an adjustment to data obtained from the American Religious Identification Survey and reported in the Statistical Abstract of the United States. See Stotzer's "Appendix—Calculating the Hate Crimes Rates."

10. Prema A. Kurien, "Mr. President, Why Do You Exclude Us from Your Prayers?" in *A Nation of Religions: The Politics of Pluralism in Multireligious America,* ed. Stephen Prothero (Chapel Hill: University of North Carolina Press, 2006), 119–38.

11. Pew Research Center, *American Muslims: Middle Class and Mostly Mainstream,* May 22, 2007, http://pewresearch.org/pubs/483/muslim-americans, accessed Mar. 21, 2008, 51.

12. For example, the North Atlantic Treaty of 1949, which established NATO, makes this statement in article 5: "The Parties agree that an armed attack against one or more of them in Europe or North America shall be considered an attack against them all and consequently they agree that, if such an armed attack occurs, each of them, in exercise of the right of individual or collective self-defence recognised by Article 51 of the Charter of the United Nations, will assist the Party or Parties so attacked by taking forthwith, individually and in concert with the other Parties, such action as it deems necessary, including the use of armed force, to restore and maintain the security of the North Atlantic area" (North Atlantic Treaty Organization Online Library, http://www.nato.int/ docu/basictxt/treaty.htm, accessed June 19, 2008). Of course, the tactics used by a religious coalition should not employ any armed response—or responses that would seem to justify the use of violence by others.

13. "Looking after One Another: The Safety and Security of Our Faith Communities," *Interfaith Network for the United Kingdom* (2005), http://www.interfaith.org.uk/ publications/lookingafteroneanother.pdf, accessed Oct. 23, 2007.

14. Rabbi Eric H. Yoffie, "Remarks as Prepared to Islamic Society of North America," 44th Annual Convention Transcript by President of URJ, *Union for Reform Judaism,* Chicago (Aug. 31, 2007), http://urj.org/yoffie/isna, accessed Sept. 21, 2007.

15. Ibid.

16. Stewart Ain, "Reform Draws Fire for Muslim Outreach," *Jewish Week* (Sept. 6, 1997), http://www.jewishweek.org/news/newscontent.php3?artid=14493&print=yes, accessed Sept. 21, 2007.

17. Audrey Hudson, "Republicans Slam Islamic Society Convention," *Washington Times* (Aug. 31, 2007), A3.

18. Ain, "Reform Draws Fire."

19. Ibid.

20. The AMPU coalition received a grant from the September 11 Antibias Project, a partnership between the National Conference for Community and Justice and the Chevron Texaco Foundation that funded new initiatives promoting antibias education and community building in local areas. The Community Foundation of Richmond provided additional support to AMPU as well.

21. I served as a faculty advisor to AMPU's grant-writing team and participated on the advisory board from 2003 to 2006.

22. The project received *Shoot Magazine*'s recognition for "The Best Work You May Never See," http://www.siddall.com/ampu/ShootArticle.pdf; see also Bob Rayner, "Message on a Shoestring; Waging War on Prejudice," *Richmond Times-Dispatch* (July 21, 2004), A1.

23. Associated Press, "An Anti-bias Campaign Is Leaving Some Virginians Unsettled," *New York Times* (Dec. 25, 2006), A23; Robin Farmer, "Arabic Signs Posted on Buses to Foster Dialogue," *Richmond Times-Dispatch* (Dec. 22, 2006), B8.

24. A More Perfect Union, "Bus Campaign Feedback," http://www.rethinkbias. org/pages/BusCampaign/feedback.html, accessed Aug. 9, 2007.

25. Tom Peters and Robert Waterman Jr., *In Search of Excellence: Lessons from America's Best-run Companies* (New York: Warner, 1982).

26. Ibid., 289.

27. For an interesting discussion see Barbara Kellerman, *Reinventing Leadership: Making the Connection between Politics and Business* (Albany: SUNY Press, 1999).

28. Bill McKelway, "Bush Stop a Coincidence? Farmer's Glad Either Way," *Richmond Times-Dispatch* (Oct. 21, 2006), B1.

29. Andrew Rosenthal, "Bush Encounters the Supermarket—Amazed," *New York Times,* (Feb. 5, 1992), A1.

30. An interesting reflection on the importance of leaders' physical presence is Joanne B. Ciulla, "Why 'Being There' Is Essential to Leadership," in *Leadership and the Humanities,* ed. Joanne B. Ciulla, 148–63 (vol. 3 of *Leadership at the Crossroads*), set ed. Joanne B. Ciulla (Westport, Conn.: Praeger, 2008).

31. With an estimated population of 6.3 million persons in Indiana, the state's Muslim population, according to the reported figure, would make up about 4.4 of all Hoosiers. This is significantly higher than the national estimate from the Pew Survey, which suggested that 0.6 percent of the national adult population is Muslim. See my discussion in chapter 4.

32. "Muslim Alliance of Indiana (MAI) Helps Organize Second Annual Governor's Iftar," Sept. 26, 2006, http://www.muslimalliencein.com/mai/enews_brief_october2. htm, accessed Sept. 21, 2007.

33. Barbara Bradley Hagerty, "Young Imam Serves as Islam's Face to Community," *National Public Radio* (Aug. 6, 2007), www.npr.org/templates/story/story.php?story Id=12532168, accessed Sept. 21, 2007.

34. Tim Craig, "2 GOP Lawmakers Allege Democrats Have Ties to Terrorism," *Washington Post* (Oct. 21, 2007), C06.

35. Tim Craig, "Republicans Seize on Muslim Appointment," *Washington Post* (Oct. 4, 2007), VA4.

36. George W. Bush, "President Bush Rededicates Islamic Center of Washington" (June 27, 2007), http://www.whitehouse.gov/news/releases/2007/06/print/2007 0627-2. html, accessed June 29, 2007.

37. Pew Research Center, *Muslim Americans*, 49.

38. Peters and Waterman, *In Search of Excellence*, 289.

39. Mac Davis, "It's Hard to Be Humble," on *It's Hard to Be Humble*, Casablanca Records (1980).

40. Richard Rorty, "Religion as Conversation-Stopper," *Common Knowledge* 3(1) (Spring 1994): 1–6. Rorty later revised his view, citing Nicholas Wolterstorff. See Richard Rorty, "Religion in the Public Square: A Reconsideration," *Journal of Religious Ethics* 31(1) (March 2003): 141–49.

41. Christopher Hitchens, *God Is Not Great: How Religion Poisons Everything* (New York: Twelve, 2007).

42. John Danforth, "In the Name of Politics," *New York Times* (Mar. 30, 2004), A17; Danforth, "Onward, Moderate Christian Soldiers," *New York Times* (June 17, 2005), A27.

43. John Danforth, *Faith and Politics: How the "Moral Values" Debate Divides America and How to Move Forward Together* (New York: Viking, 2006), 10.

44. Danforth, "In the Name of Politics."

45. Danforth, "Onward, Moderate Christian Soldiers"; Danforth, *Faith and Politics*, 17–18.

46. Danforth, "In the Name of Politics."

47. John Locke, *A Letter concerning Toleration* (Amherst, N.Y.: Prometheus, 1990).

48. Terry L. Price, *Understanding Ethical Failures in Leadership* (New York: Cambridge University Press, 2006); Terry L. Price, "Epistemological Restraint—Revisited," *Journal of Political Philosophy* 8(3) (2000): 401–407.

49. Roy P. Basler, ed., *The Collected Works of Abraham Lincoln*, 8 vols. (New Brunswick, N.J.: Rutgers University Press, 1953), vol. 5: 332–33.

50. Aristotle, *Nicomachean Ethics*, ed. Terence Irwin (Indianapolis: Hackett, 1985), book 4, chap. 3, 97–105.

51. Gustavo Gutiérrez, *The Power of the Poor in History*, trans. Robert R. Barr (Maryknoll, N.Y.: Orbis, 1983 [1979]), 13. For a discussion of feminist critiques of Reinhold Niebuhr on this point see Douglas A. Hicks, "Self-interest, Deprivation, and Agency: Expanding the Capabilities Approach," *Journal of the Society of Christian Ethics* 25(1) (Spring 2005): 147–67. For a Kantian account of the proper duties owed to the self see Thomas E. Hill Jr., "Servility and Self-respect," in *Autonomy and Self-respect* (New York: Cambridge University Press, 1991).

52. I have laid out in more detail the starting points for this approach—within the context of religion's role in the workplace—in Douglas A. Hicks, *Religion and the Workplace: Pluralism, Spirituality, Leadership* (New York: Cambridge University Press, 2003), 166–68.

53. See chapter 6.

54. James Madison, *Memorial and Remonstrance against Religious Assessments* (1785), paragraph 5, http://religiousfreedom.lib.virginia.edu/sacred/madison_m&r_1785.html, accessed Nov. 7, 2007.

CHAPTER 9

1. Jeff Stein, "Can You Tell a Sunni from a Shiite?" *New York Times* (Oct. 17, 2006), A21; Jeff Stein, "Democrats' New Intelligence Chairman Needs Crash Course on al Qaeda," *CQ.com* (Dec. 8, 2006), http://public.cq.com/public/20061211_homeland.html, accessed Oct. 12, 2007.

2. Peter Beinart, "Foreign Policymaking Requires, at Minimum, Factual Competence," *Richmond Times-Dispatch* (Dec. 21, 2006), A11.

3. "Trent Lott in His Own Words," *New York Times* (Nov. 16, 2006), A29.

4. These estimates are based on the Pew Research Center's 2007 survey *American Muslims: Middle Class and Mostly Mainstream* (May 22, 2007) http://pewresearch.org/pubs/483/muslim-americans, accessed Mar. 21, 2008, 9–10, 21.

5. See my discussion of religious identity in the United States in chapter 2, in which I cite the figure for Christian affiliation, 78 percent, from the 2008 *U.S. Religious Landscape Survey,* which differs slightly from the figure Prothero used prior to the Pew survey's publication.

6. Stephen Prothero, *Religious Literacy: What Every American Needs to Know—and Doesn't* (San Francisco: HarperSanFrancisco, 2007). See especially pp. 1–6 and 21–34.

7. Barbara Bradley Hagerty, "Understanding the Gospel according to Huckabee," *All Things Considered,* National Public Radio (Feb. 8, 2008), http://www.npr.org/templates/story/story.php?storyId=18821021, accessed Mar. 13, 2008.

8. Cited in Prothero, *Religious Literacy,* 31. Prothero treats this case as in the context of the religious illiteracy of journalists; that is only part of the question concerning communication among leaders, the media, and citizens.

9. Ibid., 1.

10. *Descubrir el Islam: Religión islámica. Primaria* (Discover Islam: Islamic Religion, First Grade), Madrid: Ediciones SM, 2006.

11. Carlos Morán, "Publicado el primer libro de religión islámica para escolares," *El País* (Oct. 18, 2006).

12. Dr. José María Contreras, interview by author, La Fundación Pluralismo y Convivencia, Madrid (Mar. 30, 2007).

13. Juan G. Bedoya, "33 profesores para 74.000 alumnos," *El País* (Mar. 27, 2007), 45.

14. "Khalil Gibran International Academy," http://Schools.nyc.gov/SchoolPortals/15/k592/default.htm. For critic Daniel Pipes's account of the controversy see his blog, http://www.danielpipes.org/blog/731, accessed Oct. 12, 2007.

15. See www.bengamlacharter.org, accessed Oct. 12, 2007; Greg Allen, "Publicly Funded Hebrew Charter School Opens in Florida," National Public Radio (Sept. 16, 2007).

16. Gary Orfield and Chungmei Lei, "Historic Reversals, Accelerating Resegregation, and the Need for New Integration Strategies," Report of the Civil Rights Project/ Proyecto Derechos Civiles, UCLA (Aug. 2007), http://www.civilrightsproject.ucla.edu/ research/deseg/reversals_reseg_need.pdf, accessed Nov. 10, 2007.

17. Council for America's First Freedom, http://www.firstfreedom.org.

18. First Amendment Center, http://www.firstamendmentcenter.org.

19. See the report and the response to critics posted at American Textbook Council, "Islam and the Textbooks," http://www.historytextbooks.org/islam.htm, accessed Oct. 13, 2007.

20. See the opening of chapter 3.

21. James Davison Hunter and David Franz, "Religious Pluralism and Civil Society," in *A Nation of Religions: The Politics of Pluralism in Multireligious America*, ed. Stephen Prothero (Chapel Hill: University of North Carolina Press, 2006), 256–73, quote on p. 271.

22. The University of Richmond's Mission Statement is available at http://presi dent.richmond.edu/mission/index.html, accessed Nov. 7, 2007.

23. Anne Colby, Thomas Erlich, Elizabeth Beaumont, and Jason Stephens, *Educating Citizens: Preparing America's Undergraduates for Lives of Moral and Civic Responsibility* (San Francisco: Carnegie Foundation for the Advancement of Teaching and Jossey-Bass, 2003).

24. Prothero, *Religious Literacy*, 141–43.

25. Laurie Goodstein, "Prisons Purging Books on Faith from Libraries," *New York Times* (Sept. 10, 2007), http://www.nytimes.com/2007/09/10/us/10prison. html?pagewanted=print, accessed Oct. 13, 2007.

26. Neela Banerjee, "Prisons to Restore Purged Religious Books, *New York Times* (Sept. 27, 2007), http://www.nytimes.com/2007/09/27/washington/27prison.html, accessed Oct. 13, 2007.

27. Duncan Williams makes this point in the video "Building Bridges," which is part of the Encountering Religious Diversity section of Diana L. Eck, *On Common Ground: World Religions in America*, CD-Rom (New York: Columbia University Press, 1997).

28. Adam Smith, *The Theory of Moral Sentiments*, III.I.46. Library of Economics and Liberty Online, http://www.econlib.org/library/Smith/smMS.html, accessed Oct. 15, 2007.

29. Ibid.

30. For a discussion of how globalization played a role in expanding the moral imagination of Westerners who offered assistance in light of the 2004 Asian tsunami, see Jonathan B. Wight and Douglas A. Hicks, "Disaster Relief: What Would Adam Smith Do?" *Christian Science Monitor* (Jan. 18, 2005), 9. I develop these points about moral imagination in Douglas A. Hicks, "Global Poverty and Bono's Celebrity Activism: An Analysis of Moral Imagination and Motivation," in *Global Neighbors: Christian Faith and Moral Obligation in Today's Economy*, ed. Douglas A. Hicks and Mark Valeri, 43–62 (Grand Rapids, Mich.: Eerdmans, 2008), 52.

31. Martha C. Nussbaum, "Compassion and Terror," *Daedalus* (Winter 2003): 10–26.

32. Christian Smith, "Religiously Ignorant Journalists," *Books and Culture* (Jan. 1, 2004): 6–7.

33. Mark Juergensmeyer, *Terror in the Mind of God: The Global Rise of Religious Violence* (Berkeley: University of California Press, 2000), 19–43.

34. Mark Trevelyan, "EU Lexicon to Shun Term 'Islamic Terrorism'" (Nov. 4, 2006) *Tiscali.co.uk,* http://www.tiscali.co.uk/news/newswire.php/news/reuters/2006/04/11/topnews/eu-lexicon-to-shun-term-34islamic-terrorism34.html&template=/news/templates/newswire/news_story_reuters.html, accessed Oct. 15, 2007; Diane West, "Call It like It Is: PC Lexicon," *Washington Times* (July 6, 2007), A17; "Abizaid: In 'The Battle of Words,' Phrases like 'Islamic Extremism' Alienate 'Mainline Islam,'" *Think Progress,* http://thinkprogress.org/2007/09/18/abizaid-extremism/, accessed Oct. 16, 2007.

35. See Juergensmeyer, *Terror in the Mind of God,* 4–10.

36. Douglas A. Hicks, *Religion and the Workplace: Pluralism, Spirituality, Leadership* (New York: Cambridge University Press, 2003), 13.

37. Ibid., 187–93.

CHAPTER 10

1. J. Thomas Wren, *Inventing Leadership: The Challenge of Democracy* (Northampton, Mass.: Edward Elgar, 2007), 216.

2. See chapters 2 and 6.

3. Robert Putnam, "*E Pluribus Unum:* Diversity and Community in the Twenty-first Century—The 2006 Johan Skytte Prize Lecture," *Scandinavian Political Studies* 30(2) (2007): 138.

4. See chapter 2.

5. Nobel laureate Amartya Sen aptly cautions that the frequent grouping of people by one aspect of their identity tends to harden lines of difference and consequently fuels communalism and even violence; Amartya Sen, *Identity and Violence: The Illusion of Destiny* (New York: Norton, 2006).

6. Max Weber, "Politics as a Vocation," in *From Max Weber: Essays in Sociology,* trans. and ed. H. H. Gerth and C. Wright Mills (New York: Oxford University Press, 1946), 77–128.

References

Abdo, Geneive. *Mecca and Main Street: Muslim Life in America after 9/11*. New York: Oxford University Press, 2006.

"Abizaid: In 'The Battle of Words,' Phrases like 'Islamic Extremism' Alienate 'Mainline Islam.'" *Think Progress.* http://thinkprogress.org/2007/09/18/abizaid-extremism/. Accessed October 16, 2007.

"ADL Troubled by National Islamic Civil Rights Organization's Failure to Condemn Terrorism by Name." *Anti-Defamation League,* August 21, 2007. http://www.adl.org/PresRele/Teror_92/5115_92.htm. Accessed September 5, 2007.

Ain, Stewart. "Reform Draws Fire for Muslim Outreach." *Jewish Week,* September 6, 1997. http://www.jewishweek.org/news/newscontent.php3?artid=14493&print=yes. Accessed September 21, 2007.

Ajemian, Robert. "Where Is the Real George Bush; the Vice President Must Now Step Out from Reagan's Shadow." *Time* 129 (January 26, 1987), 20–21.

Allen, Greg. "Publicly Funded Hebrew Charter School Opens in Florida." National Public Radio, September 16, 2007.

Allen, Mike. "Edwards Rejects 'The War on Terror.'" *Time,* May 2, 2007. http://www.time.com/time/nation/article/0,8599,1616724,00.html. Accessed November 7, 2007.

American Textbook Council. "Islam and the Textbooks." http://www.historytextbooks.org/islam.htm. Accessed October 13, 2007.

Andrews, Greg. "City's Mall Gamble Paid Off: After 10 Years, Circle Centre at Core of Rejuvenated Downtown." *Indianapolis Business Journal* (September 5, 2005): 1.

"Ann Coulter on CNBC Show: Jews Need 'Perfecting.'" *Editor and Publisher.* http://www.editorandpublisher.com/eandp/news/article_display.jsp?vnu_content_id=1003657196. Accessed November 7, 2007.

Anti-Defamation League. "Council on American-Islamic Relations." *Anti-Defamation League,* August 8, 2007. http://www.adl.org/Israel/cair.asp. Accessed September 5, 2007.

Appiah, Kwame Anthony. "The Case for Contamination." *New York Times Magazine* (January 1, 2006), 30–37, 52.

———. *Cosmopolitanism: Ethics in a World of Strangers*. New York: Norton, 2006.

Aristotle. *Nicomachean Ethics*, ed. Terence Irwin. Indianapolis: Hackett, 1985.

Associated Press. "An Anti-bias Campaign Is Leaving Some Virginians Unsettled." *New York Times* (December 25, 2006), A23.

———. "Minneapolis Airport Approves Stiffer Penalties for Cabbies Who Refuse Customers with Alcohol." *International Herald Tribune*, April 16, 2007. http://www.iht.com/articles/ap/2007/04/16/america/NA-GEN-US-Muslim-Cabbies-Alcohol.php. Accessed November 8, 2007.

———. "Tancredo: If They Nuke Us, Bomb Mecca." *FoxNews.com*, July 18, 2005. http://www.foxnews.com/story/0,2933,162795,00.html. Accessed November 7, 2007.

Banerjee, Neela. "Prisons to Restore Purged Religious Books." *New York Times*, September 27, 2007. http://www.nytimes.com/2007/09/27/washington/27prison.html. Accessed October 13, 2007.

Bárbulo, Tomás. "Ataqué al bandido porque estaba sequro de que iba a morir." *El País* (February 12, 2007).

Barton, David. "An Historical Perspective on a Muslim Being Sworn into Congress on the Koran." *WallBuilders*, January 2007. http://www.wallbuilders.com/resources/misc/ellison.pdf. Accessed June 21, 2007.

Basler, Roy P., ed. *The Collected Works of Abraham Lincoln*. 8 vols. New Brunswick, N.J.: Rutgers University Press, 1953.

BBC News. "Infinite Justice, Out—Enduring Freedom, In." September 25, 2001. http://news.bbc.co.uk/2/hi/americas/1563722.stm. Accessed March 10, 2008.

Beam, Alex. "Dean's Conversion Experience." *Boston Globe* (December 11, 2003), B17.

Bedoya, Juan G. "33 profesores para 74.000 alumnos." *El País* (March 27, 2007), 45.

Beinart, Peter. "Foreign Policymaking Requires, at Minimum, Factual Competence." *Richmond Times-Dispatch* (December 21, 2006), A11.

Bellah, Robert N. "Civil Religion in America." *Daedalus* 96 (Winter 1967): 1–21.

Berke, Richard. "With a Crackle, Religion Enters G.O.P. Meeting." *New York Times* (November 18, 1992), 23.

Blankley, Tony. "Is There a Clash of Civilizations? Islam, Democracy, and U.S.—Middle East and Central Asia Policy." Hearing before the Subcommittee on the Middle East and Central Asia of the Committee on International Relations. Serial no. 109–210. September 14, 2006.

Bowen, John R. *Why the French Don't Like Headscarves: Islam, the State, and Public Space*. Princeton, N.J.: Princeton University Press, 2007.

Bowman, Rex. "Goode Refuses to Apologize for Letter." *Richmond Times-Dispatch* (December 22, 2006), A1.

Brooks, David. "One America, Slightly Divisible." *Atlantic Monthly* (December 2001), 53–65.

Brunskill, Mary K. "Rep. Pete Stark Becomes First Congressman to Publicly Declare He's an Atheist." *All Headline News*, March 14, 2007.

Burns, James MacGregor. *Leadership*. New York: Harper Torchbooks, 1978.

————. *Transforming Leadership*. New York: Grove, 2004.

————, and Georgia Sorenson. *Dead Center: Clinton-Gore Leadership and the Perils of Moderation*. New York: Scribner, 2001.

Burns, John F. "Top Anglicans Rally to Besieged Bishop." *New York Times* (February 12, 2008), A11.

Bush, George W. "Address to a Joint Session of Congress and the American People." *White House: President George W. Bush*, September 20, 2001. http://www.whitehouse.gov/news/releases/2001/09/20010920–8.html. Accessed March 10, 2008.

————. " 'Islam Is Peace,' Says President: Remarks by the President at Islamic Center of Washington, D.C." *White House: President George W. Bush*, September 17, 2001. http://www.whitehouse.gov/news/releases/2001/09/20010917–11.html. Accessed September 24, 2007.

————. "President Bush Rededicates Islamic Center of Washington." *White House: President George W. Bush*, June 27, 2007. http://www.whitehouse.gov/news/releases/2007/06/print/20070627–2.html. Accessed June 29, 2007.

————. "President Highlights Faith-based Initiative at Leadership Conference." Omni Shoreham Hotel, Washington, D.C. *White House: President George W. Bush*, March 1, 2005. http://www.whitehouse.gov/news/releases/2005/03/20050301–4.html. Accessed November 7, 2007.

————. "President Hosts Iftaar: Remarks by the President at Iftaar in State Dining Room." *White House: President George W. Bush*, November 7, 2002. http://www.whitehouse.gov/news/releases/2002/11/20021107–11.html. Accessed September 24, 2007.

————. "President Rallies the Troops in Alaska." *White House: President George W. Bush*, February 16, 2002. http://www.whitehouse.gov/news/releases/2002/02/2002021 6–1.html. Accessed October 13, 2006.

————. "President's Address to the Nation." *White House: President George W. Bush*, September 11, 2006. http://www.whitehouse.gove/news/releases/2006/09/print/20060911–3.html. Accessed March 13, 2008.

————. "President's Remarks at National Day of Prayer and Remembrance." *White House: President George W. Bush*, September 14, 2001. http://www.whitehouse.gov/news/releases/2001/09/20010914–2.html. Accessed March 10, 2008.

————. "President's Remarks to the Nation." *White House: President George W. Bush*, September 11, 2002. http://www.whitehouse.gov/news/releases/2002/09/20020 911–3.html. Accessed March 13, 2008.

————. "White House Press Conference." *White House: President George W. Bush*, September 16, 2001. http://www.whitehouse.gov/news/releases/2001/09/20010916–2.html. Accessed October 13, 2006

Buultjens, Ralph. "India: Religion, Political Legitimacy, and the Secular State." *Annals of the American Academy of PSS* 483 (1986): 93–109.

Caldwell, Deborah. "David Barton and the 'Myth' of Church-State Separation." *Beliefnet*, 2006. http://www.beliefnet.com/story/154/story_15469.html. Accessed June 21, 2007.

Cannon, Carl M. "Bush and God." *National Journal* (January 3, 2004): 12–18.

Casey, Shaun. *The Making of a Catholic President: Kennedy versus Nixon 1960*. New York: Oxford University Press, 2009.

Catholic News Service. "Kerry Addresses Faith, Values but Rejects Bishops on Life Issues." October 25, 2004. http://www.catholicnews.com/data/stories/cns/0405879.htm. Accessed November 7, 2007.

Ciulla, Joanne B. "Leadership Ethics: Mapping the Territory." In *Ethics: The Heart of Leadership*, ed. Joanne B. Ciulla, 3–25. Westport, Conn.: Praeger, 1998.

———. "Messages from the Environment: The Influences of Policies and Practices on Employee Responsibility." In *Communicating Employee Responsibilities and Rights: A Modern Management Mandate*, ed. Chimezie A. B. Osigweh Yg, 133–40. New York: Quorum, 1987.

———. "Why 'Being There' Is Essential to Leadership." In *Leadership and the Humanities*, ed. Joanne B. Ciulla, 148–63. Vol. 3 of *Leadership at the Crossroads*, set ed. Joanne B. Ciulla. Westport, Conn.: Praeger, 2008.

———, Donelson R. Forsyth, George R. Goethals, Crystal L. Hoyt, Michael A. Genovese, and Lori Cox Han, eds. *Leadership at the Crossroads*. 3 vols. Westport, Conn.: Praeger, 2008.

Clinton, William J. "Addressing the Nation." *PBS Online Newshour*, August 17, 1998. http://www.pbs.org/newshour/lewinsky_address/address.html. Accessed March 15, 2008.

———. "Memorandum on Religious Expression in Public Schools." Public Papers of the Presidents, 31 *Weekly Comp. Pres. Doc.*, July 12, 2007.

———. "Presidential Radio Address on Prayer in School." *William J. Clinton Foundation*, May 30, 1998. http://www.clintonfoundation.org/legacy/053098-presidential-radio-address-on-prayer-in-school.htm. Accessed November 7, 2007.

———. "Religious Liberty in America." *William J. Clinton Foundation*, July 12, 1995. http://www.clintonfoundation.org/legacy/071295-speech-by-president-on-religious-liberties.htm. Accessed August 29, 2007.

———. "Remarks at the White House Interfaith Breakfast." American Presidency Project, University of California–Santa Barbara, August 30, 1993. http://www.presidency.ucsb.edu/ws/?pid=47007. Accessed August 29, 2007.

———. "Remarks by the President at Religious Leaders Breakfast." *William J. Clinton Foundation*, September 11, 1998. http://www.clintonfoundation.org/legacy/091198-speech-by-president-at-religious-leaders-breakfast.htm. Accessed March 15, 2008.

CNN, "Situation Room: Special Edition: Sojourners Presidential Forum," George Washington University (June 4, 2007), http://transcripts.cnn.com/TRANSCRIPTS/0706/04/sitroom.03.html, accessed Sept. 2, 2007.

Cohen, Arthur Allen. *The Myth of the Judeo-Christian Tradition*. New York: Harper and Row, 1969.

Colby, Anne, Thomas Erlich, Elizabeth Beaumont, and Jason Stephens. *Educating Citizens: Preparing America's Undergraduates for Lives of Moral and Civic Responsibility*. San Francisco: Carnegie Foundation for the Advancement of Teaching and Jossey-Bass, 2003.

"Correspondence of the *Boston Journal:* The President's Entry into Richmond." *Littell's Living Age,* no. 1090 (April 22, 1865), 137–38. http://cdl.library.cornell.edu/cgi bin/moa/pageviewer?frames=1&cite=&coll=moa&view=50&root=%2Fmoa%2 Flivn%2Flivn0085%2F&tif=00109.TIF&pagenum=137, accessed November 8, 2007.

Coulter, Ann. "Calvin and Hobbes—and Muhammad." *Anncoulter.com,* February 8, 2006. http://www.anncoulter.com/cgi-local/article.cgi?article=99. Accessed November 10, 2007.

Council on American-Islamic Relations. "Islamic Statements against Terrorism in the Wake of the September 11 Mass Murders." *Council on American-Islamic Relations.* http://www.cair.com/AmericanMuslims/AntiTerrorism/IslamicStatementsAgainst Terrorism.aspx. Accessed November 7, 2007.

———. "An Open Letter from CAIR to the ADL." August 30, 2007. http://www.cair. com/default.asp?Page=articleView&id=2939&theType=NR. Accessed September 5, 2007.

Cousins, Norman, ed. *In God We Trust: The Religious Beliefs and Ideas of the American Founding Fathers.* New York: Harper and Brothers: 1958.

Craig, Tim. "Republicans Seize on Muslim Appointment." *Washington Post* (October 4, 2007), VA4.

———. "2 GOP Lawmakers Allege Democrats Have Ties to Terrorism." *Washington Post* (October 21, 2007), C06.

"Cross Returned to Wren Chapel." *SaveTheWrenCross.org,* March 7, 2007. http://www. savethewrencross.org/stwcstatement.php. Accessed August 16, 2007.

Danforth, John. *Faith and Politics: How the "Moral Values" Debate Divides America and How to Move Forward Together.* New York: Viking, 2006.

———. "In the Name of Politics." *New York Times* (March 30, 2004), A17.

———. "Onward, Moderate Christian Soldiers." *New York Times* (June 17, 2005), A27.

Dawkins, Richard. *The God Delusion.* Boston: Houghton Mifflin, 2006.

Deal, Terrence E., and Allan A. Kennedy. *Corporate Cultures.* Boston: Addison-Wesley, 1982.

Debusman, Bernd. "In U.S., Fear and Distrust of Muslims Runs Deep." *Reuters.com,* February 25, 2007. http://www.reuters.com/article/topNews/idUSARM55127020070225. Accessed November 7, 2007.

Descubrir el Islam: Religión islámica. Primaria (Discover Islam: Islamic Religion. First Grade). Madrid: Ediciones SM, 2006.

Eaton, Leslie. "U.S. Prosecution of Muslim Group Ends in Mistrial." *New York Times* (October 23, 2007), A1.

Eck, Diana L. *A New Religious America: How a "Christian Country" Has Now Become the World's Most Religiously Diverse Nation,* rev. ed. San Francisco: HarperSanFrancisco, 2002.

———, Rebecca K. Gould, and Douglas A. Hicks. "Encountering Religious Diversity: Historical Perspectives." In *On Common Ground: World Religions in America,* by Diana L. Eck and the Pluralism Project at Harvard University. CD-ROM. New York: Columbia University Press, 1997.

Eck, Diana L., and the Pluralism Project at Harvard University. *On Common Ground: World Religions in America.* CD-ROM. New York: Columbia University Press, 1997.

Eckholm, Erik. "Muslim Voters Detect a Snub from Obama." *New York Times* (June 24, 2008), A1, A20.

"Education: Clinton Sets School Prayer Guidelines." *Facts on File World News Digest,* July 20, 1995. *Facts.com.* Facts on File News Services. Accessed August 29, 2007.

Elder, George R. "Crossroads." In *Encyclopedia of Religion,* 2d ed., ed. Lindsay Jones, 2070–71. Vol. 3. Detroit: Macmillan Reference USA, 2005. Gale Virtual Reference Library. Accessed June 26, 2008. http://go.galegroup.com/ps/start.do?p=GVRL&u=vic_uor.

"Ellison: Lawmaker Has 'A Lot to Learn about Islam.'" *CNN.com,* December 21, 2006. http://www.cnn.com/2006/POLITICS/12/21/quran.congress/index.html. Accessed August 20, 2007.

"The Enemy Within." *Snopes.com.* http://www.snopes.com/politics/obama/muslim.asp. Accessed October 26, 2007.

Everett, William Johnson. "Religion and Federal Republicanism: Cases from India's Struggle." *Journal of Church and State* 37 (1995): 61–85.

Farmer, Robin. "Arabic Signs Posted on Buses to Foster Dialogue." *Richmond Times-Dispatch* (December 22, 2006), B8.

First Amendment Center. "State of the First Amendment 2007: Final Annotated Survey." *First Amendment Center.org,* September 12, 2007. http://www.firstamendment-center.org/PDF/SOFA2007results.pdf. Accessed March 16, 2008.

Frommer, Frederic J. "Congressman to Be Sworn in Using Quran." Associated Press, January 4, 2007. http://abcnews.go.com/Politics/wireStory?id=2768341. Accessed August 20, 2007.

———. "Ellison Says He Was Wrong to Compare Bush 9/11 Response to Nazis." *Associated Press State and Local Wire,* July 17, 2007.

Fuller, Robert. *Religion and the Life Cycle.* Philadelphia: Fortress, 1988.

Gallup, George, and D. Michael Lindsay. *Surveying the Religious Landscape: Trends in U.S. Beliefs.* Harrisburg, Penn.: Morehouse, 1999.

Gardner, Howard, in collaboration with Emma Laskin. *Leading Minds: An Anatomy of Leadership.* New York: Basic Books, 1995.

Gergen, David. *Eyewitness to Power: The Essence of Leadership.* New York: Simon and Schuster, 2000.

Geroux, Bill. "Nichol Leaving W&M for UNC; Ex-President's Departure Would Mark the Final Chapter in His Stormy Tenure." *Richmond Times-Dispatch* (March 14, 2008), A1, A11.

Gerson, Michael. "Giuliani's Abortion Muddle." *Washington Post* (May 23, 2007), A21.

Gerth, H. H., and C. Wright Mills. "Introduction" to *From Max Weber: Essays in Sociology,* trans. and ed. H. H. Gerth and C. Wright Mills. New York: Oxford University Press, 1946, 3–74.

Gilgoff, Dan. "John McCain: Constitution Established a 'Christian Nation.'" Interview. *Beliefnet.com.* http://www.beliefnet.com/story/220/story_22001.html. Accessed October 3, 2007.

Giovanni, Nikki. "Transcript of Nikki Giovanni's Convocation Address." *Virginia Tech,* April 17, 2007. http://www.vt.edu/remember/archive/giovanni_transcript.html. Accessed March 9, 2008.

Gladwell, Malcolm. *The Tipping Point: How Little Things Can Make a Big Difference.* New York: Little, Brown, 2000.

Gleason, Philip. "The Melting Pot: Symbol of Fusion or Confusion?" *American Quarterly* 16(1) (Spring 1964): 20–46.

Goodson, Susan. "History of the Wren Cross." *Williamsburg (Va.) Virginia Gazette* (November 11, 2006), 25A.

Goodstein, Laurie. "Prisons Purging Books on Faith from Libraries." *New York Times,* September 10, 2007. http://www.nytimes.com/2007/09/10/us/10prison. html?pagewanted=print. Accessed October 13, 2007.

Gorriarán, Ramón. "El terrorismo vuelve a convertirse en la principal preocupación de los españoles." *El Ideal* (Granada, Spain), February 23, 2007, 34–35.

Gutiérrez, Gustavo. *The Power of the Poor in History: Selected Writings,* trans. Robert R. Barr. Maryknoll, N.Y.: Orbis, 1983.

Hagerty, Barbara Bradley. "Understanding the Gospel according to Huckabee." *All Things Considered,* National Public Radio, February 8, 2008. http://www.npr.org/ templates/story/story.php?storyId=18821021. Accessed March 13, 2008.

———. "Young Imam Serves as Islam's Face to Community." National Public Radio, August 6, 2007. http://www.npr.org/templates/story/story.php?storyId=12532168. Accessed September 21, 2007.

Hall, Edward T. *The Silent Language.* New York: Anchor, 1959.

Hardin, Peter "Immigration Foe Goode Says Mexican Flag 'Riles' Him." *Richmond Times-Dispatch* (May 25, 2007), B1.

Harris, Grove. "Wiccan Invocation: A Canary in the Mineshaft of the United States." Background paper prepared by the Pluralism Project at Harvard University. *Pluralism Project at Harvard University,* January 23, 2007. http://www.pluralism.org/ research/profiles/display.php?profile=73769. Accessed October 15, 2007.

Harris, Sam. *The End of Faith: Religion, Terror, and the Future of Reason.* New York: Norton, 2004.

———. *Letter to a Christian Nation.* New York: Knopf, 2006.

Hawkins, John. "Interview with Tom Tancredo." *Right Wing News,* 2007. http://www. rightwingnews.com/interviews/tancredo.php. Accessed November 10, 2007.

Hayes, Kevin. "How Thomas Jefferson Read the Qur'an." *Early American Literature* 39(2) (2004): 247–61.

Heifetz, Ronald A. *Leadership without Easy Answers.* Cambridge, Mass.: Belknap, 1994.

Herberg, Will. *Protestant, Catholic, Jew: An Essay in American Religious Sociology,* new ed., completely rev. Garden City, N.Y.: Anchor, 1960.

Hicks, Douglas A. "Ethical Diversity and the Leader's Religious Commitments." In *The Quest for Moral Leaders: Essays on Leadership Ethics,* ed. Joanne B. Ciulla, Terry L. Price, and Susan E. Murphy, 45–61. Northampton, Mass.: Edward Elgar, 2005.

———. "Global Poverty and Bono's Celebrity Activism: An Analysis of Moral Imagination and Motivation." In *Global Neighbors: Christian Faith and Moral Obligation in Today's Economy*, ed. Douglas A. Hicks and Mark Valeri, 43–62. Grand Rapids, Mich.: Eerdmans, 2008.

———. *Inequality and Christian Ethics*. New Studies in Christian Ethics 16. New York: Cambridge University Press, 2000.

———. "Public-sector Leadership, Development, and Ethics: The State of the Literature and Central Questions for Future Work." In *World Ethics Forum: Conference Proceedings*, ed. Charles Sampford and Carmel Connors, 149–69. Queensland, Australia: Institute for Ethics, Governance, and Law, 2007.

———. *Religion and the Workplace: Pluralism, Spirituality, Leadership*. New York: Cambridge University Press, 2003.

———. "Self-interest, Deprivation, and Agency: Expanding the Capabilities Approach." *Journal of the Society of Christian Ethics* 25(1) (Spring 2005): 147–67.

———. "Spiritual and Religious Diversity in the Workplace: Implications for Leadership." *Leadership Quarterly* 13(4) (October 2002): 379–96.

Hill, Thomas E., Jr. *Autonomy and Self-respect*. New York: Cambridge University Press, 2001.

Hinton, Mick. "Legislator to Find Home for Quran." *Tulsa World*, October 25, 2007, A1.

Hitchens, Christopher. *God Is Not Great: How Religion Poisons Everything*. New York: Twelve, 2007.

Hopkins, Dwight. *Religions/Globalizations: Theories and Cases*. Durham, N.C.: Duke University Press, 2001.

Hostetler, A. J. "Virginians Come Together to Mourn; Tech Victims Remembered with Moments of Silence, Tears, Bells, and Balloons." *Richmond Times-Dispatch* (April 21, 2007), A3.

Huber, Nancy S., and Michael Harvey, eds. *Leadership at the Crossroads*. College Park, Md.: James MacGregor Burns Academy of Leadership, 2006.

Hudson, Audrey. "Republicans Slam Islamic Society Convention." *Washington Times* (August 31, 2007), A3.

Hunter, James Davison. *Culture Wars: The Struggle to Define America*. New York: Basic Books, 1991.

———, and David Franz. "Religious Pluralism and Civil Society." In *A Nation of Religions: The Politics of Pluralism in Multireligious America*, ed. Stephen Prothero, 256–73. Chapel Hill: University of North Carolina Press, 2006.

Huntington, Samuel P. "The Clash of Civilizations?" *Foreign Affairs* 72(3) (1993): 22–49.

———. *Who Are We?: The Challenges to America's National Identity*. New York: Simon and Schuster, 2004.

Hutchison, William R. *Religious Pluralism in America: The Contentious History of a Founding Ideal*. New Haven, Conn.: Yale University Press, 2003.

Interfaith Network for the United Kingdom. "Looking After One Another: The Safety and Security of Our Faith Communities." *Interfaith Network for the United Kingdom*, 2005. http://www.interfaith.org.uk/publications/lookingafteroneanother.pdf. Accessed October 23, 2007.

Islamic Community in Spain. "Islam in Granada: Welcome to the Islamic Capital of Europe." Pamphlet. March 2007.

Jefferson, Thomas. *The Autobiography of Thomas Jefferson, 1743–1790,* ed. Paul Leicester Ford. Philadelphia: University of Pennsylvania Press, 2005 (1914).

Jenkins, Philip. *God's Continent: Christianity, Islam, and Europe's Religious Crisis.* New York: Oxford University Press, 2007.

Johnson, Lyndon B. "Remarks at the Signing of the Immigration Bill, Liberty Island, New York." *Lyndon Baines Johnson Library and Museum,* October 3, 1965. http://www.lbjlib.utexas.edu/johnson/archives.hom/speeches.hom/651003.asp. Accessed November 7, 2007.

"Judge: Woman Can't Cover Face on Driver's License." *CNN.com,* June 10, 2003. http://www.cnn.com/2003/LAW/06/06/florida.license.veil. Accessed November 7, 2007.

Juergensmeyer, Mark. *Terror in the Mind of God: The Global Rise of Religious Violence.* Berkeley: University of California Press, 2000.

Kaine, Tim. "Virginia Tech Shootings." Official Site of the Governor of Virginia. http://www.governor.virginia.gov/TempContent/Tech-Archive.cfm. Accessed August 10, 2007.

Kallen, Horace. "Democracy versus the Melting-Pot." *Nation* 100(2590) (1915): 190–94, 217–20.

Kant, Immanuel. "An Answer to the Question: What Is Enlightenment?" In *Kant: Political Writings,* ed. Hans Reiss, 54–60. Cambridge Texts in the History of Political Thought. New York: Cambridge University Press, 1991.

———. "Religion within the Boundaries of Mere Reason." In *Kant: Religion within the Boundaries of Mere Reason and Other Writings,* trans. Allen Wood and George di Giovanni. Cambridge Texts in the History of Philosophy. New York: Cambridge University Press, 1999.

Kellerman, Barbara. *Reinventing Leadership: Making the Connection between Politics and Business.* Albany: SUNY Press, 1999.

Kennedy, John F. Address of Senator John F. Kennedy to the Greater Houston Ministerial Association. *John F. Kennedy Presidential Library and Museum,* September 12, 1960. http://www.jfklibrary.org/Historical+Resources/Archives/Reference+Desk/Speeches/JFK/JFK+Pre-Pres/1960/Address+of+Senator+John+F.+Kennedy+to+the+Greater+Houston+Ministerial+Association.htm. Accessed November 7, 2007.

"Khalil Gibran International Academy." http://Schools.nyc.gov/SchoolPortals/15/k592/default.htm.

King, Martin Luther, Jr. "Letter from Birmingham Jail." April 16, 1963. In *A Testament of Hope: The Essential Writings and Speeches of Martin Luther King, Jr.,* ed. James M. Washington (San Francisco: HarperSanFrancisco, 1986), 289–302.

Kloppenberg, James. "Life Everlasting." *Religion and Values in Public Life, Center for the Study of Values in Public Life at Harvard Divinity School* 5(4) (Summer 1997), 1–3.

Kung, Hans, and Karl-Josel Kuschel, eds. *A Global Ethic: The Declaration of the Parliament of the World's Religions.* New York: Continuum, 1993.

Kunkle, Fredrick. "Fairfax Native Says Allen's Words Sting." *Washington Post* (August 25, 2006), B9.

———. "School's Move toward Inclusion Creates a Rift; Upset about Cross's Removal, William and Mary Alumni Mount Online Protest." *Washington Post* (December 26, 2006), B1.

Kuo, David. "John Edwards: 'My Faith Came Roaring Back.'" *Beliefnet.com*, undated. http://www.beliefnet.com/story/213/story_21312_1.html. Accessed September 1, 2007.

————. *Tempting Faith: An Inside Story of Political Seduction.* New York: Free Press, 2006.

Kurien, Prema A. "Mr. President, Why Do You Exclude Us from Your Prayers?" In *A Nation of Religions: The Politics of Pluralism in Multireligious America,* ed. Stephen Prothero, 119–38. Chapel Hill: University of North Carolina Press, 2006.

Kymlicka, Will. *Multicultural Citizenship: A Liberal Theory of Minority Rights.* New York: Oxford University Press, 1995.

Lambert, Frank. *The Founding Fathers and the Place of Religion in America.* Princeton, N.J.: Princeton University Press, 2003.

Lewis, David Levering. *God's Crucible: Islam and the Making of Europe, 570 to 1215.* New York: Norton, 2008.

Leyden, Kevin M. "Social Capital and the Built Environment: The Importance of Walkable Neighborhoods." *American Journal of Public Health* 93(9) (September 2003): 1546–51.

Lincoln, Bruce. "Bush's God Talk: Analyzing the President's Theology." *Christian Century* (October 5, 2004): 22–29.

Lindsay, D. Michael. *Faith in the Halls of Power: How Evangelicals Joined the American Elite.* New York: Oxford University Press, 2007.

Locke, John. *A Letter concerning Toleration.* Amherst, N.Y.: Prometheus, 1990.

Lynn, Barry W. *Piety and Politics: The Right-wing Assault on Religious Freedom.* New York: Harmony, 2006.

MacCullough, J. A. "Cross-roads." In *Encyclopaedia of Religion and Ethics,* ed. James Hastings. Vol. 4, 330–35. New York: Charles Scribner's Sons, 1924.

MacFarquhar, Neil. "Fears of Inquiry Dampen Giving by U.S. Muslims." *New York Times* (October 30, 2006), A1.

MacIntyre, Alisdair. *After Virtue: A Study in Moral Theory.* Notre Dame, Ind.: University of Notre Dame Press, 1981.

Madison, James. *Memorial and Remonstrance against Religious Assessments.* 1785. http://religiousfreedom.lib.virginia.edu/sacred/madison_m&r_1785.html. Accessed November 7, 2007.

Marsh, Charles. *God's Long Summer: Stories of Faith and Civil Rights.* Princeton, N.J.: Princeton University Press, 1997.

McCain, John. "McCain Speaks at Columbia University." U.S. Senate, John McCain. May 16, 2006. http://mccain.senate.gov/public/index.cfm?FuseAction=PressOffice.PressReleases&ContentRecord_id=544c3108-bec5-4951-abe6-f4501ca4dfd4&Region_id=&Issue_id=e2d83197-0adb-4a53-994a-9eb58268b452. Accessed March 14, 2008.

McGraw, Barbara A. *Rediscovering America's Sacred Ground: Public Religion and Pursuit of the Good in a Pluralistic America.* Albany: SUNY Press, 2003.

McKelway, Bill. "Bush Stop a Coincidence? Farmer's Glad Either Way." *Richmond Times-Dispatch* (October 21, 2006), B1.

McRoberts, Andrew R., and Constance B. McRoberts. "At William and Mary, Cross Becomes a Lightning Rod." *Washington Post* (February 18, 2007), B08.

Menocal, María Rosa. *The Ornament of the West: How Muslims, Jews, and Christians Created a Culture of Tolerance in Medieval Spain.* New York: Little, Brown, 2002.

Montagne, Renee. "Filmmakers Shatter Arab Stereotypes in Hollywood." National Public Radio, September 13, 2006. http://www.npr.org/templates/story/story. php?storyId=6064305. Accessed September 28, 2007.

Morán, Carlos. "Publicado el primer libro de religión islámica para escolares." *El País* (October 18, 2006).

A More Perfect Union. "Bus Campaign Feedback." http://www.rethinkbias.org/pages/ BusCampaign/feedback.html. Accessed August 9, 2007.

"Muslim Alliance of Indiana (MAI) Helps Organize Second Annual Governor's Iftar." *Muslim Alliance of Indiana,* September 26, 2006. http://www.muslimalliancein. com/mai/enews_brief_october2.htm. Accessed September 21, 2007.

Nichol, Gene R. "Nichol Discusses Cross Decision in Message to Campus Community." *College of William and Mary,* December 20, 2006. http://www.wm.edu/news/ ?id=7102, accessed August 16, 2007.

————. "Nichol Discusses Wren Cross Decision with BOV." Remarks prepared for the William and Mary Board of Visitors. *College of William and Mary,* November 20, 2006. http://www.wm.edu/news/index.php?id=7026. Accessed August 16, 2007.

Norris, Michelle. "Ellison to Take Oath on Thomas Jefferson's Quran." *All Things Considered,* National Public Radio, January 3, 2007.

North Atlantic Treaty Organization. Online Library. http://www.nato.int/docu/basictxt/ treaty.htm. Accessed June 19, 2008.

Nussbaum, Martha C. "Compassion and Terror." *Daedalus* (Winter 2003): 10–26.

O'Brien, Nancy Frazier. "U.S. Congress More Religiously Diverse; Catholics Still Well Represented." Catholic News Service, January 16, 2007. http://www.catholicnews. com/data/stories/cns/0700279.htm. Accessed November 7, 2007.

Office of Personnel Management, State of Oklahoma. "Governor's Ethnic American Advisory Council." State of Oklahoma, Minutes of Meeting, February 16, 2007. http://www.ok.gov/opm/HR_and_Employee_Services/Ethnic_American_Advi sory_Council.html. Accessed November 8, 2007.

O'Rear, Caine. "Bush Addresses Grieving Community." *Richmond.com,* April 17, 2007. http://www.richmond.com/news-features/731. Accessed March 21, 2008.

Orfield, Gary, and Chungmei Lei. "Historic Reversals, Accelerating Resegregation, and the Need for New Integration Strategies." Report of the Civil Rights Project/ Proyecto Derechos Civiles, UCLA. August 2007. http://www.civilrightsproject.ucla. edu/research/deseg/reversals_reseg_need.pdf. Accessed November 10, 2007.

Peters, Thomas J., and Robert H. Waterman Jr. *In Search of Excellence: Lessons from America's Best-run Companies.* New York: Warner, 1982.

Peterson, Kurt W. "American Idol: David Barton's Dream of a Christian Nation." *Christian Century* (October 31, 2006): 20–23.

Pew Forum on Religion and Public Life. *U.S. Religious Landscape Survey. Report 1: Diverse and Dynamic.* Washington, D.C.: Pew Research Center, February 2008.

Pew Research Center. *Muslim Americans: Middle Class and Mostly Mainstream.* May 22, 2007. http://pewresearch.org/pubs/483/muslim-americans. Accessed March 21, 2008.

Pew Research Center for the People and the Press. "Religion in Campaign '08: Clinton and Giuliani Seen as Not Highly Religious; Romney's Religion Raises Concerns." Pew Forum on Religion and Public Life, Washington, D.C., September 6, 2007. http://pewforum.org/surveys/campaign08/. Accessed March 15, 2008.

Pinsky, Robert. "Eros against Esperanto." In *For Love of Country: Debating the Limits of Patriotism, Martha C. Nussbaum with Respondents,* ed. Joshua Cohen, 85–90. Boston: Beacon, 1996.

Pipes, Daniel. "On New York's 'Khalil Gibran International Academy.'" *Daniel Pipes Blog,* March 7, 2007. http://www.danielpipes.org/blog/731. Accessed October 12, 2007.

"Pluralism—National Menace." *Christian Century* (June 13, 1951).

Prager, Dennis. "America, Not Keith Ellison, Decides What Book a Congressman Takes His Oath On." *Townhall.com,* November 28, 2006. http://www.townhall.com/col umnists/DennisPrager/2006/11/28/america,_not_keith_ellison,_decides_what_ book_a_congressman_takes_his_oath_on. Accessed March 13, 2008.

"President and Board Accept Committee Recommendation on Wren Cross." *William and Mary News,* March 6, 2007. http://wm.edu/news/?id=7456. Accessed August 16, 2007.

Price, Terry L. "Epistemological Restraint—Revisited." *Journal of Political Philosophy* 8(3) (2000): 401–407.

———. *Leadership Ethics: An Introduction.* New York: Cambridge University Press, 2009.

———. *Understanding Ethical Failures in Leadership.* New York: Cambridge University Press, 2006.

Prothero, Stephen, ed. *A Nation of Religions: The Politics of Pluralism in Multireligious America.* Chapel Hill: University of North Carolina Press, 2006.

———. *Religious Literacy: What Every American Needs to Know—and Doesn't.* San Francisco: HarperSanFrancisco, 2007.

Pulsar Research and Consulting. "*Time* Poll: Survey on Faith and the Presidential Election." May 10–13, 2007. http://www.pulsarresearch.com/PDF/TIME_Report.pdf. Accessed March 15, 2008.

Putnam, Robert. *Bowling Alone: The Collapse and Revival of American Community.* New York: Simon and Schuster, 2000.

———. "*E Pluribus Unum:* Diversity and Community in the Twenty-first Century— The 2006 Johan Skytte Prize Lecture." *Scandinavian Political Studies* 30(2) (2007): 137–74.

Ratner, Sidney. "Horace M. Kallen and Cultural Pluralism." *Modern Judaism* 4 (May 1984): 185–200.

Rawls, John. "The Idea of Public Reason Revisited." *University of Chicago Law Review* 64 (1997): 765–807.

———. *Political Liberalism.* John Dewey Essays in Philosophy 4. New York: Columbia University Press, 1993.

Ray, Jonathan. "Beyond Tolerance and Persecution: Reassessing Our Approach to Medieval Convivencia." *Jewish Social Studies* 11(2) (Winter 2005): 1–18.

Rayner, Bob. "Message on a Shoestring: Waging War on Prejudice." *Richmond Times-Dispatch* (July 21, 2004), A1.

Reuters News Service. "French Sikhs Ask Chirac to Spare Turbans from Ban." January 9, 2004. http://in.news.yahoo.com/040109/137/2atgc.html. Accessed September 21, 2007.

Robinson, Jo Ann Gibson. *The Montgomery Bus Boycott and the Women Who Started It: The Memoir of Jo Ann Gibson Robinson*, ed. David J. Garrow. Knoxville: University of Tennessee Press, 1987.

Roof, Wade Clark. *A Generation of Seekers: The Spiritual Journeys of the Baby Boom Generation*. San Francisco: HarperSanFrancisco, 1993.

Rorty, Richard. "Religion as Conversation-Stopper." *Common Knowledge* 3(1) (Spring 1994): 1–6.

———. "Religion in the Public Square: A Reconsideration." *Journal of Religious Ethics* 31(1) (March 2003): 141–49.

Rosenthal, Andrew. "Bush Encounters the Supermarket—Amazed." *New York Times* (February 5, 1992), A1.

Rousseau, Jean-Jacques. *On the Social Contract*, trans. Judith R. Masters and ed. Roger D. Masters. New York: St. Martin's, 1978.

Rubboli, Massimo. "'The Battle Is God's': Patriotic Sermons during the American Civil War." Paper presented at the "War Sermons" conference, Université de Provence Aix-Marseille 1. November 17–19, 2005.

Sacirbey, Omar. "Ellison Not First to Forgo Bible for Oath." *Christian Century* (December 26, 2006): 14–15.

Sahuquillo, M. R. "La inmigración cambia el mapa religioso." *El País* (March 31, 2007), 33.

Sandel, Michael J. *Liberalism and the Limits of Justice*. 2d ed. New York: Cambridge University Press, 1998.

Scheer, Robert. "The Playboy Interview: Jimmy Carter." *Playboy* 23(11) (November 1976), 63–86.

Schein, Edgar H. *Organizational Culture and Leadership*, 2d ed. San Francisco: Jossey-Bass, 1992.

Schlesinger, Arthur M., Jr. *The Disuniting of America: Reflections on a Multicultural Society*, rev. and enlarged ed. New York: Norton, 1998.

Sen, Amartya. *Identity and Violence: The Illusion of Destiny*. New York: Norton, 2006.

Seuss, Dr. "The Zax." In *"The Sneetches" and Other Stories*. New York: Random House, 1961, 25–36.

Shain, Barry Alan. *The Myth of American Individualism: The Protestant Origins of American Political Thought*. Princeton, N.J.: Princeton University Press, 1994.

Siegel, Jennifer. "Koch Calls for Pundit's Ouster from Shoah Council." *Jewish Daily Forward*, December 8, 2006. http://www.forward.com/articles/kock-calls-for-pundits-ouster-from-shoah-council/. Accessed August 20, 2007.

Slater, Wayne. "GOP Buttons on Their Shirts and Faith on Their Sleeves: Republican Convention Draws Religious Conservatives." *Dallas Morning News* (June 4, 2006).

Sloat, James M. "The Subtle Significance of Sincere Belief: Tocqueville's Account of Religious Belief and Democratic Stability." *Journal of Church and State* 42(4) (Autumn 2000): 759–79.

Smith, Adam. *The Theory of Moral Sentiments*. Library of Economics and Liberty Online. http://www.econlib.org/library/Smith/smMS.html. Accessed October 15, 2007.

Smith, Christian. *Christian America? What Evangelicals Really Want*. Berkeley: University of California Press, 2000.

———. "Religiously Ignorant Journalists." *Books and Culture* (January 1, 2004): 6–7.

Smothers, Ronald. "Jewish Groups Criticize Remarks by a Governor as 'un-American.'" *New York Times* (November 20, 1992).

Stein, Jeff. "Can You Tell a Sunni from a Shiite?" *New York Times* (October 17, 2006), A21.

———. "Democrats' New Intelligence Chairman Needs Crash Course on al Qaeda." *CQ.com*, December 8, 2006. http://public.cq.com/public/20061211_homeland.html. Accessed October 12, 2007.

Stotzer, Rebecca. *Comparison of Hate Crime Rates across Protected and Unprotected Groups*. Research study. Los Angeles: Williams Institute at the UCLA School of Law, 2007.

Straw, Jack. "I Want to Unveil My Views on an Important Issue." *Lancashire Telegraph* (October 5, 2006), 12.

Sullivan, Amy. "Faith of the Candidates." *Time* poll. *Time.com*, July 12, 2007. http://www.time.com/time/politics/article/0,8599,1642653,00.html. Accessed October 17, 2007.

———. *The Party Faithful: How and Why Democrats Are Closing the God Gap*. New York: Scribner, 2008.

Suskind, Ron. "Without a Doubt." *New York Times Magazine* (October 17, 2004).

"Terrorist Attack Aftermath: General's Remarks on Islam Draw Fire." *Facts.com. Facts on File World News Digest* (October 23, 2003).

Thiemann, Ronald F. *Religion in Public Life: A Dilemma for Democracy*. Washington, D.C.: Georgetown University Press, 1996.

Thompson, Robert Farris. *Flash of the Spirit: African and Afro-American Art and Philosophy*. New York: Random House, 1983.

Tigay, Chanan. "For Jews, FBI Hate Crime Report Has Some Good News, Some Bad." Jewish Telegraphic Agency, November 24, 2004.

Tocqueville, Alexis de. *Democracy in America* (Garden City, N.Y.: Anchor Doubleday, 1969).

Trevelyan, Mark. "EU Lexicon to Shun Term 'Islamic Terrorism.'" *Tiscali.co.uk*, November 4, 2006. http://www.tiscali.co.uk/news/newswire.php/news/reuters/2006/04/11/topnews/eu-lexicon-to-shun-term-34islamic-terrorism34.html&template=/news/templates/newswire/news_story_reuters.html. Accessed October 15, 2007.

Tu, Janet I., and Lornet Turnbull. "Christmas Trees Going Back Up at Sea-Tac." *Seattle Times*, December 12, 2006. http://archives.seattletimes.nwsource.com/cgi-bin/texis.cgi/web/vortex/display?slug=seatactrees12m&date=20061212&query=trees+menorah+rabbi. Accessed November 10, 2007.

"The 25 Most Influential Evangelicals in America." *Time* (February 7, 2005). http://www.time.com/time/covers/1101050207. Accessed May 21, 2007.

U.S. Commission on International Religious Freedom. "Annual Report of the United States Commission on International Religious Freedom." May 2004. http://www.uscirf.gov/countries/publications/currentreport/2004annualrpt.pdf. Accessed October 19, 2007.

U.S. Department of State, Bureau of Democracy, Human Rights, and Labor. *International Religious Freedom Report 2006*. U.S. Department of State. http://www.state.gov/g/drl/rls/irf/2006/71380.htm.

Van Biema, David. "Minnesota's Teetotal Taxis." *Time*, January 19, 2007. http://www.time.com/time/magazine/article/0,9171,1580390,00.html. Accessed February 1, 2007.

Vezner, Tad. "Request for Rare Quran Uncovers Minnesota Tie." *St. Paul (Minn.) Pioneer Press* (January 4, 2007).

Vílchez, Rafael. "Los musulmanes de Órgiva dispondrán de un cementerio propio en el municipio." *El Ideal* (Granada, Spain) (March 15, 2007), 19.

Von Drehle, David. "Political Split Is Pervasive; Clash of Cultures Is Driven by Targeted Appeals and Reinforced by Geography." *Washington Post* (April 25, 2004), A01.

Weber, Max. "Politics as Vocation." In *From Max Weber: Essays in Sociology*, trans. and ed. H. H. Gerth and C. Wright Mills, 77–128. New York: Oxford University Press, 1946.

Weigel, George. *The Cube and the Cathedral: Europe, America, and Politics without God*. New York: Basic Books, 2005.

West, Cornel. "The Democratic Soul." *Religion and Values in Public Life, Center for the Study of Values in Public Life at Harvard Divinity School* 6(1) (Fall 1997): 1, 4.

———. *Race Matters*. Boston: Beacon, 1993.

West, Diane. "Call It like It Is: PC Lexicon." *Washington Times* (July 6, 2007), A17.

Wight, Jonathan B., and Douglas A. Hicks. "Disaster Relief: What Would Adam Smith Do?" *Christian Science Monitor* (January 18, 2005), 9.

Will, George. "God of Our Fathers." *New York Times Book Review* (October 22, 2006), 10.

Williams, Rowan. "Archbishop's Lecture—Civil and Religious Law in England: A Religious Perspective." *Archbishop of Canterbury*, February 7, 2008. http://www.bishopthorpepalace.co.uk/1575. Accessed March 16, 2008.

Williamson, Thad. *Sprawl, Justice, and Citizenship: The Civic Costs of the American Way of Life*. New York: Oxford University Press, forthcoming.

Wilson, Graeme. "Brown Breaks Ranks to Back Straw over Lifting Muslim Veils." *Telegraph News*, December 10, 2006. http://www.telegraph.co.uk/news/uknews/1531106/Brown-breaks-ranks-to-back-Straw-over-lifting-Muslim-veils.html. Accessed June 16, 2008.

Wolfe, Alan. *One Nation, After All: What Middle-class Americans Really Think About*. New York: Penguin, 1999.

Wren, J. Thomas. *Inventing Leadership: The Challenge of Democracy*. Northampton, Mass.: Edward Elgar, 2007.

Wuthnow, Robert. *America and the Challenge of Religious Diversity*. Princeton, N.J.: Princeton University Press, 2005.

Yoffie, Rabbi Eric H. "Remarks as Prepared to Islamic Society of North America." 44th Annual Convention Transcript by President of URJ. *Union for Reform Judaism*, Chicago, August 31, 2007. http://urj.org/yoffie/isna. Accessed September 21, 2007.

Zahn, Paula. "Politics and Religion: Democratic Presidential Candidates on Faith." *Paula Zahn Now*, CNN, June 4, 2007.

Zangwill, Israel. *The Melting Pot: Drama in Four Acts*. New York: The Macmillan Company, 1921.

Index

connectors, 9, 88, 90, 91, 93–94, 123, 125,
    136, 155, 160, 162, 167
Constitution, Indian, 87
Constitution, Spanish, 83
Constitution, U.S., 6, 30, 54, 110, 111, 114,
    116, 117
contamination, 88–89
Contreras, José María, 85–86
convivencia, 9, 80, 83–86, 88–89, 90, 91,
    93, 94, 97, 118, 120, 128, 131, 136, 142,
    145, 152, 161, 162, 163, 167, 170
cosmopolitanism, 55, 88–89
Coulter, Ann, 5
Council for America's First Freedom, 125,
    146
Council for American-Islamic Relations
    (CAIR), 28–29, 120–21, 123
Council on Islamic Education, 147
Covey, Stephen, 173–74
creationism, 145
cross, 25, 75, 105, 108 (*see also* Wren cross)
crossing paths, 9, 80, 88–89, 92–94, 125,
    127, 145, 160
crossroads, 16, 90, 91–94, 97, 123, 125, 128,
    136–38, 145, 147, 160, 162, 164, 167, 171,
    176
crusade, 50, 51, 156
cultural pluralism, 38–39, 51, 79 (*see also*
    pluralism)
culture wars, 5, 51, 52, 53, 57, 60, 63, 79, 101,
    105, 110–11, 114, 145, 146, 148
culture, and leadership, 7, 77–78, 93, 97,
    101–18, 128, 159, 167, 170, 172

Danforth, John, 64, 133–34, 136
Daniels, Mitch, 129–30, 131, 160
Dar Al Hijrah Islamic Center, 130
Dar Al Noor Mosque, 130
Davis, Mac, 133
Dawkins, Richard, 65
Dean, Howard, 67–68, 156
deism, 54, 146
depth finder, 63–64
dhimmis, 83–84
dietary restrictions. *See* food
disaster relief, 6, 151–52
Dodd, Christopher, 69
driver's license, 16–18
Duncan, Rex, 18

Easter, 73
Eck, Diana, 41, 42, 80
economy, 6, 43, 72–73, 83, 92–93, 154, 169

Edwards, John, 53, 68
Eid-al Adha, 127
Eightfold Path, 151
Elizabeth II (England), 103
Ellison, Keith, 12–14, 101, 102, 110–13,
    117–18
Emerson, Ralph Waldo, 37
empathy. *See* sympathy
Enlightenment, the, 70
Episcopal Church in the U.S., 24
Episcopalians, 64, 133
Equal Employment Opportunity
    Commission (EEOC), 133
equality, 9, 32, 52, 55, 62, 76, 77, 94, 105,
    106, 109, 113, 117, 128, 130, 131,
    136, 138, 152, 159, 166, 171, 172
Erlich, Thomas, 149
Esperanto, 71
ETA, 20, 81, 82
Europe, 19, 29, 31, 34, 36–37, 40, 41, 48,
    51, 59, 94, 142–43, 172
Europeans, 4, 14, 20, 29, 38, 142
European Union, 81, 94, 154–55 (*see also*
    Europe)
Evangelical Left, 52
evangelicals, 4, 41, 52, 55–57, 174
evangelical tradition, 23, 51, 52, 162
Everett, William J., 87
evolution, 145
Exodus, 25
extremism, 6, 49, 77–78, 82, 124,
    131, 175

Facebook.com, 164
Fairfax County, VA, 12
faith-based organizations and government,
    31, 35, 72
Falwell, Jerry, 65, 69
fanaticism, 5 (*see also* extremism)
Farrakhan, Louis, 111, 122
Fatima's hands, 75
fear-mongering, 5
Federal Bureau of Investigation (FBI), 60,
    121–22, 139
federal workplace, 115
First Amendment, 14, 30, 53, 56, 77–78, 94,
    102, 103, 106, 113, 114–15, 116, 117, 131,
    152, 173
First Amendment Center, 95, 146
Fitzmeier, Jack, 150
flag, Mexican, 12
flag, U.S., 11
Flowers, Gennifer, 113